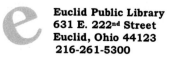

The Secret History *of the*
MONGOL QUEENS

The Secret History *of the*

MONGOL QUEENS

HOW THE DAUGHTERS OF
GENGHIS KHAN
RESCUED HIS EMPIRE

JACK WEATHERFORD

CROWN PUBLISHERS  NEW YORK

Copyright © 2010 by Jack Weatherford

Illustrations © 2010 by N. Bat-Erdene

Published in the United States by Crown Publishers, an imprint of the
Crown Publishing Group, a division of Random House, Inc., New York.

www.crownpublishing.com

CROWN and the Crown colophon are registered trademarks of
Random House, Inc.

Library of Congress Cataloging-in-Publication Data
Weatherford, J. McIver.
The secret history of the Mongol queens / Jack Weatherford.
p. cm.
Includes bibliographical references and index.
1. Genghis Khan, 1162–1227—Family.   2. Queens—Mongolia—History.
3. Daughters—Mongolia—History.   4. Women—Mongolia—History.
5. Inheritance and succession—Mongolia—History.   6. Mongols—History.
7. Mongols—Biography.   8. Mongolia—Kings and rulers—Biography.
9. Mongolia—History.   10. Mongolia—Biography.   I. Title.
DS22.W39 2010
950'.20922—dc22
2009020822

ISBN 978-0-307-40715-3

Printed in the United States of America

DESIGN BY LENNY HENDERSON
Maps and family trees by Jeffrey L. Ward

1   3   5   7   9   10   8   6   4   2

First Edition

May the Golden Light of the Eternal Blue Sky
forever bless the mothers and the daughters
of the Great Mongol Nation

CONTENTS

Map of the Mongol Empire (1206–1368) viii

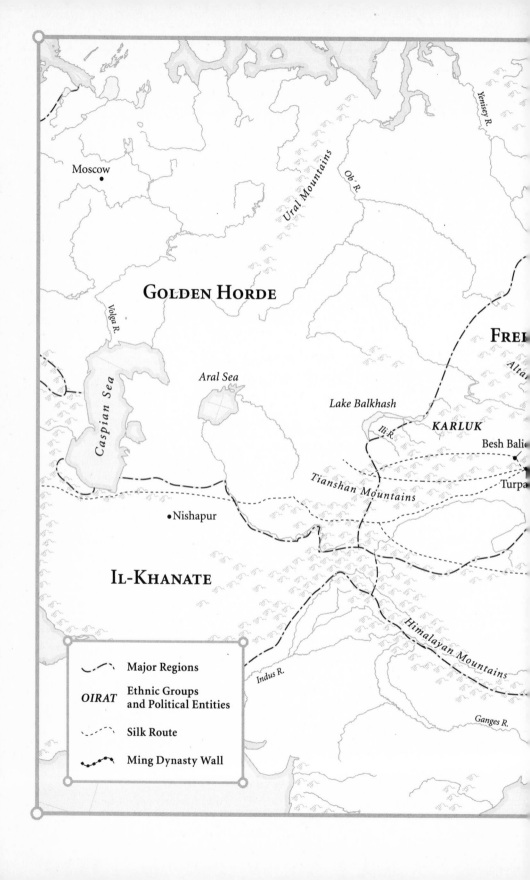

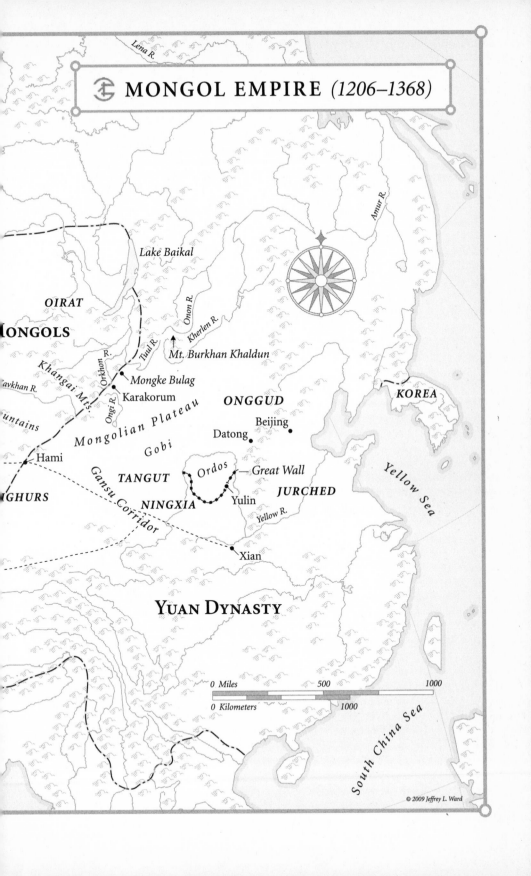

MONGOL EMPIRE *(1206–1368)*

Lena R.

Amur R.

Lake Baikal

OIRAT

MONGOLS

Onon R.

Tuul R.

Kherlen R.

Mt. Burkhan Khaldun

KOREA

Khangai Mts.

Orkhon R.

avkhan R.

untains

Ongi R.

Mongke Bulag

Karakorum

ONGGUD

Beijing

Mongolian Plateau

Datong

Hami

Gobi

TANGUT

Ordos

Great Wall

Yellow Sea

Gansu Corridor

GHURS

NINGXIA

Yulin

JURCHED

Yellow R.

Xian

YUAN DYNASTY

0 Miles   500   1000

0 Kilometers   1000

South China Sea

© 2009 Jeffrey L. Ward

The Missing Chapter

O N AN UNKNOWN DAY LATE IN THE THIRTEENTH CENTURY, an unidentified hand clumsily cut away part of the text from the most politically sensitive section of *The Secret History of the Mongols.* The censored portion recorded words spoken by Genghis Khan in the summer of 1206 at the moment he created the Mongol Empire and gave shape to the government that would dominate the world for the next 150 years. Through oversight or malice, the censor left a single short sentence of the mutilated text that hinted at what had been removed: "Let us reward our female offspring."

In the preceding section of the text, Genghis Khan bestowed offices, titles, territories, and vassals upon his sons, brothers, and other men according to their ability and contribution to his rise to power. But at the moment where the text reported that he turned to the assembly to announce the achievements and rewards of his daughters, the unknown hand struck his words from the record. The censor, or possibly a scribe copying the newly altered text, wrote the same short final sentence twice. Perhaps the copyist was careless in repeating it, or perhaps the censor deliberately sought to emphasize what was missing or even to taunt future generations with the mystery of what had been slashed away.

More than a mere history, the document known as *The Secret History of the Mongols* recorded the words of Genghis Khan through-out his life as he founded the Mongol nation, gave his people their basic laws, organized the administration, and delegated powers. It served as the biography of a tribe and its leader as well as the national charter or constitution of the nation that grew into a world empire. Only the most important members of the royal family had access to the manuscript, and therefore it acquired its name.

The *Secret History* provides an up-close and personal view of the private life of a ruling family that is unlike any other dynastic narrative. The text records the details of conversations in bed between husband and wife; of routine family problems as well as arguments over who had sex with whom; and expressions of the deepest fears and desires of a family who could not have known that they would become important actors in world history. Many episodes and characterizations, particularly those regarding Genghis Khan's early life, are unflattering. It was not written by sycophantic followers currying favor, but by an anonymous voice dedicated to preserving the true history of one of the world's most remarkable men and the empire he founded. That did not mean that the history was available to just anyone, however.

The Mongols operated possibly the most secretive government in history. They preserved few records, and those were written in the Mongolian language, which their conquered subjects were not allowed to learn. While Mongol khans gave away jewels and treasures with little evidence of covetousness, they locked their documents inside the treasury and kept them closely guarded. As Persian chronicler Rashid al-Din wrote in the thirteenth century: "From age to age, they have kept their true history in Mongolian expression and script, unorganized and disarranged, chapter by chapter, scattered in treasuries, hidden from the gaze of strangers and specialists, and no one was allowed access to learn of it." Both the secrecy of the records and the apparent chaos in which they were kept served the purposes of the rulers. With such an unorganized history, the person who controlled the treasury of documents could pick and choose among the papers and hide or release parts as served some political agenda of the moment. If a leader needed to discredit a rival or find an excuse to punish someone, there was always some piece of incriminating evidence that could be pulled from the treasury. Following the example of Genghis Khan, the early Mongol rulers clearly recognized that knowledge constituted their most potent weapon, and controlling the flow of information served as their organizing principle.

Genghis Khan sired four self-indulgent sons who proved good at drinking, mediocre in fighting, and poor at everything else; yet their names live on despite the damage they did to their father's empire. Although Genghis Khan recognized the superior leadership abilities of his daughters and left them strategically important parts of his empire, today we cannot even be certain how many daughters he had. In their lifetime they could not be ignored, but when they left the scene, history closed the door behind them and let the dust of centuries cover their tracks. Those Mongol queens were too unusual, too difficult to understand or explain. It seemed more convenient just to erase them.

Around the world, the influential dynasties of history exhibit a certain uniformity in their quest for power, and they distinguish themselves from one another primarily through personal foibles, dietary preferences, sexual proclivities, spiritual callings, and other strange twists of character. But none followed a destiny quite like that of the female heirs of Genghis Khan. As in every dynasty, some rank as heroes, others as villains, and most as some combination of the two.

Rashid al-Din wrote that "there are many stories about these daughters." Yet those stories disappeared. We may never find definitive accounts for all seven or eight of Genghis Khan's daughters, but we can reassemble the stories of most of them. Through the generations, his female heirs sometimes ruled, and sometimes they contested the rule of their brothers and male cousins. Never before or since have women exercised so much power over so many people and ruled so much territory for as long as these women did.

References to Genghis Khan's daughters have come down to us in a jumble of names and titles with a stupefying array of spellings, according to how each sounded to the Chinese, Persians, Armenians, Russians, Turks, or Italians who wrote their stories. Each source differs on the number of daughters. The *Secret History* identifies eight sons-in-law for Genghis Khan and his wife Borte in the pivotal year 1206, and it further identifies each of them as a commander of a thousand troops. The list of sons-in-law is longer than the list of daughters, due in part to multiple marriages and also to the efforts of more distant relatives by marriage to raise their status and apparent closeness to Genghis Khan in the official record.

Through the generations, Mongol chroniclers and scholars dropped the names of Genghis Khan's daughters one by one from their accounts. By the time of the Buddhist chroniclers of the seventeenth century, the number of remembered daughters had dwindled to only one, and then even she disappeared in the contorted chronicles that followed.

Four became ruling queens of their own countries and commanded large regiments of soldiers. At least one became literate, but several supported scholars, schools, and the publication of religious and educational texts. Some had children, while others died without surviving descendants. The youngest, of whom Rashid al-Din wrote: "Genghis Khan loved this one more than any of his other daughters," was treacherously assassinated by her brother soon after their father's death.

At court these noble women wore elaborate headdresses of felt and feathers that rose more than two feet above their ears so they would tower over everyone around them and "give [themselves] a great luster when they are on horseback." When they could, they raised their children in peace, but when it was necessary, they put on the helmet of war, took up the bows and arrows of battle, and went forth to defend their nation and their families. The royal Mongol women raced horses, commanded in war, presided as judges over criminal cases, ruled vast territories, and sometimes wrestled men in public sporting competitions. They arrogantly rejected the customs of civilized women of neighboring cultures, such as wearing the veil, binding their feet, or hiding in seclusion. Some accepted the husbands given to them, but others chose their own husbands or refused any at all. They lived by the rules of society when prudent, and they made new rules when necessary.

Without Genghis Khan's daughters, there would have been no Mongol Empire. Genghis Khan recognized early in his career that an empire as large as the one he was creating could not be managed by a single ruler alone. To survive it needed different centers of power that fulfilled complementary roles. Not able to rely upon his sons to guard the empire he was conquering, he increasingly turned to his daughters, who ruled a string of kingdoms along the Silk Route from northern China through Central Asia.

Yet almost as soon as Genghis Khan died, the daughters came under attack, first from the wives of their brothers. What started as a war of powerful women against one another soon degenerated into simply a war against women in power. In the next generation, their nephews, the grandsons of Genghis Khan, intensified the attack on the systematic balance of powers left by Genghis Khan and on the lineages of his daughters.

Through most of the Mongol imperial era, from 1206 until 1368, the royal women of Genghis Khan's Borijin clan mounted a persistent opposition to the centralized governments of their male relatives. Not only did the women fight outside efforts to claim their territories, but even after some faced gruesome and horrendous deaths, their daughters and granddaughters continued the struggle for the heritage bestowed upon them by Genghis Khan.

With the official role of royal women compromised and then nearly eliminated, the empire buckled, collapsed, and died. By 1368 the Mongols had lost their lands, fled back to their steppe homeland in disgrace, and resumed fighting among themselves with even more viciousness than ever. The bickering, feuding, and raiding lasted for another century, until a new queen unexpectedly appeared around 1470. Queen Manduhai the Wise lifted up the Mongol banners that had been left trampled in the dust. She awakened the forgotten consciousness of the

Mongols. She put the Mongol nation back in order, created a new government, and then, like the Mongol queens before her, disappeared back into the fog of neglect.

Words and documents can dimly reflect the truth, like shadows by a night fire or the outline of a mountain through the mist, but alone they are too small and primitive to contain all of it. While words may be altered or censored, the truth endures, even when not properly recorded. Truth can be forgotten, misplaced, or lost, but never annihilated. The human hand might erase the words, mutilate the manuscript, or chisel off a name, but that only alters memory. Such vandalism tampers with the evidence without altering the facts. Cutting part of a document still leaves an outline of what was removed, a silhouette of the missing piece.

Once an event happens, evidence will remain in some form. The land always remembers. The truth will lurk somewhere waiting for the wind to blow away the sand that hides it. A few scattered ashes tell us of a campfire from long ago; even a delicate footprint can survive in hardened mud for millions of years to permanently record a fleeting act. The world remembers long after people have forgotten.

We rarely find what we do not seek. Once we look for information on these great queens, we realize that much of the history was not hidden at all; it was merely ignored. Snippets of evidence concerning these royal women can still be found in the diplomatic reports of the Chinese court, letters to the Vatican, the elegant Muslim histories, royal Armenian chronicles, the memoirs of merchants such as Marco Polo, and carved into the stones of Taoist and Confucian temples. Once we know what we are looking for, we find the Mongol queens in the rhymes of Chaucer and the arias of Puccini, in Persian manuscript paintings and silken *thangkas* hanging in Tibetan monasteries. Those queens are still there, waiting through eight centuries for us merely to see them again.

This book is a small effort to find that lost story, to reassemble the clipped pages of the *Secret History,* to blow the dust off this neglected chapter, and to see once again what in our past has been denied to us for seven hundred years. What did those censors not want us to read? What is it about our history that we are not allowed to know? If the truth was important enough for one generation of powerful officials to go to great lengths to hide it, then it should be important for us to search for it now.

PART I

Tiger Queens of the Silk Route
1206–1241

There is a khan's daughter

Who steps on in a swinging manner

And has the marks of twenty tigers,

Who steps on in a graceful manner

And has the marks of thirty tigers,

Who steps on in an elegant manner

And has the marks of forty tigers,

Who steps on in a delicate manner

And has the marks of fifty tigers.

MONGOL EPIC POEM

Altan Urug: The Golden Family of Genghis Khan

DAUGHTERS*	INHERITANCE
Khojin	
Alaqai	*Onggud*
Al-Altun	*Uighur*
Checheyigen	*Oirat*
Tumelun	
Tolai	*Karluk*

SONS	INHERITANCE
Jochi	*Russia*
Chaghatai	*Central Asia*
Ogodei	*Western Mongolia*
Tolui	*Eastern Mongolia*

Chotan
m.
Dei Sechen — Borte Khatun
m. — **Genghis Khan**

Hoelun — Khasar
m.
Yesugei — Temuge
— Temulun

GENGHIS KHAN'S OTHER WIVES	INHERITANCE
Yesugen	*Khangai Mts.*
Yesui	*Tuul River*
Khulan	*Khentii Mts.*

Altani†
m.
Boroghul

* *Order is not certain. Borte is probably not
the birth mother of all the daughters.*

† *Kinship position uncertain*

It Takes a Hero

A RENEGADE TATAR WITH THE KNIFE OF VENGEANCE HIDDEN in his clothes slowly crept toward the camp of Genghis Khan's elderly mother, Hoelun. He sought revenge against Genghis Khan, who had annihilated the ancient Tatar clans, killed many of their warriors, married their women, and adopted their children, even changing their names to make them Mongol.

As a military and political leader with many enemies, Genghis Khan lived in a well-guarded encampment where bodyguards had strict orders to kill anyone who crossed a precise point without permission. Hoelun, however, lived apart in her own camp, and although she now had ten thousand soldiers and their families assigned to her control, at her advanced age she let her youngest son take her part of the army out on missions with her eldest son, the khan, while she stayed home.

Despite her rank, Hoelun's camp differed little from that of any other Mongol nomad. It consisted of a small collection of *gers*, the round tent of the steppes, positioned in a straight line with the doors facing south. Often called a "yurt" in the West, the Mongol *ger* was made of thick layers of felt wool pressed into large blankets, and could be packed up and moved as the seasons changed or as whim dictated.

The clearest sign that this was the imperial camp of the khan's mother was the presence of Hoelun's white camel and black cart. Women owned the *gers* and all the carts, but as befits a nomadic people, a woman was better known by her mode of transportation than by her home. Younger women rode horses; older women drove carts. Unless gravely ill or seriously injured, a man could never ride on a woman's cart, much less drive it.

Mongol carts of this time consisted of a small wooden bed above the axle and two wheels. Extending from the front were the two long shafts, between which the draft animal pulled the cart. All carts had the same black covering and looked much alike, but a woman showed her individuality in the choice and training of the draft animal. Common women drove a lumbering ox or a woolly yak before their heavily laden carts, but in her older years Hoelun had become fond of a high-stepping white camel to cart her around in the impressive manner appropriate for the mother of the emperor. She was known to travel long distances very quickly and even to travel at night. Since camels of any sort, much less white ones, were not very common north of the Gobi, her camp was easy to find and identify.

As the Tatar approached the camp, few men could be seen except her guards, Jelme and Jetei. Befitting her status, Hoelun had men rather than dogs to guard the area around her *ger,* and since her son Genghis Khan had a great fear of dogs, she kept none around to sound the alarm of an intruder. The Tatar waited until an opportune moment when the guards were distracted. The two men intended to butcher a hornless black ox, which they would do by knocking it unconscious with a single ax blow to the middle of the forehead; if that blow did not kill the animal, they plunged the knife into the back of the neck or the throat. Since such a profane act could never be done near an entryway or in the presence of the sun, the guards dragged the beast toward the shadowed north side behind the *ger.* The ox would be out of sight of the door, but so would they.

As soon as the guards passed out of sight, the would-be assassin headed straight for the door, which consisted of a felt blanket draped over an opening about four feet high. The Tatar raised the flap and entered.

Hoelun had no reason to suspect the cruel intent of the bedraggled young man standing before her, and, although the mother of the most powerful chief on the steppe, she continued to observe the simple traditions of hospitality followed by every nomadic family. Any traveler arriving at her tent could expect hot food and rest before continuing across the steppe. A gentle fire of dried animal dung, the focal point of the *ger* and the symbol of the family, burned constantly in the center of the open space beneath a smoke hole that also served as the only window in the structure. Milk and water always stood ready, awaiting the arrival of any lost hunters, chilled herders, returning warriors, and other passing strangers in need of food, warmth, or simple human companionship. If no fresh meat was available, dried beef and yak hung in the rafters; by adding these to water, Hoelun could produce a nourishing soup within minutes. She might offer the traveler a bowl of broth or a small snack of sheep tail fat that could be held over the glowing dung to cook. Soup was their staple, and the Mongols rarely added herbs, spices, or flavoring other than trace amounts of salt.

Although her husband had been killed by the Tatars nearly twenty-five years earlier, she would not have been suspicious of this Tatar now. The Tatar tribe had been thoroughly incorporated into the Mongol nation. Genghis Khan had married a Tartar queen and, at her request, had also accepted her elder sister as a wife. In an effort to set a good example for other women of the tribe, Hoelun had adopted a Tatar orphan, raising him to become one of the first people to read and write the Mongolian language, using the recently borrowed Uighur script. He had grown into a respected leader, and, although not a great warrior, he would soon become the supreme judge of the nation.

When the Tatar arrived, Hoelun was alone in the *ger* with Altani, a girl about ten to fourteen years old. Altani may have been one of Hoelun's granddaughters, or perhaps an adopted child.

Hoelun and Altani remained on the eastern side of the tent, where women did most of their work and kept their tools. By custom, even the humblest visitor could enter unannounced and sit quietly by the door on the western (the male) side of the *ger*. The Tatar did precisely that, assuming the place assigned for an ordinary man, servant, beggar, or other humble petitioner.

The inside of the *ger* was normally a quiet haven. People whispered. Gestures had to be kept to a minimum in an environment where a simple toss of the hand or flick of the wrist might hit grandmother in the head, knock over a bowl of hot tea, or even bring down a low ceiling rafter or part of the wall. To make the body as small as possible when seated, Mongols rarely stretched out their legs, and never did so in the direction of the fire. A male usually folded one leg under his body and drew the knee of the other leg up to his chest, wrapping his arm around it or even resting his chin on it. Inside the *ger,* everyone sought to become as unimposing as was practicable.

Even if Hoelun had known that the visitor carried a knife, she would not have been surprised or alarmed. Herders often concealed knives and other tools inside their garments. Men and women wore the same basic clothing, and it was ideal for hiding things. Large leather boots came up to the knees, but they were spacious enough inside to allow for thick strips of winter insulation of fur and felt. The main clothing was the *deel:* a large tunic coat held in place by a massive leather belt or cloth sash, while a few knotted buttons secured the top over the right breast. The most noted characteristic of Mongol clothing was its bulky size, as it was made for insulation and for comfort when riding in cold weather. The *deel* was always large enough to enclose a child, a lamb, or anything else requiring protection. Because of the fierce cold, herders packed an assortment of goods inside the *deel,* such as water canteens and food, to prevent them from freezing.

The sleeves were so large and long that a sword could be easily hidden in one. Because the herders' hands needed to be free for work, they did not wear gloves; instead they had wide, open sleeves that hung down several inches past the fingertips. While riding horses in the winter, a Mongol pulled the reins up into the sleeve of the coat so as to have warmth without sacrificing the sensitive details of holding the reins firmly against the naked flesh of the fingers.

Hoelun, Altani, and the Tatar would have been dressed nearly identically except for their hair. All the decorative and sexual symbolism of their appearance was concentrated on the head. Women pulled the hair high on their head and packed it with animal fat to prevent lice. To make the forehead appear large, they emphasized it by smearing it with yellow makeup. By contrast, men wore a small clump of bangs in the middle of the forehead directly above the nose. Aside from the bangs, men shaved most of the head except for two large clumps just above each ear. They never cut these tufts, but instead braided them into "horns" that hung down to the shoulders and often grew so long that they had to be looped back over the ear.

The Great Khan's mother knew how to deal with men and certainly did not fear them; she had already raised ten boys, including the four she had with her husband, two that he had with another wife, plus the four she adopted after becoming a widow. Even now she had two children staying with her, and at least one of her sons or grandsons was probably about the same age as the Tatar who was now within an arm's reach of her.

In her old age, Hoelun was raising not only Altani but also Tolui, Genghis Khan's youngest son and her youngest grandson. Tolui had just reached the age when he could run around outside the *ger* by himself. From the time children could crawl, they needed to be constrained. Infants were held gently and passed constantly from person to person or, when necessary, were tightly tied with a rope to keep them away from the flames of the fire.

At age four or five, Tolui was now old enough to go near the hearth without injuring himself. As the youngest boy, he enjoyed special privileges and was called *otchigen* or *otgon*, "the prince of the fire." Because he was the last to leave his mother's womb, he held the closest connection to the past: In him resided the honor and future of the family. One day he would be charged with caring for his aged parents, and he could inherit their animals and household. In giving him the name Tolui, which referred to the three stones used to make a fire in the center of the *ger*, his parents clearly stated the boy's symbolic importance.

Before the soup finished heating, young Tolui threw open the felt flap hanging over the door and dashed into the *ger*. With the impulsive energy of a four-year-old, he raced inside with no particular purpose and turned to run out again. At this moment, rage stirred inside the Tatar and then erupted. Without warning, and before Tolui could get through the flap a second time, the stranger lunged from his seat, grabbed up Tolui in his arms, and ran out the doorway with him. To rob a family of its youngest son was to deprive it of its heir. In addition to the emotional pain of losing the little Prince of the Fire, such a loss, akin to the departure of his ancestors' support and the blessing of the sky, carried enough supernatural importance to jeopardize the career of Genghis Khan.

Before the grandmother could scream for help, Altani jumped up and tore out the door behind the kidnapper. She chased after him, and when she drew near, the Tatar pulled out his knife. Tolui struggled to free himself, but to no avail. The assailant sought to turn Tolui slightly in his arms in order to stab the knife into the boy's jugular vein or heart.

Just as the Tatar had Tolui in position and was ready to thrust in the knife, Altani leapt on him. In the words of the *Secret History*, "With one hand she seized his plaits" (referring to the large braid over each ear), "and with the other she seized the hand that was drawing the knife." She fought to keep the Tatar's arm down and the weapon away from the boy, and "she pulled it so hard that he dropped the knife."

Even after disarming the attacker, Altani clung to him as tightly as he clutched the child, and the Tatar fought to escape her hold. She could not overpower him alone, but because of her weight and tight grip, he could not throw her off to escape with the boy.

Behind the *ger*, the guards had just slaughtered the ox and commenced butchering it when they heard the screams. Dropping the meat, they ran around the *ger* toward the sound of the struggle between Altani and the Tatar. The two men reached her, clutching their butchering tools in "their fists red with the animal's blood." The guard with the ax raised it and struck the Tatar. Altani grabbed Tolui and pulled him aside while the two guards finished off his assailant "with ax and knife."

Soon after the incident, the guards began to vie over which one of them deserved the credit for having saved the child: the one who knocked the kidnapper unconscious with the ax or the one who cut him open with the knife. With a strong tone of self-congratulation, they wondered aloud: "If we had not been there and if, by running fast and arriving in time, we had not killed him, what would Altani, a woman, have done?" The attacker "would have harmed the life of the child."

Altani heard their boastful talk and objected to their claiming credit for saving Tolui. She demanded recognition for what she had done. "I ran up and caught up with him, seizing his plaits and pulling the hand that was drawing the knife," she declared to the men. "If the knife had not dropped, wouldn't he have done harm to the child's life before Jetei and Jelme arrived?"

Although Jelme and Jetei both received awards and promotions, Genghis Khan made it clear who was the true hero of the episode, and "the chief merit went, by general consent, to Altani." Genghis Khan held her up as a model for everyone. In the Mongol perspective, challenges choose us, but we choose how to respond. Destiny brings the opportunities and the misfortunes, and the merit of our lives derives from those unplanned moments.

The Mongols, and certainly Genghis Khan in particular, placed great importance on sudden individual acts of unexpected heroism. Those are the moments that reveal not just the character of the person, but the soul itself. Many people are paralyzed by fear or, equally as debilitating, by indecision. The hero acts, and often fails, but acts nonetheless. Such a person belongs to the spiritual elite of the divinely blessed and heavenly inspired *baatar*, a person filled with a firm, strong, unyielding spirit. Usually translated simply as "hero," the word is much more important in Mongolian, containing an emphasis on the personal will behind the act; the heroes formed an honored group known as the *baatuud*.

Genghis Khan always sought out the service of the *baatar*, the hero who acts immediately and decisively without concern for personal benefit or even survival. Unlike the Greek heroes, who were males of superhuman physical strength, the *baatar* might be male or female, young or old, and frequently, as in this case, only a child. Most important, a *baatar* might spring from any family, but, in Genghis Khan's experience, the *baatuud* rarely came from rich families or aristocratic and powerful clans. He placed such importance on the spirit of the *baatuud* that he built his military and political system around them. The ideal government for him was rule by these heroic elites, by a true aristocracy of the spirit.

In this regard, Genghis Khan differed remarkably from those around him who believed in a natural aristocracy of birth. These old clans had dominated the steppe tribes for generations and claimed power as a birthright earned by the actions of their ancestors. More than any other barrier, this attitude and the actions derived from it had held Genghis Khan back in life. The aristocracy of birth had been his eternal enemy, and he sought to defeat it through his assembly of heroes: the aristocracy of brave spirits, the *baatuud*.

All his life, Genghis Khan had been treated as an outsider, as an inferior underling. The Mongols were interlopers onto the steppe. They were hunters from a far northern land of lakes and forests, where they had originally lived in temporary cone-shaped tents made of bark. Over the generations they had gradually moved out of the forests in the area of Mount Burkhan Khaldun at the source of the Onon and Kherlen rivers in the north-central region of modern Mongolia.

When the hunting was bad, they scavenged off the herding tribes, stealing animals, women, and whatever else they could before dashing back to the security of their mountainous hideouts. The older Turkic steppe tribes had herded for many centuries, and they looked down on the primitive Mongols, treating them as vassals and expecting them to bring forest gifts of fur and game. They found the Mongols sometimes useful as warriors to help them in a raid, or to herd their animals, and they sometimes stole women from them. Overall, however, the sophisticated herding tribes of the Tatars, Naiman, and Kereyid despised the Mongols.

With round faces, high cheekbones, and legs markedly bowed from their life on horseback, the Mongols' appearance set them apart from their Asian neighbors. They had extremely pale skin, kept lubricated by cleaning with animal fat, and had almost no body hair, leading a South Asian chronicler to write that the Mongols "looked like so many white demons." From frequent exposure to the bitter cold, their cheeks became so red through the nearly translucent skin that they were described as having "faces like fire."

They had wide mouths and large teeth of a uniform size, which, because of the lack of starches in the diet, did not rot or become discolored. Aside from skin color, the most distinctive Mongol trait was the eye shape. Several Chinese commentators remarked on the unusual eyelids of the Mongols, because these nomads did not have a crease or fold. Only late in life, or when they became tired, did a large wrinkle or fold begin to appear in the skin covering the eye. Persian observers referred to the Mongols as having "cat eyes." Another Muslim chronicler wrote that "their eyes were so narrow and piercing that they might have bored a hole in a brazen vessel."

Queen Gurbesu of the Christian Naiman tribe to the west summed up the attitude of civilized steppe people toward the Mongols: "The Mongols have always stunk and worn filthy clothes. They live far away; let them stay there." Only begrudgingly did she acknowledge some potential use for the Mongol women. "Perhaps we can bring their daughters here, and if they wash their hands we might let them milk our cows and sheep."

In this marginal and insignificant tribe, Genghis Khan grew up in an insignificant family of outcasts. He was born the son of a captured woman and was given the name Temujin because his father had recently killed a Tatar warrior by that name. His father belonged to the Borijin clan, and although they had once had an independent khan, they now served as virtual vassals for hire for whoever needed them. Before the boy was nine years old, the Tatars had killed his father, but his own Mongol relatives committed the worst offenses against Temujin's family. Feeling no responsibility for this captive wife and her brood of children, his uncles seized his dead father's animals and cast the widow and children out on the steppe to die of hunger and exposure in the brutal winter. When they survived against all odds, young Temujin was captured by the Tayichiud clan, who enslaved him and yoked him to a wooden collar like an ox. After escaping from bondage, he fled to the most isolated place he could find to care for his mother and siblings.

Living as a pariah with three brothers and two half brothers, but only one much younger sister, Temujin grew up surrounded by boys in a household oddly bereft of adult men or girls. From the beginning of his life, Temujin's male relatives repeatedly failed him and threatened his life at the most critical moments. At age twelve, Temujin so intensely disliked the bullying of his older half brother that he killed him.

Around 1179 he married Borte, a girl from a steppe clan distantly related to his mother, when he was about sixteen and she was seventeen. Although the couple expected to spend their lives together, enemies from the Merkid tribe stormed down on them, kidnapped Borte, and gave her to another man. Desperate to rescue his new wife, Temujin tracked and saved Borte, killing a large number of Merkid in the process, revealing a tenacious spirit and a nearly ruthless willingness to use whatever violence necessary to achieve his goals.

The kidnapping of Borte initiated young Temujin into steppe politics, with its perpetual low-grade hostility interrupted by spasms of amazing violence and destruction. In order to rescue Borte from the Merkid, Temujin made alliances with Ong Khan of the Kereyid tribe, the most powerful steppe chief at the moment, and with his childhood friend Jamuka. With new allies came new enemies, and the boy who had been raised as an outcast on the steppe found himself thrust into the maelstrom of dynastic struggles, clan feuds, and all the desperate treachery of steppe politics.

For the Kereyid, Temujin was, like his father and all men of his

Borijin clan, just one more Mongol vassal to be sent out to war when needed and consigned to perform the tasks that were too dangerous or boring. Temujin thought that through his extreme loyalty and his success in battle, he would gain the favor of his overlords.

Traditionally among the steppe nomads, related lineages united to form a clan, and, in turn, several clans united to form a tribe such as the Tatars or the Kereyid, or even a confederacy of tribes such as the Naiman. Although contracting or expanding over time, these unions lasted for generations and sometimes centuries. The Mongols repeatedly sought to unite into a tribe under one khan, but the union always failed. The Mongols were not so much a tribe as a roving set of fractious clans sharing the same language and culture but often fighting one another. Even within the same clan, families often feuded, broke away, and joined rival clans or enemy tribes.

Temujin's mother was not a Mongol, and his connection to her gave him a perceived opportunity to rise up in the steppe world by negotiating a formal marriage alliance with his mother's family in the Khongirad clan. Around 1184, when he was about twenty-two years old, Temujin arranged a marriage for Temulun, his only sister, with Botu of the Ikires. Such a marriage alliance would strengthen the tie between the two clans in the traditional way and showed Temujin's desire to maintain permanent marital alliances, known as *quda*. Because Temujin was still quite a novice in all respects, it seems likely that his mother, Hoelun, helped arrange this marriage.

Before the marriage, Botu "came as a son-in-law," meaning that he came to live with the bride's family as a form of service to them. According to steppe tradition, a potential groom or engaged boy resided with the family of his intended wife. Similarly, Temujin had been given at age eight to the family of his future wife, Borte, with the expectation that he would learn their ways of doing things, live under their supervision, and care for their animals. The boy had to prove himself as a capable herder, and after learning the basics as a child among his own family, he became an adult man under the watchful eye of his bride's parents. If the boy proved lazy or unsatisfactory, the family sent him away. If he could not endure the hard work and discipline imposed by his potential father- and mother-in-law, he might run away. If they developed a working relationship, the marriage between the engaged youths would evolve and blossom in its own natural time.

Bride service could sometimes be shortened, or occasionally avoided entirely, if the boy's family offered animals, usually horses, to the bride's family. Temujin and his future brother-in-law operated from different premises in arranging the marriage, which became apparent during a casual conversation with another man of Botu's family. Temujin sought to know more about his future brother-in-law by asking how many horses Botu owned. The man took the question as an opening for a horse negotiation for the marriage in place of service to the bride's family. He responded that Botu owned thirty horses and that he would give Genghis Khan fifteen of them in exchange for Temulun.

The offer of horses for his sister outraged Temujin, though not entirely for her sake. It showed that the prospective groom did not perceive Temujin as a worthy ally, but merely as a savage Mongol trying to sell his sister for some horses.

"If one is concluding a marriage and discusses value," Temujin angrily responded, "then one is acting like a merchant." Temujin commenced to lecture the man: "The ancients had a saying: 'Unity of purpose is a fortune in affliction.'" He then applied that proverb to the current situation. "If you, the people of the Ikires, follow Botu and serve me faithfully, that will suffice." Service always outranked wealth; loyalty always outranked payments. Despite the heated exchange between the young men, the marriage was arranged, possibly through the intercession of Hoelun and her connection to the groom's family.

With this early negotiation, the young Temujin articulated a firm principle, which he followed throughout his life when dealing with the women of his family: Women could never be traded for animals or property. Once he came to power, he made this personal affirmation into law.

Temujin's desire to make his mother's relatives his allies, or possibly even vassals, showed his ambition to rise up in steppe political life. Although only partially successful in making this first alliance, by the summer of 1189, when he was about twenty-seven years old, Temujin had enough support within his small part of the Mongol tribe to be selected as khan, their chieftain. He was still only a minor leader of a small group on the steppe, but henceforth he was known as Genghis Khan, "the Indomitable and Supreme Khan." For now, his title seemed excessive for the leader of such a small group, but over the years, he fulfilled its meaning more than anyone probably expected at the time.

As the totemic emblem of his clan, Genghis Khan used the image of the hunting falcon that had been the constant companion of one of his ancestors and had saved his life by capturing prey for him after his brothers abandoned him. The hunting falcons were always female. The female falcon attains a body weight and size 30 percent greater than the male, thus permitting her to capture larger prey and making her a more efficient mother or, in the case of captive falcons, a more valued hunter.

Over the next decade, Genghis Khan concentrated on fighting at the behest of his overlord, Ong Khan of the Kereyid. He repeatedly rescued his patron's kidnapped family members, avenged insults to the khan's honor, and struck out at allies who deserted the khan. He was not the best archer on the steppe, the fastest horseman, or the strongest wrestler, yet he proved to be the best warrior. His extreme tenacity, combined with a quick ability to try new tactics, gradually made him the most feared, if not the most respected, leader on the steppe.

Consistently triumphant on the battlefield, Genghis Khan once again sought to translate that success into social advancement for his family through marriage. Around 1201 or 1202, when his eldest son,

Jochi, was over twenty and his eldest daughter, Khojin, was about fifteen or sixteen, he felt successful and powerful enough to arrange marriages for them with the family of his lord, Ong Khan. After several
decades as loyal allies, Ong Khan and Genghis Khan had recently
sworn oaths to each other as father and son. To solidify this relationship, Genghis Khan proposed two marriages to his newly adopted
father: "On top of affection let there be more affection."

Specifically, Genghis Khan proposed that his eldest son, Jochi, marry
Ong Khan's daughter and, in turn, that his eldest daughter marry Ong
Khan's grandson. Had Genghis Khan merely offered his daughter in
marriage, the act would have been seen as homage from a vassal; she
would have been a gift. By asking for a set of marriages, Genghis Khan
knew that this would be seen as making Mongols equal to Kereyid and
himself equal to Ong Khan's other son.

Understanding the threat this posed to his own position, Ong
Khan's son Senggum, father of the potential groom, objected strenuously. With such a pair of marriages, Genghis Khan would be so
closely united with the family of Ong Khan that when the old khan
died, Genghis Khan might easily nudge Senggum out of the way and
become the new leader.

In a Mongolian *ger,* the place of honor has always been on the
northern side of the tent, directly opposite the doorway. Using the
metaphors of the *ger,* Senggum complained: "If a woman of our clan
goes to them, she will stand by the door looking in at the north of
the *ger.* If a woman of their clan comes to us, she will sit in the north
of the tent looking toward the door and fire." Persuaded by these
words, Ong Khan rejected the marriage proposals.

This refusal broke relations between Genghis Khan and his long-
time ally and mentor. After years of their working closely together, the
old khan would not recognize a Mongol as his son, nor as equal to a
Kereyid, no matter how incapable his own flesh and blood had been or
how successful and meritorious Genghis Khan was. Yet again, the
future conqueror was reminded that however good a warrior he might
be and however loyal a vassal, he was only a Mongol in the eyes of his

superiors. Now that he was well into his forties, they probably judged him as past his prime. He had done his duty, but the Kereyid could find another, younger replacement just as eager to do their bidding.

The simmering resentment turned to bitter anger, and war quickly broke out between Genghis Khan's Mongols and the Kereyid. This time, Genghis Khan was losing. Until now his bravery and skill had been exercised under the patronage of the Kereyid, but, left completely to his own devices, he found little support from other tribes. In 1203, the Kereyid routed his Mongols, and he fled with a small remnant to the east of Mongolia. It was the lowest time in the professional life of Genghis Khan. After fighting for almost a quarter of a century, he was a failed and defeated middle-aged man who had dared to rise above his position in life and think himself equal to the noble clans of the steppe. His sworn brother and childhood friend, Jamuka, had long ago turned against him. Many of his relatives had deserted him, and he had lost contact with others in the confusion after his defeat. He had not even been able to make a successful marriage for a single one of his children. His sons offered little assistance, and it now became clear that none was a hero.

During the most severe crises and gravest dangers, Genghis Khan usually fled to Mount Burkhan Khaldun. He felt a strong spiritual connection to the mountain and to its protective spirit. Mongols viewed mountains as males connected to the Eternal Blue Sky; waters were female, the sacred blood of Mother Earth. However, because of the proximity of the Kereyid court and army, Genghis Khan did not feel safe fleeing to Burkhan Khaldun this time. Instead he went far to the east in search of refuge near the Khalkh River.

Genghis Khan had only a small contingent of his army and former followers. The east, however, was the homeland of his mother, and his only sister had married there. In the intervening years, Temulun had died without children, but he hoped it might be possible to negotiate a new marriage for one of his daughters. In desperation, he sought out Terge Emel, one of his mother's relatives, in an attempt to build an alliance.

Terge Emel had never sided with Genghis Khan in the past and showed no affection for Mongols in general. He had been an ally of Jamuka and seemingly every other rival Genghis Khan had faced. Despite all this earlier antagonism, Genghis Khan believed that the offer of a marriage alliance might persuade Terge Emel to overlook those past differences and now save him.

The proposal would be a gentle plea for peace and cooperation through a marriage, but if that proposition failed, Genghis Khan was prepared to fight to bring his mother's relations into his fold. "If they do not come and join us of their own accord," he explained, in a graphic evocation of the way women gathered fuel to build a fire, "we shall go out, wrap them up like dry horse dung in a skirt and bring them here!"

"Your daughter looks like a frog," Terge Emel said to Genghis Khan, echoing one of the derisive descriptions hurled at the Mongols because of their unusual appearance. "I won't marry her."

Terge Emel's contempt for Genghis Khan indicates how low the Mongols ranked in the hierarchy of steppe tribes. At this moment, Genghis Khan resembled little more than a petty chief of an insignificant band, unlikely to be known beyond a small circle of enemies who seemed about to extinguish him and his followers forever. Even Terge Emel's kinship with Genghis Khan was no honor, having happened only because Genghis Khan's father had kidnapped his wife from her first husband in another tribe. Such a crime hardly constituted an affectionate kinship tie.

Having failed to persuade Terge Emel into a marriage alliance and having little else to lose, Genghis Khan killed him.

In the summer of 1203, after the death of Terge Emel, Genghis Khan wandered with the remnants of his army near a now unknown place in eastern Mongolia that he called Baljuna Waters. With no food left, he and his men had only the muddy water of the lake to sustain them, their single horse having already been eaten.

At this moment of dire physical need and emotional exhaustion, Genghis Khan looked out at the horizon and saw a man coming toward him on a white camel, almost like a hazy mirage breaking through the shimmering summer heat. Behind him came more camels, laden with trade goods, and a flock of sheep. The man was Hassan, a merchant who had crossed the Gobi into Mongolia leading camels and bearing food and merchandise to trade for sable furs and squirrel pelts. He happened to arrive in search of water at just the moment when Genghis Khan's army seemed threatened with a lingering death by starvation or falling into the hands of his enemies.

Hassan was identified as a member of the Sartaq, a term used by Mongols for both Muslims and merchants, but he came in the employ of a different ethnic group. He had been sent by Ala-Qush, a chief of the Onggud people, a Christian Turkic tribe from six hundred miles south, well beyond the Gobi, which marked the edge of the nomad's world.

Although the Mongols had nothing to trade at that moment, Hassan offered them sheep to eat and fresh horses in anticipation that he would one day be repaid for his generosity. The arrival of this unexpected aid seemed like divine intervention from the spirit of the lake; Genghis Khan's men certainly took the appearance of the Onggud and his supply of meat as a sign of heavenly favor on their leader and their undertaking.

The episode of Baljuna Waters marked the last moment of hopelessness for Genghis Khan, the last time that his army was defeated. From that day on, he might have occasional setbacks, but he was forever victorious, always triumphant. He never forgot his gratitude to the spirit of Baljuna, the spirit of the Khalkh River, or his debt to his new allies, the Onggud.

The summer of 1203 marked the turning point for Genghis Khan and the Mongols. They had been saved by a foreign merchant, and, now reinvigorated, they returned toward their homeland, where, by what seemed to the Mongols as divine guidance, people began to flock to Genghis Khan. He and his men had proved their hardiness, their willingness to stare defeat in the eye and still not back down. The people hailed them as a band of heroes.

Suddenly the spirit on the steppe had changed, and new followers also flocked to Genghis Khan. He quickly made his first marriage ally by negotiating an alliance with Ong Khan's brother Jaka Gambu, who hoped that with Mongol help he might depose his brother and become the khan of the Kereyid. To cement the new union, Genghis Khan accepted Jaka Gambu's daughter Ibaka as his wife. Jaka Gambu took Genghis Khan's youngest son, the ten-year-old Tolui, as a husband for his other daughter, Sorkhokhtani, who was several years older.

With his new allies among the rebel faction of the Kereyid and his supplies from the Onggud, Genghis Khan's fortunes had turned. In the next two years he quickly defeated all steppe opponents, and he was able to give his mother a white camel as a gift, possibly the same one Hassan had ridden to the rescue of the Mongols.

The episode beside the Khalkh River and the Baljuna Waters not only changed Genghis Khan's political fortunes, it appears to have produced a subtle, yet profound, change in his spirituality. He had spent most of his life in the land of his father, but he had been rescued in the land of his mother. He had spent most of his life relying on the spiritual aid of the male mountain, but it was the female waters that had saved him.

Genghis Khan's words after this time began to articulate this spiritual duality. According to his new vision, each person's destiny demanded the dual support of the strength offered by Father Sky and the protection of Mother Earth. Without one, the other was doomed to failure. Genghis Khan described the source of his success as "strength increased by Heaven and Earth." As stated in the *Secret History,* his inspiration and destiny were "called by Mighty Heaven," but they were "carried through by Mother Earth."

The Sky inspired; the Earth sanctioned. Any person might have inspiration from the Sky and be filled with longing, desire, and ambition, but only the devoted and sustained actions of the Earth could transform those desires and that inspiration into reality. The world is composed of sky or heaven above and water and earth below and the Mongols considered it a grave sin to insult or utter disrespectful words about either the sky or water. We live in the realm of Mother Earth, also sometimes called Dalai Ege, "Mother Sea," because her waters give life to the dry bones of the Earth.

Mother Earth provided or prevented success. She controlled the animals that Genghis Khan might find to hunt and eat or that might evade him entirely. She made water available or denied it. Repeatedly in the midst of some venture, Mother Earth saved his life by hiding him in the trees of her forest, in the water of her river, in the boulders on her ground, or in the cover of her darkness.

Whenever a person boasted about his achievements or bragged about his exploits without recognizing the role of Mother Earth in granting that success, it could be said that his mouth made him think that he was better than water. To avoid that characterization, Genghis Khan scrupulously acknowledged the role of both Father Sky and Mother Earth in everything that he accomplished.

The balance of male and female became a guiding principle in Genghis Khan's political strategy and tactics, as well as in his spiritual worldview. This theology formed the intellectual and religious organization of life based on the religion of Mother Earth and the Eternal Blue Sky. Maintaining the correct balance and mixture of these two forces sustained an individual, a family, and the nation. For Genghis Khan, negotiating the dualism of existence, finding the correct balance, became a lifetime quest.

In honoring the supernatural power of the Earth, and therefore her lakes and rivers, as the source of success, Genghis Khan's Mongols displayed a strong cultural and spiritual association with the female element of water. Before his nation became renowned as the Mongol Empire, his people were often called "Water Mongols," a name that seemed distinctly inappropriate for a people who inhabited an environment as dry as the Mongolian Plateau and situated so far from the ocean. European maps of Asia persistently identified his tribe by the name Water Mongols or its Turkish translation, *Suu Mongol*. This unusual designation continued to appear on Western maps until late in the seventeenth century, but seemingly without awareness of the name's connection to the important role that the Mongols ascribed to the female power of water as the life-giving substance of Mother Earth.

Years earlier, when his small tribe chose him to be their leader, Genghis Khan had chosen to receive the honor in a spiritually balanced place between the female Blue Lake and the male Black Heart Mountain. Now he would again choose such a spiritually balanced place where he would ask all the tribes of the steppe to accept him as their supreme ruler.

Rivers and mountains not only had a name and gender, they bore honorific titles as well. Mountains were the bones of the Earth and male, and the highest mountain always had the title of *khan*. Rivers and lakes that never ran dry bore the title *khatun*, "queen," and the Onon at the birthplace of the Mongols was called mother. Genghis Khan summoned the tribes to meet at the headwaters of the Onon River near Burkhan Khaldun. Here by the father mountain and the mother river, he would create the Mongol Empire.

The Growling Dragon and the Dancing Peacock

"WILL THEY COME? WILL THEY COME?" For the nomadic tribes of the Mongolian Plateau in the late winter and spring of 1206, that was the big question. Weary of the constant feuding, bickering, and raiding, Genghis Khan had sent out messengers to convene a *khuriltai*, a large political meeting or parliament of the steppes, with the purpose of getting allies and potential rivals alike to officially accept his leadership, thus allowing him to proclaim a permanent peace under a new government.

If they came, he would reorganize them into new tribes, issue new laws, and proclaim a new nation. In return, he promised peace among the tribes with greater prosperity and prestige for them all. During more than two decades of fighting, Genghis Khan had tenaciously proved his ability on the battlefield by conquering every tribe on the steppe and destroying their ruling clan, but could he now control them?

No formal vote would be held at the *khuriltai;* the nomads voted by coming or by not coming. Their arrival constituted an affirmation of support for Genghis Khan and the new government; not coming made them his enemies. Most of the people had fought on his side; some had fought against him. Many had achieved victory with him, and others had been defeated by his Mongol soldiers.

The site for this gathering was chosen with care. He needed a large, wide area with enough water and grass for thousands of animals.

Genghis Khan selected the open steppe between the Onon and Kherlen rivers, south of the sacred mountain Burkhan Khaldun, where he often hid from enemies and found a spiritual refuge. The Mongols inhabited the northern edge of the steppe and the southern side of the more forested hunting areas, and Genghis Khan wanted the meeting to be held in the territory of his birth and the land of his ancestors.

Although the site may have met the specific material requirements, it was a highly unusual place, even a strange one, for the tribes to be asked to gather. No important *khuriltai* had ever been organized in this area on the mountainous border of the steppe. For thousands of years, back through the great tribal empires of the Turks, Uighurs, and Huns, the focal point of steppe life had been farther to the west near the complex of rivers known as the Orkhon, which formed a more natural crossroads of nomadic routes. From this junction the Huns set out on their treks to distant Europe and India. Here the tribes had always traded foreign goods with the outside world and one another; here they had embraced foreign religions, first Manichaeism and later its twin, Christianity. The tribes along the Orkhon once had small cities, temples, and even a little agriculture. They erected monuments inscribed in Chinese and ancient Turkish nearly five hundred years before the Mongols' rise to prominence. In his choice of venue, away from the older cultural center, Genghis Khan violated steppe tradition and showed how different he planned the future of the tribes to be.

Since no large *khuriltai* had been held in the area of Burkhan Khaldun, it had to be prepared for the thousands of people who would be coming there for the first time. Preparations began well before the thick pavement of ice across the Kherlen and Onon began to break into large chunks and melt. Parties of men were sent into the forests in the mountains to chop down tall pines and drag them back to the staging ground with oxen teams; these trees would be trimmed into poles to hold up the large ceremonial tents for the summer activities. Piles of wood and hills of dung had to be gathered up to dry, in order to fuel the many fires that would be needed.

The main routes leading toward the meeting ground had to be

cleared of animals, to maintain grass corridors through which the participants might pass with their herds. Closer to the area, even larger tracts had to be vacated; this measure would ensure that when the melting snow allowed the first blades of grass to appear, animals would not immediately nibble them away. The broad pastures would become the feeding grounds for the herds that would accompany the nomads.

Large iron cauldrons had to be hauled in from miles around on carts pulled by oxen and yaks. These were the largest metal objects on the Mongolian Plateau; some were large enough to cook a whole horse or ox. Each was a treasure, and gathered together they not only provided the means for cooking food for thousands but made an impressive display of wealth and the organization needed to create and move it. If the people would come, the pots would remain cooking over the fires night and day.

For many miles around the assembly area, soldiers organized and prepared the grounds where the nation would camp. The Mongols used the same simple arrangement, whether for a small cluster of three *gers* or an assembly of thousands. The main *ger* stood in the middle with the others arranged in wings to the east and west. A series of twelve additional camps, each laid out on the same pattern, encircled the main camp for a total of thirteen. Each of Genghis Khan's four wives and his mother had her own separate court with retainers and guards.

Despite all the preparations, the outcome could not be determined. Could he do all that he promised? Would they have enough faith in him to try out his new government, his new nation? Would they come?

Even if they had already sworn allegiance to Genghis Khan and promised to attend the *khuriltai*, any clan could easily abstain at the last minute. They could gather their *gers* and animals and flee to some remote steppe beyond the reach of Genghis Khan. If necessary, they could take refuge with a surrounding nation, such as the territories controlled by their Chinese, Turkic, or Tibetan neighbors south of the Gobi, where Genghis Khan's power did not yet reach.

The assembly would do much more than merely give the people a leader; it would reshape their identity. In order to prevent former enemies from conspiring against him, most of Genghis Khan's subjects would be separated from their kin and assigned to groups of strangers, moved from their old homeland and assigned unknown territories, and in some cases have their names changed. The anticipated reorganization only heightened the uncertainty over who would come.

As spring turned to summer, the first few families began to arrive with their animals. They came in their carts pulled by oxen and yaks, riding their horses and camels, bringing a small flock of animals to supply their needs for the summer, but not so many that they would destroy the pastures. Their animals bore brands and earmarks from the farthest reaches of the steppe: symbols of the sun and moon, fire and water, the cardinal points and stars emblazoned on the hindquarters of their horses and on their banners.

The relatives of the Mongols came, and the families of Genghis Khan's wives arrived. The Turkic tribes and the Tatars of the steppe came dressed in felt with ornaments of exotic turquoise and coral. Delegations from the Siberian Forest People came dressed in fur and deerskin, as did the western tribes with their hunting eagles and the eastern tribes with their snow-leopard pelts, antelope-skin blankets, and bearskin rugs. The Onggud came across the Gobi mounted high on their camels and bringing garments of embroidered silk and the softest camel wool, more beautiful than anything ever seen in this remote hinterland.

The shamans came beating their drums and twirling wildly so that the long ribbons attached to their clothes seemed to lift them off the ground and made them appear to be flying in the wind. Young boys came with their heads freshly shaved for the summer and riding the finest horses, which they planned to race in the summer games that would celebrate the new nation. The girls came with pails of milk into which they dipped a long stick to throw milk into the air. Old men came with their magical rocks that they could clap together and control the weather, ushering in the ideal mixture of sun and occasional rain.

Perhaps weary from generations of feuding and anxious for peace, or perhaps just fearful of the power of Genghis Khan if they rejected him yet again, the leaders of virtually every tribe on the Mongolian Plateau arrived. They came as Tatars, Naiman, Merkid, Jurkin, Kereyid, and dozens of other names, but all those ancient and exalted designations would now be abandoned if they chose to become vassals of Genghis Khan. From this summer forward, they would all be a part of the nation that they had despised, derided, and scorned for so long: Mongol.

The people celebrated with great feasts of meat, an endless supply of fermented milk, and the usual Mongol sports of horse racing, archery, and wrestling. As the people amused themselves, Genghis Khan attended to the deadly serious business of organizing his army into the supreme weapon with which he would conquer the world. He created the new law and established a supreme judge to preside over its implementation. He rewarded his friends, allies, brothers, mother, and even strangers who had performed outstanding services for him.

Oddly, one of the first pressing pieces of business was a divorce, and even stranger was the reluctance with which Genghis Khan felt compelled to make it. His former ally Jaka Gambu had perceived Genghis Khan as the means by which he, Jaka Gambu, would replace his brother Ong Khan as the supreme leader on the steppe. Although he had married his daughter Ibaka to Genghis Khan, Jaka Gambu had no intention of sharing power, and after the defeat of Ong Khan, the two allies quickly turned against each other. The marriage had been made for political reasons, and when Jaka Gambu betrayed the Mongols, Genghis Khan's marriage with the rebel's daughter needed to be broken for political reasons.

In separating from her, Genghis Khan made one of the most emotional statements recorded in his life when he said, "You have entered into my heart and limbs." He had to divorce her to show that even the Great Khan obeyed the laws and yielded his personal desires to the needs of the state. "I did not say that you have a bad character," he explained to her, nor that "in looks and appearance you are ugly." He made the best possible marriage he could for her outside of his family by marrying her to one of his top generals and closest friends. "I present you to Jurchedei in deference to the great principle." To show the sincerity of his words and his high regard for her, he allowed her to keep her rank as queen, and he ordered his family to always honor her fully as a queen, as though she were still married to him. He ordered that even after his death they should treat her as his queen so they would remember that they, as he, must obey the law. "In the future, when my descendants sit on our throne, mindful of the principle regarding services that have thus been rendered, they should not disobey my words." As a further kindness toward Ibaka and her sister Sorkhokhtani, he allowed the latter to remain married to young Tolui, a decision that would later have dramatic consequences for the imperial dynasty.

Having punished one rival, Genghis Khan set about rewarding those who had been most loyal to him. His most pressing task as the new ruler of all the tribes was to divide up all the conquered lands and assign rulers to them. He did not give these lands to his sons or his generals; he gave all of them to his wives.

Each wife would rule her own territory and manage her own independent *ordo*, "court" (sometimes written as *ordu*). Borte Khatun received most of the Kherlen River, much of which had once belonged to the Tatars, with her *ordo* at Khodoe Aral near the Avarga stream that had formerly been held by the Jurkin clan. Khulan Khatun received the Khentii Mountains around Mount Burkhan Khaldun, which was the Mongol homeland. Yesui Khatun received the Tuul River, including the summer *ordo* of the Kereyid ruler, Ong Khan. Her elder sister, Yesugen Khatun, received the Khangai Mountains, which had been the territory of the Naiman.

Genghis Khan handed over the already conquered territories to his wives because now he was about to begin a new round of conquests, and for this he needed a new set of allies. A major part of the work that summer consisted in granting new marriages, ratifying marriages that had already been agreed to, and formally sanctifying some that had already occurred. He had won the wars by fighting, but now Genghis Khan sought to ensure peace through a thick network of marriage alliances. Traditionally, steppe khans took a wife from each of their vassal clans, but Genghis Khan never had more than four wives at a time. Borte always remained the chief one, and her children assumed precedence over all others.

Rather than taking a large number of wives, Genghis Khan sought to make marriage alliances for his children instead. Having twice failed to negotiate new alliances through marriages to his eldest son and daughter, he returned to a safer option. He negotiated another union with an already trusted ally, Botu of the Ikires, who had married Genghis Khan's sister, Temulun. Genghis Khan arranged for his eldest daughter, Khojin, to marry Botu.

This time Genghis Khan had no trouble negotiating marriages for his sons and daughters. He married three of his daughters to Mongols in the traditional system of *qudas,* marriage alliances. The three grooms were related to his mother, Hoelun, and his wife Borte. In addition to Khojin, a daughter married a relative of his wife Borte, and his fifth daughter, Tumelun, married another of his mother's relatives, though this marriage caused some confusion for chroniclers because of the similarity of her name to Genghis Khan's sister, Temulun.

Most of the participants in the *khuriltai* of 1206 came from the steppes, but a few delegations from the world beyond also participated; among these were Genghis Khan's newfound allies, the Onggud. The fortuitous meeting with the merchant Hassan at Baljuna had evidently made as deep an impression on the Onggud as it had on Genghis Khan, because some of them also became his followers. The decisive test for this impromptu alliance between the Mongols and the Onggud had come in 1205, two years after the Baljuna rescue. After rallying his followers to defeat the Tatars and the Kereyid, Genghis Khan faced only a single powerful confederation left on the steppes, the Naiman. The Naiman leader dispatched envoys to Ala-Qush, an Onggud leader, to woo him away from Genghis Khan and join them in a war against the upstart Mongols. Such an alliance might have been able to crush the newly emerging nation from opposite sides, or at least keep it from expanding further. Ala-Qush not only rejected the Naiman offer of an alliance but sent envoys to warn Genghis Khan of a planned Naiman trap.

According to tradition, when the Onggud envoys approached the camp of Genghis Khan, they brought with them a gift from civilization; this time it was wine made from grapes, a commodity previously unknown to the Mongols, but one destined to have a major impact on them and the success of their world empire. In recognition of their unique relationship, Genghis Khan agreed to a future marriage between his daughter Alaqai Beki and the son of Ala-Qush of the Onggud.

After the earlier failed marriage negotiations for his offspring, Genghis Khan always married his daughters to only the most trust-worthy of allies. He never permitted one to marry a rival, nor did he allow them to marry any of his generals or other subordinates. Despite the emphasis on rising in rank according to merit and deeds, he main-tained strict lineage segregation. His daughters married men from the aristocratic lineages of the steppes, and later he extended this practice to the ruling lineages of specially chosen neighboring kingdoms.

Genghis Khan's sons also married women from the same *quda* alliance lineages as his daughters. In addition, the sons, and Genghis Khan himself, sometimes took a different type of wife from the royal wives and daughters of defeated tribes. In each case, Genghis Khan and his sons married a widow or daughter of the dead khan, thereby unmistakably demonstrating that the men of Genghis Khan's family had replaced those former rulers. Thus Genghis Khan took two Tatar queens and a Merkid princess as wives, while arranging for his eldest and youngest sons to marry the Kereyid princesses who had been Ong Khan's nieces.

As part of the wedding ceremony, a Mongol bride stood in front of her new *ger* and put on the *boqta,* the tall headgear of a queen. She also put on all her jewelry. Before entering the *ger,* she walked between two large fires that sanctified her so that she might enter her marriage in

the purest possible state. The marriage happened without much ceremony, but for eight days afterward, people brought presents to the
couple. On the eighth day, the family would host a grand feast. As
described by Pétis de la Croix, "These feasts seldom end without some
quarrel, because they are too profuse of their liquors."

The husband had to have a place prepared for his new wife. In one
episode in which a khan brought in a new queen for whom he had not
yet prepared a home, he sought to bring her to the *ger* of his senior
wife. Out of hospitality for the younger woman, the elder queen did
not at first object and she went to sleep, apparently without suspecting
that the couple might try to consummate the marriage at that time.

However, during the night the khan became amorous with his
bride. The older queen, sleeping nearby, awoke. "How shall I watch
you two enjoying each other in bed?" she angrily asked them.

Although it was night, the senior queen ordered them out. "Leave
my *ger*!" Since there was no other *ger* in the vicinity, the khan and his
younger wife had to spend the night outside in the open. The next day,
the khan was able to make arrangements to move the young queen in
with some of his relatives until he could prepare her a place of her own.
In the *ger*, the wife ruled even if her husband happened to be a khan.

Her first felt home came from her husband's family, but through
the years she would gradually add to it by unrolling the insulating
blankets, called the "mother felt," and pounding in new wool to make
a series of fresh coverings, called the "daughter felts." In this way her
hands, her perspiration, and her soul became a part of the felt, and the
ger became more and more hers. Eventually, her sheets of daughter felt
would help to make new *gers* for her daughters-in-law; in this way,
from generation to generation, the walls of each generation would be
made from all the women who had married into the family through all
the generations.

During the festivities and business of the summer of 1206, Genghis
Khan gave a lengthy speech praising young Altani, who had saved the

life of Tolui, and arranged for her marriage to Boroghul, one of the orphans whom his mother had adopted. Of his three brothers, four sons, and four stepbrothers, Genghis Khan singled out only Boroghul as a *baatar*, or hero. When he was a young warrior of about seventeen years old, Boroghul had rescued Genghis Khan's third son, Ogodei, from the battlefield, after the prince had been shot and fallen off his horse, passing out from a lack of blood. Despite the close presence of enemies, Boroghul nursed Ogodei through the night, continuously sucking the blood from his neck and thereby preventing infection or blood poisoning. When dawn came, Boroghul loaded Ogodei onto his horse and, holding him tightly, managed to evade enemy patrols, bringing him safely home to his father.

The speech about Altani's bravery and the shorter mention of Boroghul's similar courage not only highlighted their status as heroes, but it also gently reminded Genghis Khan's own sons of their lack of achievement. His sons, even in adulthood, were still the objects of rescue, not the rescuers. They depended on others for heroism that they still had not shown. Sadly for Genghis Khan, they never would.

At the marriage of each of his daughters, Genghis Khan issued a nuptial decree making clear her responsibilities and, more important to everyone else, what her rights and powers would be. He spoke the words directly to his daughter (or in a few later cases had the text read to her on his behalf), but the true audience was not the daughter as much as the people whom she would soon join. He made no such proclamations at the weddings of his sons, and conferred no special powers or responsibilities on them beyond the normal expectations of a husband at marriage. The series of speeches to his daughters, however, provide cogent insight into his thinking and to the role that they would play in the empire. As a hint at just what innovative type of empire he intended to create, he conferred no powers on his sons-in-law in these decrees, and in fact chose not to mention them by name or address any comments to them.

Persian and Chinese chroniclers recorded the speeches for the later marriages, but the speech to his first daughter, Khojin, was apparently lost or possibly censored. One small speech survived from this time, attributed to Genghis Khan at the marriage of Altani. These words reflect his thinking at the time of his first daughter's marriage, and it is likely that he spoke similar words at her wedding.

When Genghis Khan arranged each of these marriages, he proclaimed equality between bride and groom. He conveyed his concept of the state and its government, as well as the relationship of husband and wife, through an important Mongol metaphor: Through marriage, the couple would become two shafts of one cart. As Genghis Khan described it, "If a two-shaft cart breaks the second shaft, the ox cannot pull it. . . . If a two-wheeled cart breaks the second wheel, it cannot move."

When moving, the cart transported a family's possessions, but when stationary, the cart served as the family pantry, warehouse, and treasury. The nomads stored most of their possessions in the cart so that they would be already packed and ready to flee at the first sign of trouble. As an extension of a married woman's ownership of the cart, the wife handled all issues related to money, barter, or commerce. From the first recorded observations, Mongol men showed an aversion to handling money and conducting commercial transactions. "The management of the man's fortune," according to Persian reports, "belongs to the women: They buy and sell as they think fit."

Repeatedly, when Genghis Khan wished to make an alliance with another man, he used this same imagery of the couple pulling one cart. His nuptial decree at Altani's marriage showed a creative innovation in the cart metaphor. Genghis Khan changed the system of dual leadership from two men, who called each other brother or father and son, into an image of man and woman, such as Boroghul and Altani. In this way, he sought to replicate the spiritual tradition of supernatural harmony through Father Sky and Mother Earth. Henceforth the husband would go to war, and the wife would be left in charge of running the home and, by extension, almost every aspect of civilian life. The system made perfect sense in the Mongol cultural tradition. Soon after making the nuptial speech to Altani and Boroghul, Genghis Khan sent the husband away on a military mission.

In describing his daughters and their husbands as two shafts of one cart, Genghis Khan made clear that an ancient division of labor applied to a new set of military and political goals. While the husband commanded the soldiers on defensive maneuvers or on military attack campaigns, the wife commanded the tribe at home. Genghis Khan had well-founded and unshakable faith in his daughters and the other women around him. "Whoever can keep a house in order," he said, "can keep a territory in order." As the military campaigns grew longer, the division of labor solidified into a division of command authority. At its heart, the dual-shaft system functioned quite simply. She ruled at home; he served abroad.

Even in matters of sexuality, the Mongol woman exhibited more control. Mongol men were considered sexually shy at marriage, and part of a wife's duty was to coax her husband into his role. Unlike other men whom the Mongols encountered, such as the Turks and Persians, who had a reputation for sexual skill and boldness and were the source of much good humor, the Mongol man was deemed to have other interests and responsibilities. Yet, if his wife could not persuade him to perform his marital role adequately, she had every right to publicly seek redress. In one later episode of a marriage arranged for a famous wrestling champion, Genghis Khan's son Ogodei asked the wife about her husband: "Have you had a full share of his pleasuring?"

She responded disappointedly that her husband had not touched her because he did not want to sap his strength and interfere with his athletic training. Ogodei summoned the wrestler and told him that fulfillment of his duties as a husband took priority over sporting activities. The champion had to give up wrestling and tend to his wife.

Sex within marriage was more easily regulated than love. Mongols recognized the importance of love, and they always hoped for it within marriage. One of the traditional nuptial speeches used in the twentieth century compared the marriage of Genghis Khan's daughters to the union of dragons and peacocks: "The dragon who growls in the blue clouds, the peacock who dances chanting in the green yard . . . Even when they are far apart—their songs of desire are closely united."

Duty outranked love, and the *baatar* always chose duty to family and country over love. Genghis Khan and Borte married for love, but none of their children had that opportunity. Each married for reasons of state, with the hope that love might develop from it. The emotional sacrifice demanded by Genghis Khan of his sons and daughters, however, was minor compared to that paid by the men who married his daughters.

The daughters of Genghis Khan bore the title *beki*, an honorific designation applied to either a prince or princess. The men who married them, however, did not receive the title *khan* or *beki*. They received the special title of *guregen*, generally meaning "son-in-law," but in this case the meaning was more akin to "prince consort." A man held the title only because of his marriage to the Great Khan's daughter. If he lost her, he lost the title. Because the *guregen* could be so easily replaced, the chronicles often merely used the title rather than the name. For most practical purposes in daily Mongol life, it mattered little which man was actually filling the post at the moment. If one died, another quickly stepped into his place. Usually the replacement would be a son, brother, or nephew of the last husband.

The *guregen* occupied a unique position within the Mongol imperial system. Despite the high prestige of his close kinship to Genghis Khan, he rarely held any influential military or civilian office. Genghis Khan kept the *guregen* literally close at hand; most of them received appointments within the *keshig*, the royal guard, and thus became intimate parts of Genghis Khan's personal camp. Those with superior ability became the leaders of their own military units, composed of about one thousand warriors from their own tribe or related clans, but under close supervision and never too far away from Genghis Khan. In this way, the best warriors in the *guregen*'s tribe were always separated from the majority of their tribe. A *guregen* had no chance to rise up within the hierarchy and no chance to wield independent power or launch his own campaigns. He held a prestigious but hardly enviable position in Mongol society.

The *guregen* served under their father-in-law, according to the tradition of bride service that Genghis Khan had revitalized and strengthened. Instead of herding the father-in-law's goats, camels, and yaks, these sons-in-law became herders of men; they would serve in Genghis Khan's army and fight in his wars. Genghis Khan often sent his *guregen* on the most dangerous missions, however, and they tended to be killed at a high rate. Most of them never had the chance to return home for very long. Being a son-in-law to Genghis Khan was not merely an apprenticeship phase, as it would be for a small herder; for these men it became a brief, but usually lethal, career.

A tribe acquired prestige and material benefits if Genghis Khan chose to marry one of his daughters to its leader. For the son-in-law, however, the honor was almost certainly a death sentence as well. He served virtually as the sacrificial victim in exchange for his tribe's prosperity. He would give his life in battle for Genghis Khan, and in return his tribe would benefit and his own offspring would be rewarded. A *guregen* entered into a harsh bargain.

Genghis Khan also used the marriages of his sons to further integrate the nation and to increase his own power within it. His sons, however, did not go to do bride service for their new in-laws, in part because they had too many wives and could never complete the task. Genghis Khan's daughters-in-law also came to live with the royal family, just as the sons-in-law did. Unlike the *guregen*, who lost what power he had over his tribe and was destined to quickly lose his life, the daughter-in-law acquired a much more important position. She became a *beki*, a title of honor previously used primarily for powerful men, or she became *khatun*, a queen. This was certainly more than a mere honorific.

These *khatuns* functioned as the ambassadors of their tribes. They handled negotiations, served as the communications network, and hosted visitors from their own group. As Genghis Khan's father-in-law said, his tribe's daughters acted as their "intercessors." Although not residing with her tribe, each *khatun* served as its queen away from home, representing the tribe in the court of Genghis Khan, where all major decisions were made. The tribe's success depended on her success.

The position of each wife within this ambassadorial corps reflected not only her personal relationship to her husband but also the diplomatic status of her tribe. The queens sat in careful arrangements by tiers, and where one sat relative to the other queens in the court rituals determined and publicly illustrated her tribe's position in the Mongol nation. Over the decades, the power of these daughters-in-law as queens would grow steadily until a generation after Genghis Khan's death, when they would become the contenders for the highest office in the land.

Khatun is one of the most authoritative and magnificent words in the Mongolian language. It conveys regality, stateliness, and great strength. If something resists breaking no matter how much pressure is applied, it is described as *khatun*. The word can form part of a boy's or girl's name, signifying power and firmness combined with beauty and grace. Because of the admired qualities of *khatun*, men have often borne names such as Khatun Temur, literally "Queen Iron," and Khatun Baatar, "Queen Hero."

The Mongols recognized the role of the father as the provider of sperm, which created the bones of a new child, but the mother gave meat and blood. Thus male lineages became known as the *yas,* meaning "bone of the father," while the larger kinship system was known as the *urug,* meaning "the womb." Genghis Khan gave his royal family the name Altan Urug, the Golden Womb.

Repeatedly in Genghis Khan's genealogy, the paternity of a child was in doubt. One of the most important ancestors of the Mongols, Alan Goa, had three sons after the death of her husband, but she insisted to all her sons that it did not matter from which father they came. The origin of a child's bones played a less important role than the womb from which the child sprang.

When Genghis Khan's wife Borte conceived her first child close to the time of her kidnapping, Genghis Khan insisted that, aside from the mother, it was no one's business how she became pregnant. "It happened," says the chronicle repeatedly. "It happened at a time when men were fighting; it happened at a time when men were killing. It happened at a time when the starry sky twisted in the heaven, when the nation twisted in turmoil, when people could not rest in their bed, or birds in their nest."

All that mattered was the parent's success in raising the child. The *Secret History* eloquently described a mother's devotion to her children: "She choked on her own hunger in order to feed them. She worried constantly how to make them into adults. She cleaned them and pulled them up by their heels to teach them to walk." It took the effort of a mother to transform boys into men. She "stretched them by the shoulders to pull them up to become men. She pulled them by their necks. She pulled them up to the height of other men. She did these things because she was the mother with a heart as bright as the sun and as wide as a lake."

Outlawing the sale or barter of women marked Genghis Khan's first important departure from tribal practices regarding marriage, and gradually through a series of such changes he transformed the social position of his daughters, and thereby of all women, within his burgeoning empire. His laws regarding women did not spring from an ideological position or special spiritual revelation so much as from personal experience and the practical needs of running a harmonious society. The natural accord between male and female, the sky and the earth, the sun and the moon had a practical application in the relations of men and women in the family and in society.

Genghis Khan was certainly ambitious and had much larger desires in the world than merely uniting the warring tribes of the steppe. Yet, in order to expand his empire, he needed someone to rule the newly conquered people. He had to leave someone in charge. Ideally, he would have had a stable of talented sons and given each one of them a newly conquered country to govern, but his sons were simply not capable. Without competent sons, he could leave a general in charge, but Genghis Khan had been betrayed too many times by men inside and outside his family. He probably knew well the result of Alexander the Great's overreliance on his generals, who subsequently divided the empire among themselves as soon as their leader died.

The women around Genghis Khan motivated him, and he constantly strove to make them happy. "My wives, daughters-in-law, and daughters are as colorful and radiant as red fire," he said. "It is my sole purpose to make their mouths as sweet as sugar by favor, to bedeck them in garments spun with gold, to mount them upon fleet-footed steeds, to have them drink sweet, clear water, to provide their animals with grassy meadows, and to have all harmful brambles and thorns cleared from the roads and paths upon which they travel, and not to allow weeds and thorns to grow in their pastures."

Genghis Khan's mother and wives were too old to take command of these new nations and to enjoy the full benefits of what he had to offer, but he had a new generation of women who seemed as capable as the previous one. After uniting the steppe, Genghis Khan turned his attention to foreign nations, and now women assumed a far more important role in building the empire abroad. At least three daughters had been married to closely related clans, and those marriages had helped to solidify bonds within the newly formed Mongol nation; however, now four other daughters faced a far more challenging task beyond the Mongol world, in the lands of neighboring countries.

By the end of the summer of 1206, Genghis Khan had transformed the steppe tribes into a nation, or perhaps more precisely into a large army with a small mobile country attached. Normally, at the end of a large steppe conference, the various tribes would return to their way of life with little real change in the daily routines, but after the *khuriltai* of 1206, Genghis Khan prepared them to move out and conquer the world. Now that all the steppe tribes acknowledged him as their khan, he was ready to begin his next and greatest phase of life by turning the Mongol nation into an engine of conquest. In the coming twenty years, Genghis Khan and his Mongol army conquered and ruled the largest empire in history. In these two decades they would acquire far more people and territory than the Romans, Persians, Greeks, or Chinese had been able to do in centuries of sustained effort.

How could he take such a tiny nation of 1 million people with 100,000 warriors and conquer countries of many millions with armies of many hundreds of thousands? How could he conquer territories that were more than one hundred times the size of his small nation and more than a thousand times the size of his army?

Genghis Khan had hardy horses and excellent riders well trained in archery, but the steppe had had such horses and archers for thousands of years. His unique success derived not from any secret technology; it came out of his unique charisma and his ability to organize human effort.

To achieve the conquests for which he was aiming, Genghis Khan had to use every resource available to him to the fullest extent. To confront armies several times the size of his own, he had to maximize the effectiveness of every warrior and the talents of every Mongol—including the women. Thus, when he laid down the laws and created the organization of the state in 1206, he had special responsibilities for his mother, his wives, and, above all others, for his daughters. A generation later, a Persian chronicler wrote: "After Genghis Khan had tested his sons and discovered for what each of them was suited, he had some hesitation over the throne and office of Great Khan."

The isolation of the Mongolian Plateau had protected the people for millennia. They had occasionally forayed out beyond the Gobi to attack sedentary people, but in the past, conquering meant leaving their homeland forever and settling in new places. Genghis Khan was about to permanently overcome the geographic obstacles separating the Mongols from the world. Under his system, Mongol warriors could travel back and forth, maintaining their home base on the steppe and commuting to the battlefront. The Gobi changed from an obstacle into a way station on the route to world domination.

Prior to 1206, no one outside of Mongolia seemed to pay much attention to the comings and goings of the nomads there. Whoever the barbarians selected to be their khan had no more importance to the city people than whether these savages ate rats or sheep for dinner. The great centers of civilization had much more important issues to chronicle and more important politics to play than fretting about some savage tribe of herders far beyond the protective buffer formed by the vast Gobi.

Beyond the Mongolian Plateau at the beginning of the thirteenth century, civilization languished. The world was full of frenetic activity, but little significant achievement. The twelfth century that had just ended had been a stagnant era. Theology and religion had spent their meager power to move history forward and instead left the world churning in a series of endless religious wars and silly theological disputes. The old empires of the past had crumbled, but the modern nation state had not yet arrived. The era of heroes such as Alexander and Caesar had given way to petty criminals claiming to be princes of men or designated representatives of gods. The world seemed to be searching and waiting, but no one expected that the next shaper of world history would come on horseback, dressed in fur, and smelling of milk and mutton from the frozen plains of the north.

With their central geographic position and their universalistic religions and commerce, the Muslims formed the pivot of civilization, but in recent centuries the frayed world map had been torn into hundreds of shreds and patches ruled by minor aristocrats, warlords, and bandits in a constantly changing kaleidoscope of cruel conquests, forced marriage alliances, and vicious betrayals. Each area consisted of a handful of constantly changing states with its own regional civilization, but they all lagged behind the Muslims on every measure of development. The Vikings controlled a hodgepodge of territories from America to the Mediterranean; the Turks established numerous dynastic kingdoms in Central Asia and India. Only the Arabs could claim to have a truly international civilization.

Yet, by 1206, the Arabs had begun their global retreat. The Turks pressed in on the Arabs from Central Asia, and although they adopted the Arab religion of Islam, they rejected Arab rule. The Europeans had nearly expelled the Arabs from Iberia, and their Christian crusaders mounted a massive challenge to the heart of Islam in the Holy Land.

The Arabs, with the help of Kurds and others, managed to hold the core of the Muslim lands against the Crusaders, but they had been severely wounded and gravely reduced in power.

At the time of the Mongol *khuriltai,* the knights from the Fourth Crusade were sailing back to Venice and other European ports, having utterly failed in their quest to destroy Islam but having substituted instead a thorough sacking and decimation of the Orthodox Christians of Byzantium. The Crusaders had desecrated, looted, and burned their way through the oldest centers of European civilization. They placed a prostitute on the throne of the Orthodox Patriarch, pulled the gold off the walls of the churches, pried out the jewels from the covers of ancient manuscripts, and then burned the books of the greatest library in the world. They divided ancient treasures and young virgins, including the nuns, among themselves like so many toys. Having destroyed Byzantium, they would soon begin new purges of Jews and smaller crusades against those Europeans who had not yet converted or who dared follow a different interpretation of Christianity than what was authorized in Rome.

Rival clans constantly ripped apart the social fabric of Japan, Korea, Europe, and South Asia, and society convulsed in spasms of violence as one feudal lord fought another. Secular and religious rulers struggled against one another within the same feudal order that pitted all against all; kidnapping and ransoming seemed to be the main occupation. Muslims pushed against Christians in the West, Hindus and Buddhists in the East, and pagans everywhere. Christians fought everyone, but mostly themselves, as bishops attacked bishops, popes excommunicated kings, kings created antipopes.

China would eventually become the center of world civilization during the Mongol era of history, but until then, China's role had been as a regional power largely isolated from the mainstream, as dynasties and various-sized kingdoms constantly sparred against one another, rarely allowing a single one to dominate for long. As the Mongols gathered in the north, the heart of the Chinese civilization was a kingdom of about 60 million ruled by the Southern Sung Dynasty from their capital of Hangzhou. In northern China, the Jurched tribe of Manchuria ruled over about 50 million Chinese subjects as the Jin Dynasty. The Silk Route between Persia and China was dominated by the Tangut, relatives of the Tibetans, under the Xia Dynasty, and by the Kara Kitai farther west. Tibet remained an isolated zone, as did many of the small kingdoms and independent tribes of the south. Each of them would soon fall to the Mongols of Genghis Khan.

Our Daughters Are Our Shields

T HE STEPPE ALONE LACKED THE RESOURCES THAT GENGHIS Khan needed to keep his followers happy. Now that the people had peace, milk, and meat, they longed for something more: for *tangsuqs*, those rare trinkets such as gems, golden and silver ornaments, and decorative baubles for their tents, horses, and themselves. In addition to the luster they provided, every item conveyed some spiritual property from its presumed place of origin, and the farther the *tangsuq* traveled, the stronger this essence, and therefore its beneficial power, became. Seashells emitted the magical sounds of the ocean, gold radiated the warmth of the sun, and silver the cool of the moon. Iridescent peacock feathers reflected the rainbow, and wine instantly released a fog of laughter.

Genghis Khan had united the tribes by charisma and force, but to keep them loyal required more than just a strong army and strategic marriage alliances. To show that the Eternal Blue Sky supported him and blessed him, he needed to bestow new riches on the nation. He had to provide something that they could not make for themselves, to supply things that their old chiefs could not, to bring them into the world market with its constantly changing flow of luxuries and novelties.

The Mongolian Plateau, though the perfect home for herds of horses and roaming goats, had few luxuries to offer; yet it was situated just off the most important trade highway in the world. The Silk Route was so close, but remained apart, beyond the five hundred miles of gravel, rock, and sand that the Mongols called *govi* and foreigners called the Gobi.

The Mongols found some of the merchandise of urban civilization useless or frivolous. Mongols did not need chopsticks to eat their food when they had fingers, and the porcelains could not survive the rigors of a nomadic lifestyle. With the Mongol preference for the natural flavor of meat, they had no interest in the spices or the sweets that the southerners craved. A Mongol's scent was a part of personal identity, and perfumes confusingly made everyone smell like flowers and fruits, which proved more appealing to flies and mosquitoes than to other Mongols. If the many manuscripts and religious texts sold in the markets contained anything of value, they needed to be memorized so as not to take up the preciously limited space on the nomads' carts. Besides, only Hoelun's Tatar son could read, and he was already quite busy as the supreme judge.

Yet there was much in the markets that enthralled the Mongols. The camel- and goat-wool blankets were so soft and delicate that they seemed woven from feathers. The merchants sold silk that slid along the skin like freshly falling snow, and the textiles were embroidered with brightly colored flowers and birds that looked as though they could suddenly come to life. In small bags of antelope leather, the merchants carried pearls as white as milk, coral as red as the setting sun, and ivory so soft that it seemed edible. The Silk Route brought iron for making knives, pots, and stirrups that never rotted, broke, or decayed. The people of its towns and cities could strike a flint against a steel bar and make sparks fly, and they served drinks in silver bowls that could protect against poison and counteract magic spells.

The merchants from beyond the Gobi sold delicately carved combs for fixing the hair, and they traveled with magic needles that could point out the south or north in the dark or on a day darkened by sandstorms. They played musical instruments with the voices of angels, and they frightened away demons with brass cymbals that sounded like cranes dancing on ice. They blew into horns to call the thunder, and conch shells that could summon the gods. Their medicines were said to restore sight to the blind and make the barren fruitful. The bamboo wood was light enough to float on water, but strong as metal, and light could pass through the beads of glass and colored crystal. Their cosmetics revitalized an aged woman's beauty, and their potions could return an old man's virility. Compared to the novelties of the markets, the nomad's life seemed drab, the wealth in cows and horses appeared trifling, and the herder's clothes looked coarse and plain.

To obtain the luxury goods of the south, the Mongols needed something to trade. The yaks, cows, sheep, and goats could not make the trek across the Gobi, and the horses and camels could not carry heavy loads of wool or leather. The most valuable products of the north came not from the domesticated animals, but from the wild animals: antelope hides, black and brown sable pelts, tiger and wolf skins, bear claws, and the horns of elk, reindeer, ibex, and wild sheep. The Mongols could also provide hunting hawks, as well as large supplies of feathers from cranes and tundra swans. Even the fur of marmots, squirrels, and dogs could be traded, and the southern pharmacists sought to harvest body parts of wild animals, from tongue and teeth to tail and testicles, for use in medicines.

Most of these products lay beyond the Mongol steppe world; they came from animals of the distant Amur River in the northeast or the forests around Lake Baikal in the northwest. The Mongols called the northern area Sibr, which later became Siberia, and they referred to the tribes as the Oi-yin Irged, the Forest People, eventually shortened to Oirat. These groups lived in small hunting camps among the trees adjacent to the taiga in the shadow of the Arctic. Because horses could not survive that far north, some of the bands moved on sleds pulled by dogs, and others relied on reindeer. They wore animal skins and furs, ate the wild animals of the forest, and lived in bark tents. Even the rough wool and felt of the steppe was a luxury among the Oirat, while silks and teas remained as exotic to them as bamboo or books.

In 1207, only a year after the founding of the nation, Genghis Khan dispatched his eldest son, Jochi, with an army to Siberia to subdue the northern tribes. The Oirat living along the Shishigt River, west of Lake Hovsgol, became the first to join Genghis Khan. Unlike the herding tribes living on the open steppe, the Oirat lived by hunting in a wooded zone. Prior to Jochi's campaign, they had not been very active in the steppe wars, but they owed nominal allegiance to a sequence of Genghis Khan's enemies, including Jamuka, the Merkid, and the Naiman. However, their chief quickly recognized that the Oirat's future prosperity lay with the Mongols, with whom he eagerly sought an alliance.

Genghis Khan accepted the Oirat and made a proposal of marriage with two of the chief's sons. Genghis Khan's daughter Checheyigen married Inalchi. Then Genghis Khan made the alliance deeper by marrying his granddaughter, who was the daughter of Jochi, to the chief's other son, Torolchi. With the marriage of each woman, Genghis Khan's nuptial edicts became stronger and more direct in making it clear that she was to rule. His intentions could scarcely have been more precise in the wording he chose at the time of Checheyigen's marriage: "Because you are the daughter of your Khan father, you are sent to govern the people of the Oirat tribe." This time he made no mention of a secondary ruler, co-ruler, or another shaft on the cart. She was not simply to govern the Oirat the way that they had been in the past; she would not be a mere substitute for their old khans. "You should organize the Oirat people and control them," her father demanded. "Your words must show your wisdom."

"You are going to pitch a tent there," he told her, "but do not be a stranger in your mother-in-law's family!" The omission of the name, or any mention of her husband or his father's lineage, further indicated that not only would the new son-in-law surrender power over the Oirat, but he would not even be living among them in his homeland. He would be removed to follow Genghis Khan and fight with the Mongol army, leaving Checheyigen there among her husband's female relatives.

As usual in the nuptial edicts, Genghis Khan added some more personal advice. "Be sincere always," he was quoted as saying. "Maintain your soul as one in the night and the day." And with fatherly concern he added, "Get up early and go to bed late."

Checheyigen's position over the Oirat gave the Mongols control of the northern trade routes all the way into the Arctic. Even with this new source of trade goods, Genghis Khan still needed access into the Silk Route.

The "Silk Route" or "Silk Road" referred to the network of trade connections between the three main civilizations of China, India, and the Mediterranean, with the Muslim countries dominating the center of this intercontinental triangle. The core consisted of some five thousand miles, but the inclusion of alternative, secondary, and connecting routes doubled or tripled the size. In the east, the route began with the ancient Chinese city of Xian, but in the west, where the route fingered out into dozens of streams, almost any major Mediterranean or Indian city could be called the termination point.

Trade routes usually follow the path of least geographic resistance. They move around mountains and deserts when possible. Travelers on the Silk Route had to cross two difficult barriers in western China: the Tianshan Mountains and the treacherous Taklamakan Desert. Farther to the east, they faced two more equally formidable obstacles in the Tibetan Plateau and the Mongolian Plateau, but fortunately for the traders, a narrow strip of lowland called the Gansu Corridor runs between the two, and virtually all trade funneled through this area like water through a canyon. The only place that the Silk Route is actually a single route is the easternmost area of the roughly one thousand miles from Dunhuang into the heartland of China via Xian.

Whoever commanded this passageway held a stranglehold on the entire Silk Route. Through millennia, the three main contenders had been the Chinese on one side and the Turkic and Tibetan tribes on the other. At the time of Genghis Khan's rise to power in Mongolia, the Tangut occupied the corridor and doggedly defended their control of the lucrative trade routes.

The Tangut, who referred to themselves as the Great White Nation, were essentially a Tibetan people who had come down off their high plateau in the tenth century, giving up nomadic herding to exploit the trade corridor. In contrast to the earlier Central Asian traders such as the Sogdians, the Tangut acquired a heavy overlay of Chinese civilization, as exemplified in their use of their own language written with Chinese characters. They were dedicated Buddhists resisting the press of Islam along the Silk Route, but within Buddhism, they encouraged a wide diversity of theological schools and institutions.

The Tangut recognized that Genghis Khan was not a merchant, but a conqueror seeking to control the trade. As soon as he united the steppe, he dispatched forces south to attack the Tangut cities closest to the Mongol nation. As early as 1205, he had sent small bands of his cavalry south to probe the Tangut defenses. Attacking a walled and heavily fortified Tangut city proved far more difficult than capturing a herder's camp, but through persistence and trial and error, Genghis Khan managed one small victory after another. Each triumph forced new contributions of camels and merchandise from the Tangut, but it did not produce a constant supply of goods. With each defeat the Tangut earnestly vowed to send more animals and wares in future tribute, but as soon as the Mongols disappeared back north of the Gobi, the defeated cities stopped payment. Genghis Khan's campaigns, while proving militarily successful and giving his army good practice in laying siege to cities and maneuvering back and forth through the Gobi, were not producing the material results he sought.

Unable to succeed by military force alone, Genghis Khan devised another strategy that depended upon his daughter Alaqai Beki, whom he had promised in marriage to the family of the Onggud leader Ala-Qush. With Alaqai now around sixteen or seventeen years old, he decided to send her to the Onggud.

Alaqai was born to Genghis Khan and Borte around the year 1191, about the time that Borte turned thirty years old. Some scholars believe that her name means "Siberian Marmot," but others offer a more mysterious origin tied directly to the birth of her father. According to this etymology, the name means "Palm of the Hand," in reference to some now unknown event at the time of her delivery. Such an origin for the name closely parallels the account of her father's birth, when Genghis Khan emerged from the womb clutching a small blood clot in the palm of his hand. This was taken as a sign that he would one day rule the world. Whether true or not, the connection of these birth stories for the father and daughter show that some people place her in an important position comparable to his. No such story exists for any other member of the royal family.

Mongol tradition strongly maintains that Borte refused to hand over the rearing of her children to any of the many retainers she acquired as her husband's power expanded. She and her mother-in-law, Hoelun, are attributed with raising their children, and she, much more than Genghis Khan, instilled in their daughters the duty to serve the nation. Borte came from the Khongirad, and in contrast to the Mongols' nearly exclusive reliance on force and violence, her tribe had a far more subtle approach to public life and diplomacy. As Borte's father explained: the Khongirad did not depend on the strength of their sons; they trusted instead in the beauty and cleverness of their daughters to protect them. He said that their daughters rode on carts pulled by black camels, and that they married powerful men and became queens to negotiate, intercede, and protect them. "From ancient time," he said, "the Khongirad people have queens as our shields."

Having grown up in the tribe that expected such a role for its daughters, Borte transmitted those same values and expectations to her female offspring. Her daughters were bred to rule.

Alaqai Beki was the first of her Borijin clan to come off the Mongolian Plateau to impose Mongol rule over the sedentary civilization of China. As she rode down the steep embankment that separated the Mongol steppe world from the agricultural and urban world of the Chinese, she faced more than 100 million people who, through generations of fighting, had come to loathe and fear everything she represented.

The steppe society where Alaqai grew up differed markedly from the land she went to rule. The Onggud lived south of the Gobi on the borderland between the zones of herding nomads and the settled farmers of China. They had trading towns surrounded by high, thick walls. They lived in buildings for part of the year and in felt *gers* for the other part, and they worshiped in temples. The Onggud formed one of the oldest civilizations of northern Asia.

To remove competition against the rule of his daughters, Genghis Khan not only removed their husbands to his army, he dismissed all their other wives. Only the Mongol wife would preside. If the *guregen* already had wives, he had to divorce them in order to marry a royal Mongol woman, and once married he could not take another wife without a rarely issued dispensation from the Great Khan.

Divorcing the other wives did not impede the status of their children. Unlike societies that employed baroque procedures for distinguishing between legitimate and illegitimate children, the Mongols accepted all children as equal. No child could be born without the consent of the Eternal Blue Sky. No earthly law or custom could presume to declare the child illegitimate.

The wives might be dismissed and their power curtailed, but the children, particularly the sons, could not be easily displaced as future sources of power. In other societies, such heirs and potential rivals faced nearly certain death, but Alaqai Beki took control of her husband's other children in order to protect them, and to keep them close enough to prevent one from being set up as a rival ruler.

Alaqai Beki took literally the Mongol nation's first step from its pastoral homeland into what would become one of the greatest conquests in Asian history. In his nuptial edict, her father charged her with an amazing mission. In preparation for the coming invasions, he told her: "You should be determined to become one of my feet." He left no doubt that this was a major military assignment. She was not there merely to administer, but to rule—thereby beginning the expansion of the Mongols from a tribal nation into a global empire. "When I am going on an expedition, you should be my helper, when I am galloping, you should be my steed!"

Despite her youth, the importance of her mission demanded that Alaqai Beki act on her own young judgment. "No friend is better than your own wise heart!" Genghis Khan told her. He elaborated on this need for self-reliance, despite what complaints she might hear from those around her. "Although there are many things you can rely on, no one is more reliable than yourself," he explained. She held ultimate power, and therefore, ultimate responsibility. "Although many people can be your helper, no one should be closer to you than your own consciousness." He warned her to be careful because her survival was of the highest importance. "Although there are many things you should cherish, no one is more valuable than your own life."

He also gave her more fatherly advice to protect herself and to foster good habits. He stressed the importance of constant learning as the key to being a successful ruler. He told her to be "prudent, steadfast, and courageous." In perhaps his most important words, he said, "You have to remember life is short, but fame is everlasting!"

No Mongolian description survives of the coronation of the Mongol queens. The only hint comes from foreign accounts that Mongols raised their queens up to office while they were seated on a white felt rug, which would make their installation identical with that of a newly proclaimed khan.

The departure from home was simple for Alaqai and for each sister leaving her mother's *ger* for a new life far away. The mother and daughter stood in front of the *ger*, and the daughter presented first her right cheek and then her left so that her mother might sniff each one in the traditional kiss of the Mongols. This sniff would help the mother to remember the smell of the child until they met again. Sometimes the mother declined to sniff the second cheek, saying, "I will sniff the left one when you return." So great is the power of words that by saying it and visualizing it happening, the mother hoped to ensure that they would meet again.

When the daughter mounted her horse to ride away, she did not look back at the *ger* of her past but had to stare straight ahead into the future. Borte, like any Mongol mother, watched her daughter ride away but never shed a tear. A Mongol mother was never supposed to cry in the presence of her child. Of all the fluids from a mother's body, tears were the most dangerous. The mother's blood gave life to the infant growing in the womb, and her milk nourished the baby after birth. Her saliva moistened the food that the mother chewed and put into the child's mouth, and she used her urine to wash and sterilize her offspring's wounds. The tears of a mother, however, contained dangerous power; no matter how great the pain the mother felt, she could not shed them in the presence of the child for fear of causing future harm.

Instead of crying, the mother performed an ancient ritual of the steppe. She brought out a pail of milk, and as her child rode away, she stood before the door of her *ger* and threw milk into the air with a *tsatsal*, a wooden instrument resembling a large perforated spoon. With an upward and outward toss of her right arm, the mother waved the *tsatsal* and aspersed the milk into the air until her child passed out of her sight. The milk constituted a special prayer, and it carried the hope that the mother could pour out a white road ahead of her child. Because a route made of white stones and sand can reflect the moon and stars, it could be traveled at night as well as day. Particularly for Alaqai passing south across the Gobi, night travel would help her animals not to overheat and would thus require less water. A white road offered freedom, but it also posed far greater danger than the usual black road of day. Because it was traveled in the darkness of night, the white road could easily lead into the land of temptation, error, and sin. By sprinkling the milk, the mother reminded her offspring of their obligation to behave properly.

Once her daughter passed beyond the horizon, the mother put down her pail of milk, and then after walking far away from her *ger* and her family, she lay facedown on the earth and cried her pain and her tears onto the ground. Mother Earth always understood the sorrow of a mother and would hide her tears.

As long as her children remained away from her, the Mongol mother came out every morning with her pail and *tsatsal* to sprinkle milk in the direction of each one of them and any other family member away from home. For a people without ownership of land, the milk aspersions of the *tsatsal* also served to mark a territory of occupation. Her ritual sought a blessing and permission from the spirits of the land for her family to use all the land, waters, and pastures within sight in every direction. The *tsatsal* ritual located the family in space and in relation to one another, and it simultaneously established geographic location, spiritual connection, and social orientation.

According to the diplomatic procedures of the age, Genghis Khan sent Alaqai Beki to rule by marrying her to Ala-Qush, the leader of the neighboring kingdom, or the leader's son, or nephew. The exact identity of her first husband remains unclear, but in time she married each of the men in succession, as needed or as she preferred. The confusion over her husbands' identities frustrated generations of scholars, but the vagueness further illustrates the unimportance these men had in her administration. The identity of the Mongol queen mattered; the identity of her consort did not.

Alaqai's kingdom occupied a large swath of land in what is now Chinese Inner Mongolia. Like the future empire that her father would create, Alaqai Beki's multicultural kingdom spanned the Mongol, Turkic, and Chinese worlds. Because of her position at the intersection of these three civilizations, two of which were literate, we know more about her than her sister, Checheyigen of the Oirat. This information derives not from the Mongol chronicles, but from those of her neighbors, who exercised an intense curiosity about the Mongol queen.

As a leader of the Onggud, Alaqai Beki headed a tribe that had never been a powerful conquering or independent force, yet their history stretched back much farther than that of the Mongols. The Onggud formed one of the Turkic-speaking groups that had dominated the history of China's northern borderlands over the previous two thousand years. They entered the pages of recorded history in the eighth century, when they constituted a part of the powerful Turkic empire based on the Mongolian Plateau during China's Tang Dynasty, between the years 618 and 907. They roamed in the long region between the inhabitable Gobi to the north and the agricultural lands of the Yellow River to the south.

Their neighbors called the Onggud by different names, but each name revealed a certain aspect of their identity, location, or relation with stronger powers around them. Although large and scarcely populated, the area has a consistent ecological appearance that is succinctly summarized in the Chinese name for the Onggud. They call them the Shatuo, meaning "the Sandy Gravel tribe," in reference to this transitional zone between the desert and farmland. The Chinese also referred to the Onggud as the White Tatars, a benign designation that distinguished them from the wilder Mongols, whom they called Black Tatars.

The Mongols consistently called them the Onggud, and according to the etymology recorded by a thirteenth-century Persian chronicler, they acquired their name from a word for wall. They were therefore the People of the Wall, representing their occupational status and geographic location under the Jin Dynasty of the Jurched. Whether the etymology was true or not, this designation "People of the Wall" accurately encapsulates their history: They traditionally manned the forts and protected the Chinese settlements from the other, wilder tribes of the steppes. Another etymology derives from the word for gate or opening, and this designation also shows that for the Mongols, they were not so much a barrier to China as the entrance into it.

Because of their loyalty to a series of northern Chinese dynasties, the Onggud also had an official designation as a military prefecture called the Tiande Jun, a type of border patrol. Although willing to guard the frontier and work for their Chinese or other employer, the Onggud carefully maintained their own Turkic language, and they repeatedly embraced foreign religions, such as Christianity; that set them firmly apart from the Chinese population and from the ruling dynasty of both the Song and the Jin.

Marco Polo wrote that these people called themselves Ung, which is the singular form of the name Onggud. He, however, preferred to call them by their more official designation as the Tenduc, his rendering in Latin letters of the title of Tiande Jun, referring to the militarized border zone where they lived. After the travels of Marco Polo, the Onggud became known in the West as the Tenduc. As Dutch mapmakers began to chart the most distant parts of the Asian interior, they consistently used this name, giving the tribe a prominent position located in various places from the Pacific Coast to the Arctic Sea.

Through contacts with the civilizations of China and the Silk Route, the Onggud developed an early tradition of literacy long before the Mongols and most of the other steppe tribes. Depending upon the political climate and the changing weather patterns, they sometimes farmed and other times herded. They lived in settled communities and occasionally built cities, but then returned to nomadic life when necessary or advantageous. The combination of agricultural and herding lifestyles provided the materials for their most desired trade goods. They manufactured and marketed camlet, a luxuriously soft fabric made from a combination of fine camel hair from the steppe and silk from China in the south.

Onggud leaders exercised a special skill for detecting and befriending the next rising power on the steppe. The success of their leaders derived from their demonstrated ability to make themselves useful enough that each new dynasty needed their immediate assistance against the steppe tribes. At no time did the Onggud skill in picking the future power become more obvious, or more advantageous to them, than when they allied with the rising conqueror Genghis Khan and his Mongols. Yet the decision lacked unanimity, and Onggud opinion divided sharply between those who favored the new alliance and those who wanted to preserve their older relationship with the richer and far better established Jin Dynasty of the Jurched.

The movement of Alaqai Beki off the Mongolian Plateau began Genghis Khan's expansion into the vast civilizations and kingdoms south of the Gobi. Cities and kingdoms stretched out in a seemingly infinite array before the Mongols: the Jurched kingdom with its millions of Chinese peasants and craftsmen; the small but productive kingdoms of Korea; the exotic and mystic land of Tibet; the degenerate but luxurious miniature Song Empire of South China, the isolated and varied kingdoms of Yunnan, and still more whose names and people remained completely unknown to the Mongols.

Before the Mongols could taste the wealth of any of these distant lands, they needed a beachhead to the south of the Gobi. The Gobi loomed like a large ocean of rock and gravel protecting the southern kingdoms from the northern tribes. Under good conditions, crossing the Gobi required six weeks, but they had to be very carefully chosen weeks. A small error could easily lead to the death of hundreds of warriors and horses.

The Mongols could not cross in the spring because the horses and men were usually too weak to withstand the harsh trip, and the horrific sandstorms of the spring could bury a whole army. Summer was too hot and winter too cold. The fall provided the best weather for travel, but only in years with enough rainfall to supply the minimum needs of grass and water. Even in a good fall season, a miscalculation might see the army severely hampered by an unseasonably late heat wave or, even more likely, an early arrival of winter.

At the end of even the best crossing, the army would be at its weakest and thereby most vulnerable to foreign attack. Crossing in the fall meant that they arrived in the south at the start of winter, a time when Mongols liked to attack, but not an auspicious time for the horses to graze and regain their strength after the hard trek through the Gobi. The army needed a large supply of fresh horses to replace the worn-out ones that would need months to recover, and the men needed food after the deprivations of nearly two months in the desert. While the men and animals recovered, they needed protection from any southern army that might seize this moment to expel them back into the harsh Gobi.

Alaqai overcame each of these obstacles for the Mongol army. By controlling the Onggud lands, she supplied the army with provisions and new horses while protecting it from southern attack. Alaqai's kingdom was a fortress built in enemy territory.

Because Genghis Khan's army of about 100,000 soldiers was approximately one-tenth the size of the Jurched's to the south, he devised a plan that emphasized tactical retreat as much as attack. For such a strategy to succeed, he required a place to which he could withdraw and be guaranteed protection. Alaqai provided that cover for his army. She was both the vanguard of the Mongol army and its security.

Two of Alaqai's sisters rapidly followed as queens over two other Turkic groups: the Uighurs in what is now the Xinjiang region of western China and the Karluk to the northwest in what is now Kazakhstan. Like soldiers being deployed to the front lines, his daughters were hurriedly assigned to their marriages as Genghis Khan planned a large-scale assault on China.

Genghis Khan's policy of benign treatment of people who voluntarily joined his empire, plus his harsh treatment of those who resisted, lured many minority groups with a grievance against their rulers to rebel and ask him for help. Despite the strict conditions of military commitment that accompanied membership in the Mongol Empire, Genghis Khan's cultural and religious tolerance especially attracted people who felt abused by a class of rulers speaking a different language or practicing a different religion than their subjects. The most poignant plea came from the Uighur people, who had originated centuries earlier in the Orkhon River area of central Mongolia but had relocated to the oases of western China in the eighth century.

The Uighurs, many of whom had converted to Islam, had lost their independence to the Kara Kitai under a staunchly Buddhist dynasty, also known as the Western Liao, since they were an offshoot of the Liao Dynasty, which ruled northern China from 926 to 1125. Their Kara Kitai rulers took the region's wealth to their capital city, Balghasun, on the Chu River to the west of Lake Issyk Kul in modern Kyrgyzstan. In 1209, the Uighurs revolted by killing their local Kara Kitai officials, and the Uighur leader sent a passionate and urgent plea for protection to Genghis Khan. At this time, Genghis Khan was living along the Kherlen River, preparing for the invasion of China. The Uighur leader had the title *Idiqut,* meaning "Divine Majesty."

"As if one saw Mother Sun when the clouds disperse," pleaded the Idiqut's envoy, according to Mongol history, "as if one came upon the river water when the ice disappears, so I greatly rejoiced when I heard of the fame of Genghis Khan." The Persian chronicle recorded almost the same words: "It seemed to me as though the sky had been cleared of clouds and the bright sun had come out from behind them and broken up the ice that had frozen on the rivers, and pure clear water could be seen."

The Idiqut made an exceedingly servile request. "If through your favor," he said, groveling, "I were to obtain but a ring from your golden belt, but a thread from your crimson coat, I will become your fifth son and will serve you." The Persian chronicles described the marriage of the Idiqut to Genghis Khan's daughter Al-Altun as making a slave into a noble.

Twentieth-century Japanese archaeologists working in Gansu Province discovered an inscription in Mongolian and Chinese from the Uighur prince Hindu recounting the history of that family. It gave an additional account of how the Uighur family became *quda* to Genghis Khan, and in so doing provides a few lost details.

"Whereas, by the Protection of Eternal Heaven," began the inscription, "the Sovereign of the Great Mongol Empire had been predestined to unite all nations . . . in accordance with the Will of Heaven, had gone campaigning, executing the great work . . . [and] assembling the nations, the Idiqut of the Uighurs submitted with the people of his realm . . . under Fortunate Genghis Khan."

The request to become a fifth son betrayed the true aspiration of the Uighur leader; thus Genghis Khan sent word for the Idiqut to come in person. He came, bringing tribute of "gold, silver, small and big pearls, silks, brocades, damasks, and satins." In addition to these precious items, he brought gifts of symbolic meaning for the Mongol royal family, which he sought to join through marriage. He brought black sable furs, the gift that Borte had brought with her to Genghis

Khan when they first married, and which he subsequently used to make his first ally, Ong Khan. The Uighur Idiqut also brought white gyrfalcons and white geldings.

Genghis Khan accepted him since he came voluntarily and without a Mongol invasion, "by submitting gracefully without causing the men of the Fortunate Genghis Khan to suffer and without causing his horses to sweat," according to the inscription. The Idiqut served Genghis Khan faithfully, fighting honorably in several campaigns against the Tangut and Muslims. According to the inscription about him, "He rendered service in gratitude to the Emperor, punishing deeds which were harmful to the Empire; he performed ones which were useful."

Unlike the accounts of Alaqai Beki's court, we lack direct reports of how Al-Altun ran the Uighur kingdom; however, the surviving information points to a role similar to that of her sister Alaqai. The bilingual Chinese and Mongolian inscription of Prince Hindu describes the Uighur leader as the one who "protects and defends the state and wards off invasion" for Genghis Khan, and as the barrier "to ward off and repel evil enemies." The words echo literally the words of the *Secret History* in describing the role of the women of Genghis Khan's family: They are the shields to defend the empire.

Genghis Khan dispatched his daughter Al-Altun to the Uighurs with a clear message. He told her that, as a Mongol queen, he gave her three husbands. Her nation was her first husband. Her second husband was her own reputation. In third place came the earthly man to whom she was married. Of the three, he wanted it clear that her priority was to her duty and her nation. "If you can take your nation as your husband and serve him very carefully, you will earn your reputation." If she maintained these priorities, her relations with her flesh-and-blood physical husband would find their own place. "If you can take your reputation as your husband and carefully protect it," her father explained, "how can the husband who has married you ever forsake you?"

As with all of Genghis Khan's daughters, it is difficult to know if the name we have for Al-Altun was her birth name or a new name-title, of the kind Genghis Khan often gave his men. Al-Altun, especially in some of the varied spellings such as Il-qaltun, Il-khaltun, and Il-galtun, appears to be a title. The Mongolian term *il* designated a subordinate people. In the time of Genghis Khan's grandsons, the Mongols in Persia and Iraq took the name Il-Khanate, meaning "Vice-Khanate," and the ruler became known as the Il-Khan, or "Viceroy." Al-Altun seems to be a predecessor to that title, meaning "Vice-Royalty." The recording of so many of the daughters with names or titles beginning with *Al* further indicates the possibility that several of them were new but related name-titles of this order.

In ruling the Uighur, Al-Altun performed an important function similar to that of Alaqai in the Onggud territory and equally important for the next stage of empire. The Uighurs occupied a series of oases in the desert—including their capital at Besh Baliq, meaning "Five Cities," northeast of modern Urumqi in western China—as well as the oasis settlement of Turfan, protected by its heavily fortified military base of Gaochang, surrounded by an earthen wall nearly forty feet thick and three miles in circumference. Another wall in the inner core of the city protected the ruler and his military retinue.

The settlements such as Hami and Turfan, scattered far apart across the vast deserts of the Silk Route, formed literal oases of civilization supplying a variety of delicacies from melons and raisins to alcohol. Turfan consisted of a large depression covering an area of about five thousand square miles in one of the most inhospitable places on earth. In the middle of the Eurasian continent, it lay as far from the ocean as any place could be. With two thousand miles separating Turfan from the Pacific Ocean, and much of that desert, the oasis lay much too far away for the Chinese officials to control. At an average altitude of 262 feet below sea level, with some places more than 500 feet below sea level, daily temperatures rose to above 100 degrees Fahrenheit in the summer and fell to well below freezing in the winter. With almost no measurable rainfall, Turfan constituted a virtual Death Valley that sustained life only because farmers managed to irrigate it with underground water.

Over the generations, the inhabitants of this isolated spot found ways to access snow melting off nearby mountains, which they directed through a system of deeply dug irrigation channels. Under normal circumstances, the high daily temperatures, dry air, and relentless sun would have caused irrigation ditches to quickly run dry. Known as *karez,* and similar to the *qanat* system of Central Asia, Turfan's irrigation tunnels kept the water from evaporating and carried it wherever it was needed.

A Chinese description of the settlement at Turfan by an earlier Sung envoy in 982 probably applied equally to all the oasis settlements of the Uighur territory: "The area has no rain or snow and is extremely hot, and when the hottest season arrives the inhabitants all move into caves dug in the earth . . . Their houses are covered with white clay, and water from Jinling, Golden Mountain, flows through them and is circulated through the capital city to water the gardens and turn mills. The area produces the five cereal grains, but it lacks buckwheat. The nobles eat horse-meat and the common people eat goat or fowl." The report then described the people as "fond of archery and riding." The women "wear oiled caps. . . . They are fond of excursions and always take along musical instruments."

The Uighur aristocracy maintained the nomadic lifestyle with large herds of horses. They summered in their yurts in the Tianshan Mountains and moved back to the oasis cities for cooler months. The peasants under their command stayed in the oases to cultivate melons, fertilizing them with cow dung and covering them with mats at crucial times to protect them from the powerful sun or extreme evaporation from the soil.

Compared with the simplicity of the Mongol court or with the courts of her sisters, Al-Altun entered a luxurious setting. With their position along the Silk Route and their small but highly cosmopolitan markets along the oases, the Uighur cities offered connections to major civilizations and had adopted goods, customs, and words from across Eurasia. The Uighur ruler was described as wearing a red robe and a golden crown while presiding at official functions from a golden chair, placed up high on a platform decorated with pearls and jewels.

The cultural contacts show clearly in this description because the platform under the throne came from China, while the Uighur word for crown, *didim,* came from Greek *diadéma,* showing the lingering influence of the Greeks from the invasion of Alexander the Great more than one thousand years earlier.

The cosmopolitan fashions of the Uighur court combined influences from throughout the Mongol empire, including Chinese textiles, Central Asian designs, Mongolian tastes, and Turkic craft ingenuity, in a unique product. Archaeological excavations have uncovered well-preserved textiles in the dry conditions. They reveal luxurious robes with intricate but quite subtle geometric patterns woven into them with golden threads. Simple color combinations, such as gold on yellow contrasted with the brighter colors popular in China as well as in the Muslim world, and the high level of craftsmanship showed a sophisticated craft industry, most likely from within the Uighur nation itself.

The inner lining design of one robe depicted a floral motif framing two rampant lions, each of which had a human head bearing a crown. The twin monarchs appeared identical, without any sign of gender. Just such a robe may have been worn by Al-Altun as she presided over the official ceremonies of daily life, receiving and dispatching envoys to the distant reaches of the Mongol Empire, whose center she controlled.

The abundance of grapes grown in the Uighur oases created a lucrative commerce in raisins and wine. Wine made from grapes developed a higher alcohol level than the fermented beverages to which the Mongols were accustomed. Grapes had to be harvested at the appropriate time, but once they were made into wine, the alcohol could be stored for years and thus consumed without regard to season.

The Mongols already had a mildly alcoholic drink in the form of fermented mare's milk, known as *airag,* or to other people by the Turkic name of *koumis.* For the traditional Mongols, *airag* had been a seasonal drink of August and September, when the mares produced copious amounts of milk but the colts already could feed themselves by grazing. The herders milked the animals in a nearly unending routine throughout the day and into the night. They stored the milk in large skins and churned it frequently as it fermented. Within a few days, the *airag* reached the ideal state. Men, in particular, drank it without moderation because it had only a small amount of alcohol and because it would last for only a few months. During the fall months, men who owned enough horses boasted that they lived exclusively on *airag*, supplemented by the meat of the occasional marmot. Because of this particular tradition, no one learned, or needed, moderation. Throwing up and having diarrhea served as emblems of masculine camaraderie in the plentiful months of autumn before the harshness of winter.

The Onggud lands under Alaqai Beki provided Genghis Khan with the base for conquering the many kingdoms of China; the Uighur kingdom tightened his grip on the Silk Route. This control provided the Mongols with a much needed commercial base, and it also gave them some military advantage in controlling the commerce in and out of China. However, China could largely supply its own needs and did not depend heavily on exports, so this control of the Silk Route could inflict only relatively minor damage on the centers of Chinese civilization.

In the spring of 1211, the Year of the Sheep, Genghis Khan gave an unidentified daughter in marriage to Arslan Khan of the Karluk Turks, who had been ruled by the Kara Kita like the Uighurs, but lived farther to the west. Their capital was on the lower Ili River in modern Kazakhstan when Arslan submitted to the Mongols. The name Karluk may have meant "Snow Lords," in reference to the snowy mountains of their home in the Tianshan. Arslan meant "Lion," and thus Arslan Khan meant "the Lion King."

When Arslan Khan married the Mongol princess, Genghis Khan took away his title, saying, "How can he be called Arslan *Khan*?" If he had been allowed to keep the title of *khan*, some of his subjects might have presumed that he outranked his royal Mongol wife or was at least equal to her. Genghis Khan changed the Karluk leader's name to Arslan Sartaqtai, meaning "Arslan of the Sart," a general term used by Mongolians for the people of Central Asia, but which had the connotation of a merchant. Genghis Khan also gave him the new title *guregen,* son-in-law, or prince consort.

In the censorship of the *Secret History,* this daughter's name disappeared. Some scholars concluded that she was Tolai, a name that formed a euphonious set with Tolui, the youngest son's name. The Chinese *Yuan Shi,* the history of Mongol rule, compiled by their successors during the Ming Dynasty, mentioned a woman of a similar name, Tore, later being married to Arslan's son. With the occasional confusion of *r* and *l* sounds in the recording of names, it is quite possible that this was the name of the queen who first married the father and then the son.

Just as Genghis Khan placed Alaqai at the Mongol entry into China, his marriage of his younger daughter to the Karluk placed that area under her control, allowing it to serve as the Mongol gateway to the Muslim lands to the south, to the Turkic steppe tribes of the west, and on into Russia and Europe. Accepting his duty as a *guregen,* Arslan joined Genghis Khan at war while the Mongol princess took up her place in his homeland. Arslan is mentioned as fighting with the Mongol army at the siege of Balkh in Tokharistan (modern Afghanistan) around 1220 and in other cities in 1222–23.

Of all the daughters, Checheyigen had the least prestigious marriage and the hardest life, since the Oirat of the northern forest was the least powerful and least important tribe. Three of her sisters became queens along the Silk Route, ruling over the grand Turkic nations of Onggud, Uighur, and Karluk. They ruled countries with walled cities, ancient histories, written languages, sacred scriptures, brick temples, and commercial and diplomatic relations all around them. They wore garments made from fine camel and goat wool and sometimes imported silks from China and brocades from Persia. They sipped hot tea in the winter and nibbled on cool melons in the summer. One even had a specialist in making refreshing sherbet drinks.

Checheyigen's other sisters married into herding tribes of the steppe who were relatives of her mother and her grandmother. Even if they did not have all the luxuries of the Silk Route cities, they had vast herds, and in the summer they drank rich yogurt and bowls of heavy cream, and ate an array of dried and fermented dairy products; in the winter they kept vast stores of frozen beef, mutton, goat, and yak, from which they enjoyed steaming bowls of nourishing hot broth.

Yet Checheyigen maintained such close social ties with the Mongols that the Oirat and the Mongols borrowed heavily from each other's culture, language, and lifestyle. Through these intermarriages, the Oirat thus became the first nonherding tribe to join Genghis Khan, eventually creating a single nation with two major lineages.

The daughters of Genghis Khan formed a phalanx of shields around their Mongol homeland. They marked the nation's borders and protected it from the four directions as they ruled the kingdoms of the Onggud, Uighur, Karluk, and Oirat. With his daughters in place as his shields surrounding his new nation, Genghis Khan could now move outward from the Mongol steppe and conquer the world.

Queens at War and Commerce

WITH ALL THE SMALLER KINGDOMS SECURELY UNITED behind him and under the control of his daughters, and with an adequate, if not entirely amicable, alliance with the Tangut in control of the Gansu Corridor of the Silk Route, Genghis Khan could move and challenge one of the larger kingdoms. For the remainder of his life he would pursue two major operations: first, the North China campaign from 1211 to 1215, and then the Central Asian offensive against the Muslims from 1219 to 1224. His daughters played critically important, but different, roles in each of these two massive quests.

In 1211 Genghis Khan attacked the Jurched rulers of North China, but his perfect plan failed almost immediately. As soon as his cavalry became hotly engaged with the Jurched forces, the Onggud erupted. The disgruntled faction suddenly revolted against young Alaqai. The rebels tried to kill her, and although they failed to capture her, they assassinated Ala-Qush and many of the other Mongol sympathizers. Alaqai barely escaped the rebels, but in addition to saving her own life, she managed to take both of her stepsons to the temporary refuge of her father's army.

While Genghis Khan had fostered a close alliance with a single Onggud clan, the others resented kowtowing to a foreign queen, particularly one from such a wild people as the Mongols. When Genghis Khan's daughter dismissed the other wives, she also destroyed the power base for their clans. The families of the old wives failed to share in the prestige and rewards of the new system and turned against her. They did not realize that because Ala-Qush was Genghis Khan's faithful ally in marriage, killing him constituted one of the gravest crimes against the Mongols.

Only twenty years old, Alaqai Beki faced these enemies at a time when it still remained unclear how successful the Mongol army would be and how powerful her father would become. Although Genghis Khan had made Ala-Qush the ruler of the Onggud, the old elite still favored their traditional alliance with the Jurched rulers of northern China, who had supplied them with a constant flow of silks and trinkets, as well as invited them to feast at grand political events at the imperial court. Those Onggud shared the more general Chinese view of the Mongols as unwashed savages who dressed in ragged wool and the skins of beasts, lived in felt tents, and gorged on unflavored meat boiled in large cauldrons that contained whole animals from the eyeballs to the tail.

When the Onggud revolted, Genghis Khan was campaigning with his army near the modern city of Datong in northern China's Shanxi Province. His soldiers had passed through Onggud territory on the way to invade China. By installing his daughter as the ruler of the Onggud, he thought that he had securely protected his rear and sides before launching the invasion. The Onggud rebels also understood this strategy, and they saw clearly the danger they posed to him. The bulk of the Mongol army now confronted the Jurched to their south and east and the Onggud to their north and west. If the Onggud rose up in rebellion, they could trap the Mongol forces between the two enemies. At the least, an Onggud rebellion would distract the Mongol forces and thereby relieve pressure on the Jurched.

Genghis Khan would tolerate no such act against his daughter, who ruled in the name of the greater Mongol Empire, nor could he afford to have such a dangerous enemy at his back. He dispatched an army with her to fight the rebels, whom they quickly vanquished.

After the suppression of the Onggud rebels, Genghis Khan favored the same kind of massive retaliation against the Onggud that he had become accustomed to using against the rebellious steppe tribes, such as the Tatars. The punishment meant killing every rebel and all the males in their family taller than the wheel of a Mongol cart, then redistributing the women and children among the tribes of the Mongol's loyal allies.

Alaqai prevented the massacre. Instead of condemning the whole nation, she persuaded her father to punish only the specific assassins who had attacked Ala-Qush. Genghis Khan wanted an investigation of the killing of Ala-Qush. "Who killed our *quda*?" he demanded to know, "so that I can extract vengeance." He demanded that the specific "person who violated his person" be brought to him. Genghis Khan then ordered the execution of the assailant and his family.

The Onggud ranked as possibly the luckiest people who ever rebelled against Genghis Khan, and their good fortune derived exclusively from having Alaqai as their ruler. As the empire grew larger and the army spread thinner and ever farther from home, Genghis Khan could not afford to tolerate any dissent or show any mercy. The Onggud were the only people whom he allowed to continue to exist as a nation after they revolted against him. Alaqai seemed determined to prove that he had not made a mistake in sparing the Onggud; she kept them loyal to the Mongols and integrated them into the heart of Mongol imperial administration.

Alaqai resumed her rule and took her stepson Jingue as her husband. She set about knitting the Onggud society back together again, but clearly within the realm of her father's growing Mongol Empire. Over the next four years, while her father fought in one city after another across northern China, she ran the Onggud nation. After she had proved her loyalty to the Onggud by protecting them from the wrath of her father, her subjects never again contested her rule.

Conquering an empire is difficult; ruling it even more so. For the Mongols the task was especially challenging since they had been a nation for a mere twenty years and had had a written language for only two years longer than that. They could turn to no single group of administrators on whom to rely in the same way they counted on merchants to operate the commercial system. Muslim administrators lived by much different rules than the Chinese administrators, and both differed from the Christians. In the marketplace one could creatively combine items from different cultures: a silk gown from China, a damask belt from Persia, a sable collar from Siberia, a peacock feather from India, beads from Venice, and turquoise chips from Afghanistan. Governmental systems, administrative practices, and law, however, could not be picked apart and recombined so readily. Muslim law derived from the Koran, which could only be read in Arabic and depended on a calendar based on the flight of Muhammad; thus for the Mongols to adopt the Muslim system of administration required accepting a whole different language and religion. Similarly, Chinese administration could not be separated from the Chinese written language and calendar. Governments were far more complexly integrated than markets.

Unable to merely pick up an existing system, the Mongols had to invent a new one, and with the men busy in perpetual war, this task fell primarily to the daughters ruling the string of kingdoms along the Silk Route. As the senior queen among the Mongols and as ruler of the largest segment of the empire, Alaqai led the way in creating a government. One of her first requirements was to learn to read and write. Where or how she did so is not known. A Chinese envoy sent by the Sung royal court in South China compiled an extensive report of his visit to the Mongols, and he wrote that Alaqai had not only mastered the rudiments of literacy, she spent a lot of time reading each day. He even specified her fondness for religious scripture, but he does not state which kinds. According to the Sung envoy, she was particularly learned in medicine. She also organized medical facilities in the lands where she ruled.

From the archaeological investigations of the ruins of Olon Sume in modern Inner Mongolia, we now know that her capital contained Christian, Muslim, and Buddhist religious structures, and it probably had Confucian and Taoist institutions and clergy. The presence of so many different religions and languages within one small city illustrates the cosmopolitan and often eclectic cultural mix that became a hallmark of the Mongol Empire. The Mongols had no universal religion that they sought to impose on their subjects; instead they encouraged all religions to flourish. Mongols such as Alaqai picked and chose what appealed to them from various religious ideas, objects, and practices with as much individual taste as they expressed when they selected from local foods. Such a right of personal preference applied not merely to the queen; every Mongol enjoyed the same opportunity.

Alaqai Beki fashioned a powerful form of Mongol internationalism. As the first member of her family and nation to rule a sedentary civilization, she invented the cultural and organizational model that grew into the Mongol Empire. On a steadily increasing scale, her capital would later be used as the prototype for Ogodei's capital of Karakorum in Mongolia; then to Khubilai Khan's building of Shangdu in Inner Mongolia, known more commonly in the West as Xanadu; and finally to Khubilai Khan's capital Khan Baliq, which the Chinese called Tatu and which would become Beijing.

Genghis Khan conquered northern China, and the Jin Dynasty of the Jurched surrendered to him but then fled farther south, leaving the Mongols in control of the north and with the Jurched as a buffer between them and the Southern Sung. Genghis Khan had anticipated that the Jurched would, as his new vassals, continue to administer northern China, so their flight south left him in control of the north but without a government to manage it. He could not stay in China and had no intention of administering the country himself. He turned to his daughter Alaqai, who, after her father, was already the highest-ranking Mongol south of the Gobi. When he withdrew back to Mongolia in 1215, Genghis Khan left her in charge of the Mongol territories in China. He left his garrison army of occupation under the leadership of General Muqali of the Jalayir clan, whose members constituted the majority of his warriors and who had long been loyal followers of the Borijin family, but Alaqai reigned.

As Genghis Khan became more occupied arranging the next major invasion, this time of the Muslim lands of Central Asia, he devoted less attention to northern China and depended increasingly on Alaqai, who proved progressively more capable. She acted independently, yet always in the best interests of the whole Mongol world no matter how far away she was from her father's mobile court. Knowing that he would be away for several years, Genghis Khan designated responsibility for managing the already conquered lands in the hands of two people. He put the Mongolian Plateau, the lands north of the Gobi, under the control of his youngest brother, Temuge Otchigen, and he left the newly conquered lands south of the Gobi under the control of his daughter Alaqai Beki, giving her the title "Princess Who Runs the State." Her authority had expanded from command of the Onggud nation of only about ten thousand members, concentrated in what is now Inner Mongolia, to being responsible for millions of people spread across northern China.

Under Alaqai's rule, troops were regularly dispatched to aid her father in his campaigns in China and Central Asia. These troops from China included medical personnel, who did much to spread the reputation and practice of Chinese medicine to the Muslim world and the West.

Through the installation of his three daughters as queens along the Silk Route, Genghis Khan controlled the territory and the fragile commercial links connecting China with the Muslim countries. With his invasion into Central Asia in 1219, Genghis Khan began a new phase of not merely capturing the trade links, but expanding them deep into the manufacturing heart of the Middle East. Just as his conquests of China started the process of taking over Chinese manufacturing industries, his armies targeted the craft centers of the Muslim world, thereby expanding control to the two major terminuses of the Silk Route.

Throughout Genghis Khan's career, the roles played by his sons remained fairly limited and stagnant, but the role of his daughters continued to develop as they matured and their experience expanded. The conquest of varied new countries and ecological zones constantly brought new military and administrative demands on the Mongols.

It was difficult for the Chinese to understand the role of Genghis Khan's daughters, though their power evoked a puzzled respect, but the Persian encounter with another daughter produced bewilderment, at best, and otherwise disgust and horror. The Chinese scorned the behavior of Mongol women as contrary to sophisticated etiquette, but the Muslims condemned them as immoral affronts to religion and, perhaps more presciently, as threats to civilization.

Although Genghis Khan lost many sons-in-law in battle, such a loss at the hands of rebels usually provoked a particularly vicious response. The fortunate fate of the Onggud rebels contrasted markedly with the fate of the rebellious citizens of Nishapur, who killed another son-in-law ten years later at a time when Genghis Khan's bloody Central Asian campaign was at its height but its ultimate victory not yet certain.

Located in what is today eastern Iran, Nishapur ranked among the primary cities of Khorasan at the time of the Mongol invasion. Khorasan, though dominated by Persian culture, was actually a part of the Turkic empire of Khwarizm, including what are now Uzbekistan, Afghanistan, Turkmenistan, and Tajikistan. Located near rich turquoise mines, Nishapur was the source of the iconic blue-green color that symbolized Persian culture. The city produced the beautifully glazed porcelains that epitomized the art and technology of the era. The most beloved of all Persian poets, Omar Khayyam, was born there in 1048 and was buried there; through his verses, he cloaked the city and Persian literature in a nearly magical aura of beauty sculpted in words. The city of turquoise, poetry, and ceramics exemplified the highest level of Persian civilization, and its destruction by an army under the leadership of a pagan princess marked the ultimate insult against all Islam. In the eyes of the Muslim world, this event came to symbolize the whole of the Mongol era.

The story was first offered in detail in the chronicle of the Persian writer Juvaini, the most accurate and informed of the Muslim historians despite his being active in the political life of the Mongols and therefore a highly partisan chronicler. Juvaini participated in many of the events and situations that he described, and he talked to the witnesses, many of whom he knew intimately.

When the Mongols captured Khwarizm's main cities of Bukhara, Samarkand, and its capital, Urgench, the sultan of Khwarizm fled to Nishapur; but instead of preparing for war, he wallowed in wine and debauchery. "He recognized no business but merrymaking," as Juvaini wrote. "Because of arranging the jewels of women he could not concern himself with the training of men, and whilst pulling down the garments of his wives he neglected to remove the confusion in important affairs." The sultan and his servants gave in to drinking and feasting, so that when the Mongols approached, he was totally drunk and his servants had to throw cold water on his head to rouse him. He abandoned the city on May 12, 1220, and fled west toward Iraq.

The people of Nishapur wisely offered no resistance to the Mongols. They obeyed the orders to surrender and agreed to assist the Mongols in the hunt for their former ruler, the sultan. The army of the Mongol general Subodei came, and the Persians fed the men and horses. For Mongols, accepting food was a highly symbolic act that not only demonstrated the submission of the conquered people but, more important, indicated that the Mongols would accept their submission and let them live as vassals. The people of Nishapur also supplied subsequent Mongol army units passing by in their hunt for the sultan.

For a short time the Mongols stopped coming. As the Mongol units became fewer and as the rumor spread that the sultan had defeated the Mongols, the people grew anxious for revolt and revenge. They thought that the Mongol wave had passed, and they were glad to be rid of both them and the sultan who had ruled them. As Juvaini described the situation, "The demon of temptation laid an egg in the brains of mankind."

The Muslims seemed not to realize that the main Mongol army had not yet arrived. Thus, in November 1220, when Tokuchar, a son-in-law to Genghis Khan, arrived with a *tumen*, a unit of ten thousand warriors, he was the vanguard of the main army under the command of Genghis Khan's youngest son, Tolui. On the third day, an arrow fired from the ramparts struck Tokuchar and quickly killed him. According to Juvaini, the Persians had no idea who the unknown fallen warrior was, and thus when his army withdrew, they thought they had defeated the Mongols. Throughout the remainder of the winter of 1220–21, the people of Nishapur seemed to believe that they had successfully and permanently driven the Mongols away. The defenders of Nishapur had three thousand crossbows, three hundred seige engines, and a supply of naptha that they could set afire and hurl from their ramparts against the Mongols.

The Mongols attacked on the morning of Wednesday April 7, 1221. By noon prayers on Friday, they had filled the moat, breached the wall for the first time, and brazenly raised their flag on a piece of the wall that they now controlled. The fighting raged on, and the Mongols continued to press onward through the night and the next day, until they controlled all the walls and fortifications around the city. According to a potentially accurate account written much later, seventy thousand defeated warriors lost their lives in the battle for Nishapur.

The people of Nishapur found themselves trapped inside their own walls. For the Mongols, this was precisely the way that they hunted wild animals—forming a fence around them and then killing them off at will. First, Tokuchar's widow, one of Genghis Khan's daughters, shut off the flow of water into the city and ordered the people to leave. After Nishapur had been evacuated onto the plains, she entered the city with her escort of warriors to round up those who had refused the order to evacuate.

When Mongols hunt, they always let some animals escape in order to reproduce. In a similar way, even when a whole city was condemned, a few people would be allowed to live. Tokuchar's widow separated out the craftsmen who might be useful in the future. Mongols had a great respect for people with any skill, from metalworking or writing to carpentry and weaving, but they had no use for defeated soldiers or people without skills, and in this category they included the rich.

In comparison with Alaqai Beki, who defended her nation even after it had rebelled against her and killed her husband, this daughter felt no connection with the rebels who had killed her husband. She ordered the burning of the empty city and then the execution of everyone except the selected workers. In the words of the chronicler known as Khwandamir, "She left no trace of anything that moved." Although the reported number of 1,747,000 executed exceeded credibility by a factor of about one hundred times the actual number, it nevertheless shows the horror felt for the Mongols. In the words of the Persian chronicler

Juvaini, who loved the cities of his homeland, "In the exaction of vengeance not even cats and dogs should be left alive." By the time the Mongols finished with Nishapur, he wrote, the "dwelling places were leveled with the dust," and "rose gardens became furnaces."

Muslim scholars believe that this daughter was likely Tumelun, but the original Persian records do not mention her name. The Mongols conquered so many cities that they did not keep a written record of them, and thus the account does not appear in their documents either. Unless some hitherto unknown text surfaces, her name will possibly never be known.

In the long list of cities conquered by the Mongols, the fall of Nishapur lacked much strategic importance, but it produced profound terror in the Muslim world because of the cultural importance of the city and its horrifying fate at the hands of an infidel woman. Any educated Muslim of the era would have keenly felt the looming doom promised by the Mongols, which seemed to have been presaged in the words of the beloved Persian poet Omar Khayyam: "Whether at Nishapur or Babylon, the Wine of Life keeps oozing drop by drop; the Leaves of Life keep falling one by one."

Muslim and Christian chroniclers used the story of the unnamed Mongol princess as the defining illustration of Mongol barbarism in war, with accounts of skulls piled up into pyramids according to sex and age, and of conquerors so ruthless that they even killed the cats and dogs of the defeated city. Despite the repeated use of these images in recounting Mongol warfare, the histories that seemed to record so precisely the number of dead never bothered to mention the name of the woman who so terrified enemy soldiers and civilians alike. The chroniclers described her merely as the daughter of Genghis Khan, the elder sister of the general Tolui, and the widow of the warrior Tokuchar.

Genghis Khan encouraged the terrifying stories about the Mongols. With such a small army compared with those that he faced and with the massive populations that he sought to conquer and control, he learned to win by propaganda and public relations as much as by his army. From the terrible abuse around him in his childhood, he mastered an uncanny ability to discern what people most wanted and most feared. He managed to use both in building his empire.

Of all civilizations to crumble before the Mongol onslaught, the Muslims certainly suffered the most and benefited the least from the Mongol invasion. After the extensive carnage of their conquest by Genghis Khan between 1219 and 1224, the Muslim states of the Middle East never again reclaimed their economic and cultural prowess at the center of the world commercial system.

For thousands of years, the people who settled in the deserts of Inner Asia traded via the unhurried flow of goods from one oasis to the next. Chinese silks slowly made their way to Rome to be unwoven and sold thread by thread, and, just as gradually, silver coins bearing the portraits of the Roman emperors drifted across the deserts toward China. Small caravans of camels—or donkeys in some areas—connected the oasis villages, and goods traveled primarily from one village to another. The traders of each oasis carefully maintained trade relations with the next, but each community and many intertwining and alternative routes prospered and withered according to local weather and political patterns. This amorphous system of small but jealously guarded routes prevented merchants from traveling in a single caravan along one entire route. Every item had to be traded dozens of times as it slowly wended its way along these multiple routes.

With the fall of Nishapur, the destruction of the Khwarizm Empire, and the conquest of the Persian cities, the Silk Route had become a Mongol highway. For the first time in the thousands of years of trade and commerce, one power controlled the Silk Route all the way from northern China across Central Asia, south to the Indus River, and west to the Caucasus Mountains at the threshold of Europe. Trade flowed uninterrupted from the Arctic Circle to the Indian Ocean, from inside the workshops of China to the cities of Persia. Except for the crucial distance of the Gansu Corridor, ruled by the Tangut kingdom, which lingered on as only a semi-vassal state of the

Mongols, Genghis Khan's daughters controlled all the states between China and Muslim Central Asia. With the aid of his daughters and his mighty army, Genghis Khan had accomplished what Alexander the Great had attempted and failed to do and what the Romans, Arabs, and Chinese had only dreamed of achieving.

The Mongols exercised ownership of the trade system, but since they knew nothing about commerce, they let the merchants run it. Mongols reaped the rewards and enjoyed the luxuries while opening up all the trade routes under a unified system and consistent policies. The Mongols simply supplied the infrastructure of safe routes, frequent resting stations, ample wells, relief animals, a speedy postal service, stable currency, bridges, and equal access for merchants, without regard to their nationality or religion.

The daughters of Genghis Khan did not create the interlocking network of trade routes, but they made it work much faster. Mongol protection and the organization of an intercontinental system of rest and relay stations permitted new supercaravans that were not only much larger than the old ones but could travel considerably farther by obtaining supplies and replacing animals as needed. Genghis Khan opened new routes, bypassing smaller settlements, and he destroyed whole cities that served as roadblocks. The Mongol routes, like modern superhighways, allowed large caravans to connect not just one oasis with the next but the entire string of oases, as merchants could now travel thousands of miles on a single journey.

The string of Silk Route kingdoms of Genghis Khan's daughters depended on controlling the points of contact and the direction of movement rather than occupying large areas of land. Gradually the Mongols developed a system of investment similar to those in modern corporations. Thus Alaqai Beki in China had shares of animals in Iraq and furs from her sister Checheyigen in Siberia; Al-Altun had claim on part of the silk production of China, and they all received wine from the Uighur oases of Al-Altun.

During the lifetime of Genghis Khan and his daughters, the Mongol enterprise was not so much an empire as a vast global corporation in which each son and daughter had the assignment to manage one part that provided a particular set of goods. The daughters operated a world financial organization that benefited almost everyone it touched. Through this interlocking set of kingdoms ruled by the daughters of Genghis Khan, the Mongols created a new world system based on a faster flow of goods and information than had been previously practical.

The Silk Route had grown slowly over several thousand years; yet suddenly, under the administration of Genghis Khan's daughters, it attained a level of complexity and global importance far beyond that of any earlier era. Alaqai Beki and her sisters transformed the chain of competing city-states and nations spread across Asia into an interlocking set of political and commercial units with a new specialization of labor that made them mutually interdependent rather than rivals. Under the control of the Mongol queens, the Silk Route reached its zenith.

In this extensive commercial system, each daughter's kingdom had its own particular role. Al-Altun's Uighurs operated the communications center of the Mongol Empire. Their location between China to the east, Mongolia to the north, and the Muslims to the southwest put them in the geographic center of the extensive Mongolian postal relay system that united the empire and made possible the rapid dispatch of messages throughout its length and breadth. The Uighurs did not serve as riders in the system; instead, they worked as translators, scribes, and clerks. From this specialization they became important in information gathering and general intelligence for the Mongol authorities.

Genghis Khan did not permit military information to be written down; it had to be delivered orally. Thus the messengers had to learn to compose and recite military orders through "rhetorically ornate rhyming words and cryptic expressions." Occasionally the people receiving an order might not understand it, but the messenger could interpret it. This special form of military poetry served the most strategic type of communication, but for more mundane affairs, the government used the Mongolian language written in Uighur script. Under the Uighur influence, the Mongols began a steep intellectual ascent. The Uighurs already had extensive libraries of hand-copied manuscripts translated from Sanskrit, but under the Mongols many Tibetan manuscripts were also translated into Uighur.

Uighur script became the Mongol script and thereby the official script of the empire. For the next seven centuries, until 1911, it remained the official script in its Mongol and Manchu forms. Even during the Ming Dynasty, which favored Chinese writing, the Chinese court had to use Mongol script for communication with many parts of its empire and foreign nations as far away as Turkey.

When Genghis Khan left on his campaign against the Muslims, he had taken Alaqai Beki's stepson Boyaohe with him as part of his personal detachment. The boy was ten or twelve years old when he set out with the army, and subsequently grew up on the campaign in Central Asia, where he performed very well and grew into an excellent soldier. By the time the Mongols conquered Muslim Central Asia and the army returned to Mongolia, Alaqai's husband, Jingue, had died. In 1225, Genghis Khan then gave the precocious Boyaohe to Alaqai to be either her third or her fourth husband. At the time of his marriage to his stepmother (who was, of course, also his sister-in-law), Boyaohe was seventeen years old, and Alaqai was in her mid-to-late thirties.

Alaqai's only child, Negudei, the son born from her marriage to Jingue, had inherited his late father's title Prince of Beiping, and she groomed him to succeed her in power. She arranged an excellent marriage for him with a daughter of her brother Tolui. During the 1230s, after nearly a quarter of a century ruling northern China, Alaqai suffered one of the cruelest blows of her life; her recently married teenage son went to fight the Song army in southern China and was struck down in battle. This ended her dynasty, and she was too old to bear more children. With the same spirit she had shown throughout her life, she devoted herself to the care of Boyaohe's other children, offering them a secure future by arranging the best marriages for them that she could within the ranks of her own Mongol family.

In the absence of her own son who could follow her, Alaqai improvised a new system that would set the pattern for Onggud rule for the next several centuries; she arranged a series of marriages of Onggud male subjects to women from her Borijin clan of the Mongols. Since Alaqai ruled for a long time, she arranged many similar marriages, which grew into a permanent part of the Mongol kinship system. When Marco Polo came to China more than half a century after Alaqai's death, this system still functioned. He explained that the leaders of the Onggud, whom he called Tenduc, "always obtain to wife either daughters of the Great Khan or other princesses of his family."

Throughout her twenty-year career, Alaqai Beki remained loyal both to her father, who sent her to rule, and to the Onggud people over whom she reigned. She laid much of the foundation for the later expansion of the Mongolian Empire into China, and she became a major conduit for selectively designating parts of Chinese civilization to be emulated by the Mongols and choosing aspects of it to be incorporated into their culture. Yet, in the end, without sons to follow her, the name of Alaqai Beki would fade quickly.

By 1226, Mongol queens controlled the Silk Route, with the exception of one small area, the still troublesome Tangut kingdom occupying the Gansu Corridor. Genghis Khan had grown tired of the perfidy of the Tangut, who promised obedience one year only to disregard it the next, sending tribute at one time and then refusing to later. Determined to finally remove the Tangut ruler, destroy his dynasty, and fully incorporate his subjects into the Mongol Empire, Genghis Khan launched a new invasion.

His principal wife, Borte, had too many responsibilities and too large a family to go with him, but on each campaign he chose one of his other three wives to accompany him. For this campaign he chose Yesui Khatun, the Tatar queen and younger sister of the second-ranking queen, Yesugen. The fourth wife, Khulan, had become the emotional favorite of his old age, but he chose Yesui because of her superior intellect and better education. It turned out to be a prescient choice.

Soon after beginning the campaign, Genghis Khan fell ill, and, unable to lead the campaign but unwilling to leave the front, he relied on Yesui to administer the government without either his enemies or his soldiers knowing of his debilitating condition.

In his final public words before his death, Genghis Khan addressed his nation as "My people of the Five Colors and Four Foreign Lands." The five colors referred to the Mongol territories he left to the five men of his family—his four sons and one surviving brother. The four foreign lands were the kingdoms of his four daughters.

At the end of his final talk, one of his retainers was quoted as making a dark prophecy. "The jade crystal that is your realm will shatter," he said. "Your many people brought together and collected together, will be scattered in all directions. Your lofty rule will be abased."

Upon hearing these words, Genghis Khan asked his people to help his children whom he was leaving behind, to offer them "water in the desert" and "a road through the mountains." He ended with the plea of his people and his descendants to "guard the good rule of the future."

"I leave you the greatest empire in the world," he said to his children. "You are the peaceable possessors of it." He begged his children to preserve his empire by remaining united: "Be then as but one tongue and one soul."

Genghis Khan greatly disliked cities, and usually just before a city surrendered, even after the hardest-fought campaigns, he departed from the scene to begin the next campaign while his officers finished the last one. Thus it was, in August 1227, just prior to the fall of the Tangut capital and the surrender of their khan, that the spirit of Genghis Khan abandoned his body. Genghis Khan's followers took his body back to the sacred mountain in Mongolia for burial in a hidden place, but they erected his *sulde,* the "spirit banners" made from the manes of his horses, to blow eternally in the wind.

His four wives had their territories occupying most of Central Mongolia. His son Ogodei acquired western Mongolia; Chaghatai received Central Asia. Tolui, the youngest son, received the ancestral homeland of eastern Mongolia. Jochi, the eldest son and the one whose brothers doubted that he was their father's son, had already died, but his heirs received Russia, the most distant part of the empire, in the hope of keeping them far removed from the rest of the family who did not recognize their father's legitimacy.

The daughters also had their lands: Checheyigen ruled the Oirat territory of Siberia. Alaqai ruled northern China. Al-Altun ruled the Uighur. Presumably Tolai was still alive with the Karluk, but too little is known about her fate. Yesui Khatun ruled the Tangut in addition to her original *ordo* along the Tuul River of Mongolia.

Genghis Khan left his Mongol nation rich and well protected.

Genghis Khan used sequences of spiritually meaningful numbers to organize his empire. Each number had a particular use: a social and cultural role in addition to its numerical value. Practical matters were organized in even numbers: two shafts of the cart or ten men to a military unit. Odd numbers held much greater supernatural power. Seven was to be avoided whenever possible, but nine and thirteen were the two most important numbers for him.

Genghis Khan's father was named Yesugei, which meant "With Nines," a name thought to bestow good fortune because its bearer would always be at the center of the eight directions and thus never be lost.

Mongols are often called by the name of the parent; thus Genghis Khan was "Son of Yesugei," or "Son of Nines." Mongols considered a name or title to carry a fate and a mission with it. Genghis Khan took his name and his patronymic seriously and literally. He structured life so that he was always the ninth, surrounded by eight. He had his primary group, known as Yesun Orlus, the "Nine Companions," or the "Nine Paladins." This set comprised the most talented and powerful men in the empire, including the four principal army commanders, known as the Four Dogs, plus the commands of his personal guard, known as the Four Horses. As always, Genghis Khan occupied the pivotal ninth position in the formation.

His personal guard originally consisted of eight hundred by day and eight hundred by night. After 1206 he adopted the older Turkic decimal system of organizing the lower military ranks into units of ten, building to the largest units of ten thousand. At this time he also increased his guard to ten thousand, but he arranged the army into eight units; the guard around him became the ninth.

In his arrangement of family government, he divided power and responsibility among eight of his children—four sons and four daughters. He had other sons and daughters, but he placed the future of the empire in the hands of these eight. Four sons held the steppes of the nomads, four daughters held the sedentary kingdoms, and Genghis Khan, the ninth in the system, ruled over them all. The system was simple, practical, and elegant. With the placement of four of his daughters as queens and four of his sons as khans, Genghis Khan had fulfilled the destiny bestowed upon him by his father's name.

Genghis Khan, however, sought to surpass his father, and for this the number thirteen had a special, but largely secret, importance for him. In the formation of his nation in 1206, he organized the *khuriltai*, and thereby the empire, into thirteen camps, and he sometimes referred to his nation as the Thirteen Ordos, or Thirteen Hordes. His four dowager queens controlled the territory surrounding the mountain in the first circle, and then in the outer circle lay the territories of his four daughters and four sons. Thus in death, precisely as at the moment of creating his empire, Genghis Khan was in the center, the thirteenth position.

In the summer of 1229, two years after Genghis Khan's death, all his offspring and the other officials of the Mongol Empire gathered to ratify Ogodei, the third son, as the Great Khan. The area of the 1206 *khuriltai* now lay a little too close to Genghis Khan's burial site on Mount Burkhan Khaldun, but the family still wanted to be near to the area. Ogodei chose an open steppe on the Kherlen River, a little to the south of the original *khuriltai*, near a spring where, according to oral tradition, his mother had nursed him, and possibly where he was born.

All the officials, generals, and Borijin clan members came. The daughters and the sons of Genghis Khan affirmed Ogodei, since their father had told them to do so. He had been chosen not because he was the smartest or the bravest, but because he was the most congenial to the largest number of people in the family, a situation created, at least in part, by his apparently being the heaviest drinker of all the heavy-drinking sons.

During the summer, as the family and officials gathered at Khodoe Aral, the supreme judge, the Tatar orphan raised by Mother Hoelun, began to write down the history of the Mongols. He gathered the stories and legends of the past, compiled the accounts of witnesses to the life of Genghis Khan, and wrote down his own memories. If he gave the record a title, it was lost, but it became known eventually as *The Secret History of the Mongols.*

At the end of the summer, Ogodei took his position at the geographic center of Mongolia, from where he would preside as the Great Khan over the eight kingdoms that constituted the Mongol Empire of Genghis Khan. Despite the mediocrity of Ogodei's leadership, the generals of Genghis Khan still commanded the army. With them in charge of the military campaigns, the empire continued to grow, adding Russia, Korea, and the Caucasus, and pushing ever deeper into China.

In terms of conquests and military expansion, the empire had not yet reached its zenith. Yet, paradoxically, it was already beginning to fall apart, and that collapse came from the center. The system left by Genghis Khan was too delicately balanced to survive. It began to totter even before all the delegates reached their homelands.

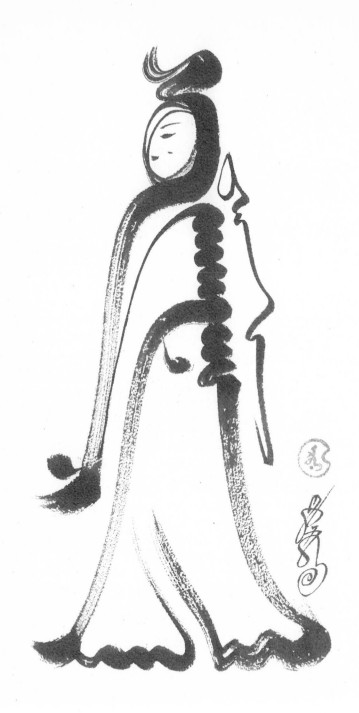

PART II

The Shattered Jade Realm
1242–1470

As the age declined, we fell into disorder,

abandoned our cities and retreated to the north.

LETTER FROM A MONGOL KHAN
TO THE KING OF KOREA, 1442

Rulers of the Mongol Empire

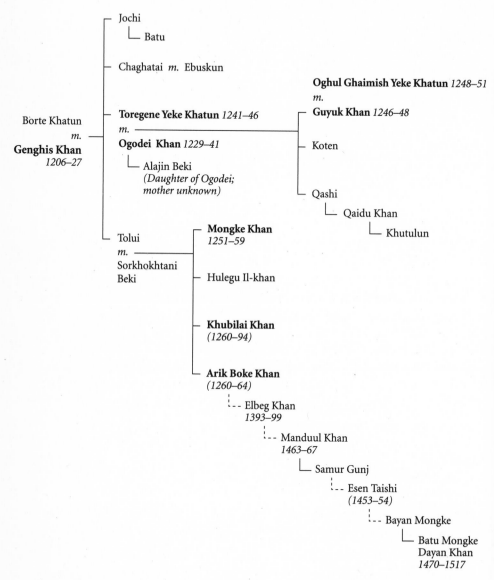

Khan *Rulers of the World Empire*

1393–99 *Dates of reigns*

(1260–64) *Contested reign as Great Khan, approximate dates only*

- - - - - *Indicates one or more omitted names or generations*

War Against Women

I N THE FALL OF 1237, AFTER EIGHT YEARS IN OFFICE, OGODEI Khan ordered the most horrendous crime of his twelve-year reign and one of the worst Mongol atrocities recorded. The nearly unbearable horror was committed not against enemies, but against the nation's daughters.

His soldiers assembled four thousand Oirat girls above the age of seven together with their male relatives on an open field. The soldiers separated out the girls from the noble families and hauled them to the front of the throng. They stripped the noble girls naked, and one by one the soldiers came forward to rape them. As one soldier finished with a screaming girl, another mounted her. "Their fathers, brothers, husbands, and relatives stood watching," according to the Persian report, "no one daring to speak." At the end of the day, two of the girls lay dead from the ordeal, and soldiers divvied out the survivors for later use.

A few of the girls who had not been raped were confiscated for the royal harem and then divided up in comically cruel ways—given to the keepers of the cheetahs and other wild beasts. The pride of Ogodei's reign had been the international network of postal stations constructed across Eurasia. He decided to augment the services of the system by sending the less attractive girls to a life of sexual servitude, consigned to the string of caravan hostels across his empire to cater to the desires of passing merchants, caravan drivers, or anyone else who might want them. Finally, of the four thousand captured girls, those deemed unfit for such service were left on the field for anybody present who wished to carry them away for whatever use could be found for them.

Somewhere in their wanderings the Mongols had learned the power of sexual terrorism. Muslim chroniclers charge that the Mongols had used a similar tactic only a few years earlier when Ogodei sent an army into North China. The Mongol force of 25,000 defeated a Chinese army of 100,000. The Mongol commander, according to the Muslims, permitted the mass sodomizing of the defeated soldiers. "Because they had jeered at the Mongols, speaking big words and expressing evil thoughts, it was commanded that they should commit the act of the people of Lot with all the Khitayans who had been taken prisoner." Even if the account was exaggerated, its existence shows that people had the idea of using mass rape as a weapon.

Even in a world hardened by the suffering of a harsh environment and prolonged warfare, nothing like Ogodei's transgression had been known to happen before, and nothing could excuse it. The chroniclers, long accustomed to reporting on rivers flowing with blood and massacres of whole cities, seem to choke on the very words they had to write to record the Rape of the Oirat Children. The Mongol chroniclers could only speak in vague terms that acknowledged a crime by Ogodei without admitting the horror of what the khan did to his own people.

The Persian chroniclers recorded the full cruelty and sheer evil behind the crime inflicted on these innocent, "star-like maidens, each of whom affected men's hearts in a different way." Everyone knew that this barbarous act violated in spirit and in detail the long list of laws Genghis Khan had made regarding women. Girls could be married at a young age but could not engage in sex until sixteen, and then they initiated the encounter with their husbands. They could not be seized, raped, kidnapped, bartered, or sold. Ogodei violated every single one of those laws.

The chronicles explain that the episode was punishment against the Oirat for not sending girls for Ogodei's harem. Ogodei's debauched appetites at this stage of his life, however, favored alcohol over girls, and while this excuse may have been proffered, the rape of the Oirat virgins was part of a much larger assault against the power of Genghis Khan's daughters and their lineages. Depraved as the violence against the girls was, it did not spring from the mindless lust of a wicked old man. The atrocity grew from a calculating greed and the desire to expand Ogodei's wealth and power. He used this ordeal to seize the lands of his sister Checheyigen, who most likely had recently died. This act brought the Oirat under Ogodei's control.

Many of the girls raped that day had been born after the death of Genghis Khan in 1227. They lived in a much different Mongol Empire from the one he founded and left to his people, and the mass rapes, although only a decade later, showed how quickly the world was changing.

The rape of the Oirat girls was the opening move in a long political, diplomatic, and terror campaign against the women of Genghis Khan's Borijin clan. Through the attack, Ogodei was taking away the powers left to his sister and imposing his own authority over her lands, her people, and her family. His crime was the beginning of the ruination of everything that his father had accomplished for his family and nation. Without the father's restraining hand, the stronger of his children began to pick off the weaker ones.

Genghis Khan's unusual system of political organization had placed Ogodei in the geographic center, surrounded by the territories of his brothers and sisters. The empire as a whole continued growing at the outer edges, but the central location of Ogodei's personal holdings prevented him from expanding without moving into the territory of his siblings. He began encroaching on their lands almost as soon as he came to power. Since he outranked them as Great Khan, it was hard to resist him. The Oirat kingdom of Checheyigen disappeared first, but the lands of the other sisters would soon follow. The unprecedented violence Ogodei had committed against the family of one sister would now expand into a struggle against all of them.

Ogodei managed to find or invent a variety of excuses to expand his power at the expense of other members of the Borijin royal family.

He moved into the territory of his father's widows Yesui and Yesugen in the Khangai Mountains and along the Tuul River. As the youngest son, his brother Tolui, had inherited their mother's land on the Kherlen, but Ogodei had tried to take it as well after Tolui died.

One day in 1232, the forty-three-year-old Tolui had stumbled out of his *ger* and in a drunken tirade collapsed and died. Some observers surmised that Ogodei had orchestrated the death with the help of shamans who drugged the alcoholic Tolui. No matter the cause, Ogodei immediately sought to benefit from his brother's death by arranging a marriage for his son Guyuk with Tolui's widow Sorkhokhtani. Knowing precisely what Ogodei was trying to do, she politely, but firmly, refused on the grounds of devoting her life to her four sons, but the refusal meant that she could never marry anyone else.

Having failed to gain the eastern lands through this marriage strategy, Ogodei sent Guyuk on a European campaign under the leadership of his cousin, Jochi's son Batu, who was expanding his family's holdings from Russia into Poland and Hungary up to the borders of the German states, and south into the Balkans. The plan, later denied by Ogodei after it failed, seemed to have been for Guyuk to take control of some of the new territories for himself, thereby giving Ogodei's family a hold in Europe from which they could slowly absorb the lands of their relatives who controlled Russia. Batu firmly rejected Guyuk's attempts to claim part of the conquests, and after a night of raucous drinking, crude mocking, and angry arguing, Batu chased Guyuk away in fear for his life.

In addition to her central Mongolian territory along the Tuul River, Yesui had been granted the Tangut kingdom astride the crucial Gansu Corridor of China's Silk Route. Ogodei sent his second son, Koten, to take those lands. Koten proved more successful than his brother Guyuk, occupying part of the Onggud lands that had once been controlled by his aunt Alaqai Beki and the Tangut lands ruled by Yesui Khatun. Koten used these lands as a base for the conquest of Tibet, and he became the first Mongol patron of Tibetan Buddhism.

Had Ogodei's plan worked, his sons would have occupied Manchuria to the east and Tibet to the south, as well as Hungary, Poland, and Ukraine to the west, thereby encircling the Mongol Empire with his personal lands all around the edges.

As each of Genghis Khan's wives died in the coming years, her territory was seized by one of Genghis Khan's sons. Just as a man's earthly spirit lived on in the hair of his horses, a woman's spirit lived on in the wool that she pressed to make the felt walls of her *ger*. The sons seemed afraid to confiscate the actual *ger* that had been the queen's *ordo*. The *ger* had been given to her by Genghis Khan, and it was there that he had lived and slept with his wives. As each queen died, she was sent to Burkhan Khaldun for burial there, and her *ordo* was sent to the former territory of Borte at Khodoe Aral, where the Avarga stream flows into the Kherlen River. Here the four structures were erected as permanent memorials to Genghis Khan and his empire. Known as the Four Great Ordos, they became a mere symbolic relic of the empire Genghis Khan had created.

Genghis Khan's death left a power vacuum that his weak and quarrelsome sons exploited but failed to fill. Although Genghis Khan's daughters and their families suffered greatly during the reign of Ogodei, a new set of women came into power; these were the wives of the khans, the daughters-in-law of Genghis Khan. Ogodei's wife Toregene was the first to take command, while her husband sank deeper into his wine. Although not the first wife, she gradually assumed the title *yeke khatun*, "empress." The oldest surviving use of that title is from an order that she issued under her name and her seal on April 10, 1240, while her husband was still alive. The text indicates that she controlled part of the civilian administration of the empire. She pursued her own activities of supporting religion, education, and construction projects on an imperial scale.

In a similar way, even before his death, the alcoholic Tolui had effectively abdicated power to his wife Sorkhokhtani because he "used to weep a great deal." Recognizing his own inability, "he commanded that the affairs of the *ulus* [nation] and the control of the army should be entrusted to the counsel of his chief wife, Sorkhokhtani Beki." After the death of Chaghatai, khan of Central Asia and the only one of Genghis Khan's sons not to succumb to alcoholism, his widow Ebuskun assumed power.

Until their sudden arrival on the political scene, very little is known of these women; they had married into the family without, in most cases, anyone noticing them enough to mention who they were or where they came from. Mongol chronicles do not specify Toregene's origin, but according to Chinese chroniclers, she had been born a Naiman. Before her marriage to Ogodei, she had been married to the son of the Merkid chief. The Merkid had been the first enemies of Genghis Khan, responsible for kidnapping his wife Borte, and through the decades he had found and defeated them several times, only to see them strike up the feud again. When Genghis Khan conquered the Merkid for the final time in 1205, the Year of the Ox, he decided to destroy the tribe—killing off the leading men and dividing up the rest. In the distribution of the remaining tribe, Genghis Khan gave the soon-to-be-widowed Toregene to Ogodei as a junior wife.

These queens such as Toregene and Sorkhokhtani had been princesses before marrying Genghis Khan's sons. Their fathers, husbands, and brothers had been killed, but as women of the aristocratic clans, they had grown up at the center of political and diplomatic life and been exposed to the intrigues that simmer and periodically explode in every power center. In addition, the most powerful daughters-in-law of Genghis Khan came from the western tribes of Mongolia and were Christians. It is uncertain if any were literate, but being raised as Christians, they at least knew the importance of written documents, and they had a larger worldview that made them proponents of religion and education in general. Sorkhokhtani supported Muslim schools in central Asia, and Toregene patronized the Taoist monasteries in China.

In her position as empress, Toregene was by far the most powerful of all the women, but she provoked angry opposition within the Mongol court on two primary accounts. She sought to increase tax revenues from wherever she could, but in a seemingly contradictory policy, she also sought to diminish the powers of the central administration, or at least to reduce the authority and power of the ministers and officials who managed the imperial court and oversaw the bureaucracy. In 1240, a dispute arose over how to produce more tax revenue from northern China, and Ogodei moved in Mahmud Yalavach, one of his experienced Muslim administrators from Central Asia, to take over as supreme judge. Toregene, however, did not like him, and at the same time she had one of her favorites, Abd-ur-Rahman, appointed as chief tax collector. The resulting rivalry sustained enormous dissension for twenty years.

In 1241, Ogodei died, probably paralyzed from an alcoholic binge. Toregene assumed complete power over the Mongol Empire as *yeke khatun*. In pursuit of her own policies, she dismissed all her late husband's ministers and replaced them with her own. Despite being the mother of five sons, she chose not to move them into high positions of critical importance in her new government. Instead, the highest position went to another foreign woman, who had been a servant in Toregene's household. She was Fatima, a Shiite Muslim Tajik or Persian captive from the Middle Eastern campaign. The Persian chronicler Juvaini, who seemingly disapproved of women involved in politics, wrote that Fatima enjoyed constant access to Toregene's tent, and she "became the sharer of intimate confidences and the depository of hidden secrets." Fatima played a political role while the older "ministers were debarred from executing business, and she was free to issue commands and prohibitions." So enormous was Fatima's reputed power that the Persian chroniclers referred to her as a *khatun*, a "queen," of the Mongols.

Toregene maintained her nomadic court in the vicinity of the capital city, Karakorum, built by her late husband in the fertile steppes near the Khangai Mountains and adjacent to the Orkhon River in central Mongolia. By Mongol standards, the area encompassed a beautiful, well-watered series of steppes, covered with green pastures in the summer and providing nearby mountains to shelter the herders and their animals in the harsh winter; for visitors, the area presented untold hardships. One of the educated Persian officials working with the Mongols wrote of Karakorum: "And the wind has pitched over our heads tents of snow without ropes or poles. Its arrows penetrate our clothes like an arrow shot by a person of great bulk."

The newly erected capital of Karakorum consisted of a small cluster of buildings constructed in both Chinese and Muslim styles, but they were hardly more than a series of warehouses for the tribute sent from around the empire. The city also provided housing and work space for the numerous captured workmen producing goods for Ogodei's followers, and it contained a large contingent of foreign clerks translating documents and helping to handle the poorly organized administration of the massive empire.

With the usual Mongol dread of solid walls of wood or stone, Ogodei always lived in his *ger* camp, which moved four times a year in a large patterned migration within a radius of about a hundred miles around his capital. To maintain the continuity of her husband's and Genghis Khan's adherence to traditional Mongol patterns, Toregene continued to run the country from her mobile court.

She reigned as *yeke khatun* from 1241 until 1246 because it took that long to orchestrate her son Guyuk's succession as Great Khan. She had to overcome the stated preference of Ogodei for another heir, as well as the opposition of most of the officials appointed by her husband. She could not persuade these men, so she reorganized the administration of the court and the newly conquered territories, appointing new administrators from China to Turkey. In the cases of recalcitrant officials who did not heed her words, she resorted to extreme measures of public punishment. The Uighur scribe Korguz, who had been quite loyal to her husband and had been given administration over eastern Iran, angered the empress; she had him arrested and executed by stuffing stones in his mouth until he choked to death.

One of her most problematic issues derived from northern China, where she repeatedly had trouble exerting her authority over the Mongols in charge there, particularly over her second son, Koten. He harbored ambitions to take power from his mother and to become Great Khan; so when she began persecuting his father's former officials, many of them escaped to Koten's court for refuge.

Toregene continued and intensified her husband's struggle for land within the Mongol Empire. The lands closest to hers were those of Ogodei's sisters. Just as Ogodei had moved against the lands of his sister Checheyigen on an unconvincing pretext, Toregene now moved against his sister Al-Altun.

Al-Altun had ruled the Uighur territory under the aegis of Genghis Khan. It is not known what type of dealings Ogodei had with his sister while their father lived, but around the time of Ogodei's death, someone from his faction executed her. According to the Persian chronicle of Rashid al-Din, this was done in violation of laws of Genghis Khan and the Mongols. "They put to death the youngest daughter of Genghis-Khan, whom he loved more than all his other children . . . although she had committed no crime."

The official excuse for executing Al-Altun seems to have been the accusation that she poisoned her brother Ogodei. She "had killed his father [Ogodei] with poison at the time when their army was in Hungary, and it was for this that the army had retreated from those countries. She and many others were judged and killed." Accusing her of such a crime against her brother at least partially justified killing her since she would have been the first to break the law against killing a member of the family. The claim, however, did not convince the family, as evidenced by a subsequent speech made by Tolui's son Khubilai Khan at the trial of some of the retainers of Ogodei demanding to know why they killed her without a trial, as mandated by Genghis Khan.

Ogodei's daughter Alajin Beki assumed power over the Uighurs. She first married the eldest son of the old Idiqut, who had been married to her aunt, and when he died, she married his younger brother.

Like their father, each of them inherited the title of Idiqut upon marrying the daughter of the Great Khan.

In 1246, five years after her husband's death, Toregene had gained sufficient control of the empire to summon a *khuriltai* to select Ogodei's successor and to have her son named Great Khan. It had been almost two decades since the last *khuriltai* in 1229 to elect Ogodei, but this *khuriltai* contrasted markedly with the last one. The *Secret History* specifies that the princes of the family as well as the princesses and the imperial sons-in-law attended the *khuriltai* of 1229, but the role of the imperial daughters-in-law at that time was so negligible that their presence was not even mentioned. By 1246, these women had risen so quickly in power that they completely controlled the *khuriltai* and managed every detail of its agenda.

By the *khuriltai* of 1246, all four of Genghis Khan's sons were dead. None of his daughters remained in power, and it is not certain that even one was still alive. The empire of eight kingdoms had been reduced to four, corresponding to the territory of the now dead sons, but three of these were ruled by women. Ebuskun, the widow of Genghis Khan's second son, Chaghatai, ruled Central Asia or Turkestan. Sorkhokhtani served as regent for eastern Mongolia and her sons' expanding territory in northern China. Toregene ruled the territory of her late husband in the center of Mongol territory, and as empress she presided over the whole empire. Only the Golden Horde of Russia, under the control of Batu Khan, remained under male rule.

Women ruled from Korea to the Caucasus Mountains, from the Arctic to the Indus, but not one was a daughter of Genghis Khan, a member of the Borijin clan, or even technically a Mongol. Never before, or since, had, or has, such a large empire been ruled by women. Yet these women were not allies; they were rivals, as each sought more power and lands for herself and her sons.

In anticipation of the great gathering on the steppes of Mongolia in 1246, foreign dignitaries arrived from the distant corners of the empire to the capital at Karakorum or to Toregene's nomadic imperial camp, where she held court in a large and elegant tent. Friar Giovanni

DiPlano Carpini, the first European envoy to Mongolia, seemed surprised both that she had a court of her own and that the tent could contain such an enormous entourage. Guyuk, Toregene's son, "sent us to his mother where a court was solemnly held, and when we had arrived there, so great was the size of the tent which was made of white fabric, that we reckon that it could hold more than two thousand men." In addition, each of the khan's wives maintained her own court as well. Guyuk's "wives had other tents, however, of white felt which were quite large and beautiful."

Emirs, governors, and grandees jostled along the same roads as princes and kings. The Seljuk sultan came from Turkey, as did representatives of the caliph of Baghdad, and two claimants to the throne of Georgia: David, the legitimate son of the late king, and David, the illegitimate son of the same king. The highest-ranking European delegate was Grand Prince Yaroslav II of Vladimir and Suzdal, who died suspiciously just after dining with Toregene Khatun in the fall of 1246.

Even after Toregene installed Guyuk as Great Khan, he initially showed little interest in his position. As Juvaini wrote, "He took no part in affairs of state, and Toregene Khatun still executed the decrees of the Empire." Within a short time, however, he decided to consolidate his power, and a disagreement arose between them concerning Fatima, his mother's close confidante.

Guyuk wished to remove Fatima, and he sent soldiers to arrest her at his mother's court. Toregene refused to surrender her.

Toregene had twice been married to foreign men whom she had not chosen. Each time, she complied with the demands the world put upon her to be a wife, mother, and queen. With Ogodei, her second forced marriage, she had produced and reared five sons, and despite their incompetence and frequent defiance and disregard for her, she had promoted their interests. Against all odds and the express wishes of his father, she had made Guyuk emperor, but she had received no thanks from her sons or anyone else.

Now in her old age, she found some solace in and emotional attachment to Fatima. Willing to forgo political life, the two women wanted to live in peace and quiet. Their close relationship may have stemmed from nothing more than having the shared experience of being foreign women forcefully brought into the Mongol court. Despite repeated efforts by Guyuk to arrest Fatima, Toregene continued to defy her son and would not yield. The court focused on this emotional struggle of wills between Toregene the empress and her son Guyuk the Great Khan. As with so many such episodes in Mongolian history, the details are missing, but the outcome is clear. She lost.

The Muslim historian Abu-Umar-I-Usman implied that her son assassinated Toregene in order to seize total power. They sent the "Khatun to join Ogodei," he wrote, "and raised his son to the throne of sovereignty, but God knows the truth." The chronicler certainly seemed to think that she deserved her fate because "she displayed woman's ways, such as proceed from deficiency of intellect, and excess sensuality."

Fatima's fate was far worse. Guyuk hated her and wanted a public confession that she had bewitched his mother. He brought her to his court, naked and bound. Although Genghis Khan had forbidden the use of torture as part of a trial or as a punishment, Guyuk found a simple way around that law on the grounds that Fatima was not a Mongol, much less a member of the royal clan. He made her torture into a public spectacle as interrogators beat and burned her in ways designed to inflict the greatest pain without shedding her blood, which might pollute the court. For days and nights the ordeal continued, with brief periods of rest so that she might regain enough strength to suffer yet another round.

Other women may have been arrested at this point and brought to trial as well. "And then they sent also for their ladies," wrote the French envoy Rubruck in order that "they might all be whipped with burning brands to make them confess. And when they had confessed, they were put to death." Who they were or to what they confessed remains unknown.

In the end Fatima also confessed to every sin and crime that her torturers demanded, but then rather than letting her just die from her wounds or executing her quickly, Guyuk subjected her to one final ordeal. He ordered the torturers to sew up every orifice of her body to ensure the most agonizing death possible. Wrapping her carefully in felt to prevent blood escaping from the stitches, the executioners then threw Fatima into the river.

Fortunately for Mongolia and the world, Guyuk died a little more than a year later. The circumstances were not clear, but he had accumulated too many enemies to speculate on which one may have brought his life to a close. In the continuing political struggles at the center of the empire, the fringes began to unravel. With his limitless love of colorful metaphors, Juvaini wrote: "The affairs of the world had been diverted from the path of rectitude and the reins of commerce and fair dealing turned aside from the highway of righteousness." He described the land as being in darkness, "and the cup of the world was filled to the brim with the drink of iniquity." The Mongol people and their subjects, "dragged now this way, now that, were at their wits' end, for they had neither the endurance to stay nor did they know of a place to which they might flee."

Ogodei's incompetent reign had ended with the cruel rape of the Oirat girls; Guyuk's sadistic reign began with the death of his mother and the public torture of Fatima. Rather than satisfying some mysterious need for revenge, these two episodes had unleashed the wicked forces of total moral corruption. The lines of authority and power shifted rapidly and are difficult to discern with precision yet certain patterns seem clear. While many men faced execution or highly suspicious deaths, once powerful women increasingly bore the brunt of the violence. Rashid al-Din recorded, with seeming approval, that when one of Chaghatai's queens disagreed with a minister in her husband's court, the minister publicly chastised and humiliated her. "You are a woman," he told her, and therefore "have no say in this matter."

No one defended the queen, and the minister continued his campaign to limit the power of the women in the court. After rebuking the queen, the minister executed one of Chaghatai's daughters-in-law for adultery without any legal proceeding or requesting permission from anyone. Genghis Khan had left a law that no member of the family, the Altan Urug, could be executed without the agreement of a representative from each branch of the family. The minister made clear that this law did not apply to daughters-in-law. The execution of the daughter-in-law at the court of Chaghatai indicated an expanding resentment against the daughters-in-law in general. The climax of their era was about to erupt in a violent clash between two of them, Oghul Ghaimish and Sorkhokhtani.

Following Guyuk's brief and chaotic eighteen months as Great Khan, his widow Oghul Ghaimish stepped forward to take control of the empire just as her mother-in-law Toregene had done seven years earlier. She was either from the Merkid tribe or possibly was the daughter of Queen Checheyigen, who had ruled the Oirat, and thus would have been a granddaughter of Genghis Khan. Her name derived from the Turkish phrase meaning "a boy next time," given by parents who have several daughters and hope for a son. Names have a strange way of creating their own destiny, and this name proved prophetically accurate. She was the last empress to nominally lay claim over the whole empire.

Aside from her constant struggle within the royal family, we know little of Oghul Ghaimish other than from a mission report from a Dominican friar, Andrew of Longumeau, sent by Louis IX of France. He arrived with a small delegation bringing a tent chapel equipped with everything that they might need to convert the Mongols to Catholicism. Fortunately this delegation did not need to travel the whole distance to Mongolia, as the regent Oghul Ghaimish kept her camp and stronghold in modern Kazakhstan, south of Lake Balkash.

The quotes Longumeau gathered and attributed to the queen show a more thoughtful ruler than the one portrayed in the Muslim histories. According to this report, she said to the French: "Peace is good; for when a country is at peace those who go on four feet eat the grass in peace, and those who go on two feet till the ground, from which good things come, in peace."

Yet most of her comments were far blunter. She followed these philosophical musings with a very simple, pragmatic point that showed her political goals. "You cannot have peace," she told the French envoy, "if you are not at peace with *us!*" She then told him to "send us of your gold and of your silver so much as may win you our friendship." Otherwise, "We shall destroy you!" She then wrote a letter to Louis IX, ordering him to come to Mongolia to surrender to her. The Eternal Blue Sky willed that she rule over the French, and if he accepted this, she would reappoint him to his office as king. This was not what the friars had in mind when they brought her the nice chapel tent, but it is unlikely that either she or the French delegates realized how soon she herself was about to be consumed in the conflagration of Mongol imperial politics.

All the diplomats and ambassadors at her court seemed to despise her. Another French envoy, Rubruck, wrote of Oghul Ghaimish: "As to affairs of war and peace, what would this woman, who was viler than a dog, know about them?" He also eagerly passed on the gossip he heard about her. He wrote that Mongke Khan, the eldest son of Tolui and Sorkhokhtani, "told me with his own lips" that Oghul Ghaimish "was the worst kind of witch and that she had destroyed her whole family by her witchcraft."

Oghul Ghaimish was empress, but her nemesis, Tolui's widow Sorkhokhtani, only had the title of *beki*, "lady." Over the next three years, the two women fought a vigorous contest for control of the empire. The inexperienced *khatun* was no match for Sorkhokhtani, whom Christians, Jews, Muslims, and Buddhists praised effusively for her cunning. She was probably the most capable woman of the Mongol era, and she had been preparing her entire life for the moment when she had the chance to seize power for her sons. Her role in shaping the form and fate of the Mongol Empire far outweighs that of any other person of her era, and in historical impact, she stands second only to Genghis Khan himself.

By the time she faced off against Oghul Ghaimish, Sorkhokhtani had spent nearly two decades as a widow devoted solely to the task of molding her four sons into outstanding men of respected aptitude. Her sons were probably the best educated and, aside from Batu in Russia, the most talented men in the Mongol Empire. She instilled in her sons an abiding respect for her Christian faith, and they often accompanied her to celebrate the holy days. The sons also maintained portable chapels in tents that went along on the Mongol campaigns, but none of them publicly accepted baptism into her faith.

Sorkhokhtani insisted on their strict adherence to Mongol law, but at the same time, she combined this with extensive education about the civilizations around them, particularly the Jurched, Uighurs, and Chinese. She made sure that in addition to knowing traditional steppe culture, her sons learned to speak, read, and write excellent Mongolian. She had them taught to speak colloquial Chinese, although apparently not to read or write the classical version so prized by scholars and bureaucrats. Throughout the reign of Ogodei's family, she had tightly controlled her sons' behavior to keep them beyond any sort of suspicion for misconduct or disloyalty to whichever Great Khan happened to be in power. All accounts agree that she did this by making them scrupulously obey the law and the ruling khan without providing him a reason to suspect or an excuse to punish any one of them. Sorkhokhtani spent her life preparing for the *khuriltai* of 1251.

By contrast, Oghul Ghaimish was clumsy and awkward in her public role. Despite Oghul Ghaimish's decisive advantage of control over the imperial capital of Karakorum and all the lands around it, she lacked the skills to keep her immediate family, much less the whole Ogodei lineage, united under her. According to Juvaini, her work "amounted to little except negotiations with merchants, the provisional allocation of sums of money to every land and country, and the dispatch of relays of churlish messengers and tax-gatherers." In the disjointed politics of the time, "her sons held two separate courts in opposition to their mother"; and thus there were three rulers in one place. And elsewhere also, "the princes made dealings in accordance with their own wishes, and the grandees and notables of every land attached themselves to a party according to their own inclination." Confusion reigned, "and the affairs of Oghul Ghaimish and her sons got out of control because of their differences with one another and their contentions with their senior kinsmen; and their counsels and schemes diverged from the pathway of righteousness."

Despite her need to cultivate public support, Oghul Ghaimish Khatun apparently felt a deeper desire for more revenue. In July 1250, just prior to the election for the new khan, she issued an edict to increase the taxes on herders from 1 percent to 10 percent, thereby making the tax for Mongol herders the same as for conquered farmers. Such an act alienated the people whom she most needed to support her, and it revealed her poor sense of political timing.

With the full support of her four capable sons and a lifetime of preparation and waiting, Sorkhokhtani organized the campaign to elect her son to the office of Great Khan. Sorkhokhtani conspired with her nephew Batu Khan of the Golden Horde to bypass the authority of Oghul Ghaimish, call a new *khuriltai,* and orchestrate the election of her eldest son, Mongke, as Great Khan. This would be the last election in which the women of the family had a public voice. Batu Khan's invitation went to all the queens. "He sent messengers to the wives of Genghis Khan, the wives and sons of Ogodei Khan, the wife of Tolui Khan, Sorkhokhtani Beki, and the other princes and emirs of the right and left." On July 1, 1251, the assembled Mongol throng proclaimed the election of Sorkhokhtani's son, the forty-three-year-old Mongke, as Great Khan of the Great Mongol nation.

After securing the election for her son, Sorkhokhtani personally presided over the trial of her defeated rival, the ousted queen Oghul Ghaimish. Guyuk had interpreted the law to allow torture of people who were not members of the Borijin clan, and this now applied to her. Even if Oghul Ghaimish had been the daughter of Checheyigen, and thus the granddaughter of Genghis Khan, by the rules of patrilineal descent she was not a member of the Borijin clan but of the clan of her father. Her husband and her children were all Borijin members and unquestionably Mongols, but she was neither.

In a show trial similar to the one endured by Fatima, Oghul Ghaimish had to face her accusers naked, her hands sewn together with strips of rawhide. The ordeal was more public torture and interrogation than a judicial proceeding, and other women of the Ogodei branch of the family also had to face similar torture and judgment. The outcome was always the same. The condemned woman was executed in some gruesome manner and thrown into the river.

Mongke conducted the trial of the men. He sat on a chair in front of a shrine to Genghis Khan and had each man brought in for questioning. Since it was still, at least for now, against the law of Genghis Khan to torture a member of the Borijin family, Mongke ordered that their retainers be brought in and beaten to make them confess the crimes of their former masters. As part of the spectacle, one of the ministers decided or was forced to commit suicide with his own sword during the proceedings. Tanggis, an Oirat son-in-law of the late Guyuk, was beaten until the flesh fell from his thighs; yet he was a lucky one, because he survived. In yet another sign of how far they had drifted from the laws of Genghis Khan, the new generation of Mongol rulers seems to have lost its abhorrence of public bloodletting.

After the main trials in the central Mongol court concluded, regional officials were ordered to hold similar trials of members of Ogodei's lineage and their former administrators. The purge reached a climax in a literal hunt for dissenters who had escaped from the court to the countryside and found refuge from the first round of reprisals. In the traditional hunts, men formed a large circle, and by tightening it drove the prey toward the center for slaughter. In this enormous hunt, Mongke's court ordered ten units of ten thousand men each to sweep through the land in a large military formation, searching for sympathizers of the deposed branch of the family. The hunt yielded some three hundred families who had fled from the authorities. They suffered the same fate as those before them. They were beaten with heated brands until they confessed. Then they were executed.

We know nothing of most of the victims or of their alleged crimes.

They survive in the historical record only because their deaths left a warning to future generations. One queen called Toqashi Khatun was tried and convicted, in the presence of her husband, by a former political rival serving as judge. The judge "ordered her limbs to be kicked to a pulp." According to Rashid al-Din, the judge thereby "relieved his bosom filled with an ancient grudge."

Sorkhokhtani had emerged victorious, but her sons then channeled their fury against the survivors, including women who had once been their allies and helped them attain power. The worst era for royal Mongol women followed the election of Mongke Khan. Once such a purge destroys its original target, the sponsors of the persecutions often find it difficult to stop the violence. Having destroyed their enemies, they turn their fury toward one another and thus make enemies of their former confederates. The killers began to kill one another. Soon women within the victorious side came under attack.

Rubruck reported that when a wife of Mongke Khan had two people executed, he became angry with her. Then "he forthwith sent to his wife and asked her where she had found out that a wife could pass a death sentence, leaving her husband in ignorance of what she had done." As punishment he had her sealed up in solitary confinement for a week "with orders that no food be given her."

As for the queen's two retainers, a brother and sister who had carried out the executions, Mongke first killed the brother. Then he ordered the man's head be removed and hung around his sister's neck. Soldiers then chased her around the camp beating her with burning brands. When they finally tired of the torture, they killed her. Mongke also wanted to have his wife executed but did not. "And he would have had his own wife put to death had it not been for the children he had of her."

Every successful purge needs a complicit judge or judiciary, and the family of Sorkhokhtani found him in Menggeser Noyan of the Jalayir clan, whom they appointed to be supreme judge of the Mongol Empire. Since he came from neither the ruling Borijin clan nor any of their marriage ally clans, he should have been fair and impartial in reviewing cases and imposing judgments, but according to the Persian chronicles, "He was pitiless in executing offenders." Initially, Menggeser Noyan arrested the members of Guyuk's family, oversaw the interrogation, passed judgment on them, and then executed them. In this way, he insulated Mongke Khan and his family from some of the personal blame, since it was still too grave a crime for one member of the Borijin clan to execute another.

The purge expanded and continued until 1252, and most of the arrests occurred far from the main court. Still, in such cases the accused had a theoretical right of appeal to the court, particularly for a capital crime. Menggeser Noyan decided not to review any of the appeals until after execution of sentence. It remains unknown, but also unlikely, that he found anyone innocent after execution.

In the terror and chaos created by the purge, Sorkhokhtani's victorious faction confiscated the lands and property of the accused. Sorkhokhtani's sons annexed the entire kingdom of Alaqai Beki, who had ruled the Onggud and all of northern China. She claimed these lands on the legal grounds that her daughter had been married to Alaqai's son who had been killed in the southern campaign. Around 1253, Mongke Khan gave control of the Onggud and surrounding area toward the west to his younger brother. Thus, Khubilai Khan peacefully absorbed the Onggud kingdom of his aunt Alaqai Beki, but the other acquisitions for him and his brothers proved much more difficult and usually bloody.

Whereas the ruling family managed to take control of Alaqai Beki's Onggud nation by politics, they found it much harder to seize the Uighur territory, ruled by the late khan Ogodei's daughter Alajin Beki and her husband the Idiqut. Since the Idiqut was obviously loyal to the Ogodei faction, Menggeser Noyan ordered his arrest and personally oversaw the questioning of the Uighur leader.

He faced a brutal interrogation, but it probably was similar to many others presided over by the judge. They twisted the Idiqut's hands until he passed out from pain. When he revived, they placed his head into some type of wooden press. Menggeser departed from the scene of the interrogation, but he left the Idiqut in the press with guards. During Menggeser's absence, one of the guards took pity on the Idiqut and loosened the press. When Menggeser returned and saw what had happened, he had the guard seized and delivered "seventeen stout blows upon the posterior."

For a time, the Idiqut persisted in denying any involvement in a vague plot and heresy, but in the end, he and his companions succumbed and admitted to anything required of them. One of Mongke Khan's partisans summarized the interrogations very simply. "After sipping the unpalatable cup of the roughness of the Tatar rods," the accused ones always "vomited forth and declared what was hidden in their breasts." The Mongols sent the Idiqut and his men back to the Uighur territory with orders that on the Muslim holy day of Friday, the Idiqut's brother cut off the unfortunate leader's head and saw his two companions in half. To prove that his loyalty to Mongke Khan surpassed that to his own family, the new Idiqut complied.

Although he was Great Khan during this time, Mongke may have been less involved with the purge than his mother, Sorkhokhtani, and her allies. Persian chroniclers portray him as a merciful man who opposed the killing of Mongols by Mongols. In other aspects of his eight-year reign, Mongke Khan showed consistent and seemingly genuine respect for the Great Law left in place by his grandfather Genghis Khan. Of all the grandsons, he and his cousin Batu Khan of Russia seemed the most capable and the most dedicated to following the spirit of that law. The layers of officials may have shielded him from some of the worst atrocities, but he could not have been totally ignorant, no matter how preoccupied with other issues.

The purges subsided slightly when Sorkhokhtani became desperately ill. As a Christian, she feared that the illness might be related to the wretched evil she had unleashed. In an effort to attain forgiveness and prolong her life, she began to pardon the convicted. While technically sparing the life of the condemned, she and her family still sought to inflict the maximum punishment on them and to offer a lesson to anyone else who might oppose her family's rule. The condemned's "wives and children, his servants and cattle, all his animate and inanimate possessions, were seized and distributed." As a secondary form of punishment for those whose lives were spared, she sent them into the most dangerous assignments of the military, "arguing that if he is fated to be killed he will be killed in the fighting." In the case of others: "They send him on an embassy to foreign peoples who they are not entirely certain will send them back: or again they send him to hot countries whose climate is unhealthy such as Egypt and Syria." Sork-hokhtani died in February or March of 1252, while the campaign of retribution still raged through the empire.

Although Mongke Khan continued to appoint some women as queens and gave them limited power to rule over subservient areas, he made certain that they had no independent power and prevented any-one else from giving power to women. Mongke Khan issued a decree that no woman could be made *khatun* by a shaman or one of Guyuk's former officials. If any shaman or other official recognized a woman as *khatun,* Mongke Khan ordered the penalty of death, using the uniquely Mongol expression "They shall see what they shall see."

What Genghis Khan had spent a lifetime creating was destroyed within another lifetime. The Mongol Empire lingered for another cen-tury—at first growing fatter and fatter through conquest, then slowly decaying into a twisted shadow of its once noble origin. It would never again be the empire of its founder, who imposed a strict code of laws and lived an unadorned life of austerity and hard work. The delicately balanced system of men and women sharing similar powers had proved too fragile to survive. Though occupying the largest empire, the Borijin family had become just one more bloated and decadent dynasty spilling out across the pages of world history.

Like a drunk who tears down his own *ger* in some unfathomable rage, the Borijin clan destroyed everything that had made it grand and powerful. They sank into a prolonged degeneracy surrounded by the broken pieces of their once glorious Mongol Empire.

The chronicler Abu-Umar-I-Usman reported that years earlier, in 1221, during Genghis Khan's Central Asian campaign when his sons Jochi and Chaghatai conquered the capital city of Urgench, they seized the women they wanted to keep for themselves and then gathered all the remaining women outside the city walls on an open plain. They divided the women into two groups and ordered them to strip naked. According to this story, Genghis Khan's sons then gave the order for one group to attack the other.

"The women of your city are good pugilists," one of the sons was quoted as saying to the conquered city officials. "Therefore, the order is that both sides should set on each other with fists." The women, thinking that the victorious side would be allowed to live, set to fighting each other with tremendous fury. The soldiers watched the spectacle, cheering some fighters on and jeering at others. Many women killed other women in the course of the day, but eventually the audience tired of the match. At the end of the game, the generals ordered the soldiers to kill all the surviving women.

Such stories, especially from anti-Mongol sources, can never simply be accepted as fact based on only a single account. Yet the report always teaches us something, even if it is nothing more than that the idea of such an event existed; it was conceivable, and thus someone might do such a thing. Sometimes even the most implausible stories from one decade or generation become the realities for the next one. In the generation after Genghis Khan, many of the powerful women of the empire expired fighting one another much like the women of this story. And, like them, the Mongol queens ended up killing one another, only in the end to be killed themselves.

The violence did not end with the overthrow of the queens; it continued to spread and became endemic to family politics. Sorkhokhtani had kept her four sons united and focused on rivals outside their family, but, with her gone, the sons turned on one another. Within eight years, in 1259, Mongke died during a campaign in China, and his two younger brothers, Khubilai, based in northern China, and Arik Boke, based in Mongolia, began a battle for power. Khubilai captured Arik Boke and sought to put him on trial for treason, but when other members of the Borijin clan refused to attend the trial, Arik Boke died mysteriously in captivity in 1266, almost certainly a victim of his brother's quest for power.

The Mongol Empire was soon to reach its maximum territorial extent, but it could not long survive the family fighting that was destroying its ruling family. Khubilai commanded the greatest army, but it was more Chinese than Mongolian, and although he claimed the title of Great Khan in 1260, he had been elected in only a sham *khuriltai* held in China rather than Mongolia and without support from the Borijin clan or other Mongols.

While continuing to worship the spirit of their grandfather Genghis Khan and making him into a virtual god, his heirs destroyed everything he created. Yet the more they destroyed, the more ritually important they made him. Khubilai Khan created the office of *jinong*, meaning "Prince of Gold," or "Golden Prince," and assigned him "to guard the northern frontiers and to govern 'the Four Great Ordos' of the Founding Emperor, the military forces, the Mongols and the homeland." With this responsibility, the *jinong* controlled the most sacred objects in the Mongol world: the black *sulde*, Genghis Khan's horsehair banner in which a part of his earthly soul remained after he ascended into heaven, and the four *gers* of his four wives.

Mysteriously, however, over the coming years, what began as only four *gers* increased to eight. They were explained as being the shrines of his horse or his milk pail, but the structures housing them had once belonged to some woman since milk pails and saddles did not own *gers*. The most plausible explanation is that just as the *ger* of each of Genghis Khan's four wives was brought to Avarga after she died, these were quite possibly the *gers* of his four deposed daughters. Since the felt contained part of the departed woman's soul, none of the sons claiming her land wanted her soul left behind to haunt him. The solution was to collect them all together. Thereafter, they were known as the Eight Gers or Eight Ordos of Genghis Khan.

Granddaughters of Resistance

At the height of the Mongol Empire, around 1271, young Marco Polo set out from Venice to the Mongol capital at Beijing with his father and uncle, who had just completed the same round-trip. The era of conquests begun by Genghis Khan had concluded, and although its shape differed radically from what he had intended, the Silk Route still bustled with caravans, merchants, and exotic wares. Marco Polo easily made his way overland from the Mediterranean to the Mongol court of Khubilai Khan, making almost the entire trip within the Mongol Empire and under the protection of Mongol soldiers.

Yet, by the time he left Beijing to return home around 1291, the middle part of the empire had collapsed; and because he could not cross the continent, he had to sail from China around South Asia to the Persian port of Hormuz. Within the time of his trip, the empire had broken into three large pieces, and the center had shattered.

Instead of a string of khanates around the central one in Mongolia, three miniature empires emerged. In 1271 Khubilai Khan ruled most of Mongol East Asia and had declared a new Chinese dynasty that he called the Yuan. His brother Hulegu had created a soon-to-be Muslim dynasty known as the Il-Khanate over the Middle East. The only one of the three that survived in something approaching the manner created by Genghis Khan was the Russian territory given to the family of Jochi and known eventually as the Golden Horde.

The Il-Khanate of Persia, the Golden Horde of Russia, and the Yuan Dynasty of China formed three points of a large triangle, and although they tried, none of them could control the middle of the continent. This central zone of mountains and adjacent deserts extending roughly from Afghanistan to Siberia became the gathering point for all the disaffected lineages, the deposed Borijin members, dreamers bent on becoming the new Genghis Khan, and those who simply wanted a refuge from the rapidly changing world. Some of the granddaughters of Genghis Khan took up the struggle against the aggression of Sorkhokhtani's lineage, and they found new allies in the other defeated lineages of Ogodei and Chaghatai. Together they formed a vortex of resistance in the center of the Asian steppe in what is now Kazakhstan, Kyrgyzstan, and the western parts of Mongolia and China. These factions directed most of their anger against the newly formed China under Khubilai Khan, since he claimed to be the new Great Khan of the whole empire, but they pitted one part of the empire against the other when possible and rapidly changed sides when advantageous.

Between 1250 and 1270, Orghina, one of Checheyigen's Oirat daughters who had escaped the mass rape, became the center of resistance. After serving as regent in Central Asia from 1251 to 1260, but unable to form a powerful independent force, she switched sides back and forth among the contenders for the office of khan over the following decade. Orghina Khatun, described as "a beautiful, wise, and discerning princess," maneuvered through a succession of power struggles, changing allegiances and religions as needed, sometimes coming out on top and sometimes temporarily losing everything and starting again.

Inner Asia provided a constant refuge for the enemies of the large Mongol states around it. After Khubilai defeated his youngest brother, Arik Boke, who as *otchigen* had ruled the family homeland of Mongolia, he seized the courts from the widowed queens and dispersed their gers and other possessions to his male allies. In this way, Arik Boke's wives and their courts were treated more as booty from a defeated foe than as defeated members of the royal family. Such actions produced a constant flow of rebels and refugees into the free zone of the interior of the continent.

The hostile tribes of the interior would have constituted little more than a nuisance for the three Mongol factions ruling except for one important factor. All trade goods had to pass through their territory. Under the Mongols, the trade of the Silk Route had grown from transporting mere luxuries into an important international commerce at the core of the world economy. The importation of silks, bronze mirrors, and medicines from China made the Muslims more willing to tolerate the Mongol Il-Khanate as their overlords. The Golden Horde used Chinese silks and Persian carpets to maintain the loyalty of the Russian nobles, who in turn kept the peasants from revolting. The Mongol emperors of China needed Damascus glass and steel, Indian jewels, and Siberian furs as well as Muslim and European technology to sustain their power. Gold brocade became the Mongol fashion throughout the empire, and huge quantities passed back and forth, as did more prosaic items such as asbestos and dried insects used to manufacture exotic dyes.

Just as important as the trade commodities, the Silk Route carried the information that the empire needed to function: diplomatic correspondence, intelligence, tax receipts, census summaries, and conscription reports, all of which required paper to keep the bureaucracy functioning. Accompanying the merchants and camel drivers along the route was a constant flow of priests, mullahs, doctors, astronomers, engineers, brewers, printers, metalsmiths, scribes, weavers, soothsayers, translators, munitions specialists, architects, miners, and tile makers. Never before in history had so many goods and so much learning and cultural influence traveled so quickly from city to city and civilization to civilization.

The Mongols outside of Mongolia had become more of a ruling aristocracy spread out over Eurasia than a tribe of warriors. They maintained a vaguely Mongol theme to their lifestyle, but the underlying substance had shifted. The simple Mongol *gers* of felt and fur turned into mobile palaces of linen and silk with rich embroidery, plush carpets with intricate designs, and flowing curtains and door covers offering a more dramatic framing for the pageantry and staged events in the daily life of the royal elite. As Juvaini described one used for a Central Asian tiger hunt: "It was a large tent of fine linen embroidered with delicate embroideries, with gold and silver plate."

As the Mongol men married local women who preferred life in palaces, the *ger* quickly changed from the focal structure of domestic life owned and controlled by women into accoutrements of manly activities such as hunting and drinking. Although they still controlled the most powerful fighting army in the world, the Borijin men sometimes seemed more interested in designing and decorating novel tents than in obtaining necessary military equipment. According to the Persian record for making one such special *ger*, "The master craftsmen had been called together and consulted, and in the end it had been decided that the tent should be made of a single sheet of cloth with two surfaces," with both sides boasting identical designs and capped by a golden cupola. "They feasted and reveled here, and the access of mirth and joy to their breasts was unrestricted." The tent was judged so beautiful that it made the sun envious and made the moon sulk.

Marco Polo's path home across Central Asia was barred by two of Genghis Khan's most unusual descendants, a father-and-daughter fighting team. Marco Polo called the daughter Aijaruc, derived from Aiyurug—meaning "Moon Light" in Turkish. She is better known from other sources as the warrior Khutulun, which came from Mongolian Hotol Tsagaan, meaning "All White." Born around 1260, she was the great-granddaughter of Ogodei, and her father, Qaidu Khan, was the regional ruler in Central Asia.

Qaidu Khan and Khutulun lived in the interior of the continent and allied with a large number of Mongols and tribes opposed to the central rule of Khubilai Khan. After Khubilai Khan proclaimed the existence of a Chinese-style dynasty, the Yuan, in 1271, the disaffected family members in the interior increasingly portrayed themselves as the true Mongols. Their land around the Tianshan Mountains and adjacent steppes became known as Moghulistan, meaning "land of the Mongols," although it was not in the original homeland on the Mongolian Plateau.

Qaidu Khan was described as a man of average height who held himself quite erectly. According to the Persian chronicle, he had only nine scattered hairs on his face. He was as strict in his habits as in his posture. Almost unheard of in the Mongol royal family, Qaidu Khan drank no alcohol, not even the beloved *airag,* fermented mare's milk, and he ate no salt. He seemed equally as strict in his relations. When another of his daughters found her husband having an affair with her maid, Qaidu Khan executed him.

Charitably described as beautiful and much sought after by men, Khutulun had a large and powerful figure. She excelled in all the Mongol arts: riding horses, shooting arrows, and even wrestling. She became known as a champion wrestler whom no man could throw. Since Mongols frequently bet on wrestling matches and other competitions, she often won horses as a result of her wrestling victories. In time, she came to have a herd of more than ten thousand horses won in such a manner.

Her father gave her a *gergee* as a sign of her power and independence. Called a *paiza* by Marco Polo, the *gergee* was a large and heavy medallion of office, consisting of an engraved disk or rectangular plate worn on a chain around the neck. Made of silver or gold, it stated the power of the holder and that it was granted by the khan under the will of the Eternal Blue Sky. Since the earlier queens had used seals, or *tamghas,* to signify their status, Khutulun is the only woman mentioned as owning her own *gergee,* an authority usually reserved for men.

Although Khutulun had fourteen brothers, she outperformed

them all. While his other children assisted him as best they could, Qaidu Khan relied highly on his daughter Khutulun for advice as well as for support. She was her father's favorite child and helped him to administer the government and affairs of his kingdom. Rashid al-Din, definitely not a sympathetic chronicler, wrote that "she went around like a boy," though he also said that she "often went on military campaigns, where she performed valiant deeds." Despite the apparent unusualness of the relationship between Qaidu Khan and Khutulun, in some ways their cooperative work probably reflected that of Genghis Khan and his daughters.

Khutulun followed an unorthodox method of confronting the enemy. She rode to the battlefield at her father's side, but when she perceived the right moment, in the words of Marco Polo, she would "make a dash at the host of the enemy, and seize some man thereout, as deftly as a hawk pounces on a bird, and carry him to her father; and this she did many a time."

Qaidu Khan commanded an army of around forty thousand warriors. They fought all along the frontier with Khubilai Khan's China and controlled much of the interior of the country along the oases of the Silk Route and the western mountains. In addition to numerous local spats with other members of the family, Qaidu Khan's army reached toward the northeast as far as the traditional Mongol capital of Karakorum and had at least one campaign in the Khentii Mountains farther east.

Because of Genghis Khan's law that every branch of the family had to approve the granting of the title, the opposition of Qaidu Khan and Khutulun together with other disgruntled members of the Borijin clan served as a constant reminder that Khubilai Khan lacked universal Mongol approval. On both sides, the campaigns often showed more propagandistic bravado than genuine military achievement. One of Khubilai's allied cousins, a renowned archer named Toq-Temur, rode off to war on a gray horse. "People choose bays and horses of other colors so that blood may not show on them, and the enemy may not be encouraged," he is quoted as saying. "As for me, I choose a gray horse, because just as red is the adornment of women, so the blood of a wound on a rider and his horse, which drips on to the man's clothes and the horse's limbs and can be seen from afar, is the adornment and decoration of men."

Despite all the big words, the boundaries changed little. No army secured a decisive victory. The low-grade but persistent hostility continued with periodic violent flare-ups. Caravans sought out routes around the violence, but as the years passed, fewer managed to get through.

Marco Polo also became caught up in the propaganda. Having never seen the Mongols under Genghis Khan and being a young merchant rather than a seasoned soldier, he accepted and repeated many of the grandiose stories of military triumphalism heard around the Mongol court in Beijing. When Qaidu Khan fought Khubilai Khan's army at the largely abandoned capital of Karakorum in Mongolia, Marco Polo mistakenly described it as one of the hardest fought in Mongol history. "Many a man fell there," wrote Marco Polo. "Many a child was made an orphan there; many a lady widowed; many another woman plunged in grief and tears for the rest of her days." Qaidu Khan eventually withdrew, and the battle settled nothing.

Khubilai Khan faced great difficulty in combating Qaidu Khan and the tribes of the interior because his largely infantry Chinese army could not travel far and was not trained in the appropriate kind of warfare needed against mounted tribesmen in the desert and mountains. Even worse, his Mongol and other tribal warriors could not be trusted to fight people who were their own relatives or with whom they had much more in common than they had with the distant and increasingly alien Mongol court in Beijing.

Unable to depend on the Chinese and unwilling to rely on the Mongols for his protection, Khubilai Khan made one of those temporarily convenient decisions that over time produces totally unexpected results with tremendous implications. Khubilai requested and received soldiers from the west via his relatives in the Golden Horde. Fifty years earlier, the Mongols had moved an army of Saxon miners to work in northern Asia, and now Khubilai brought in soldiers who would have no kinship or cultural ties to either the Mongols or the Chinese, presuming that they would therefore be totally dependent and loyal only to him.

Although from various western origins, the recruits came from two main groups: the European Ossetians of the Caucasus Mountains and the Turkic Kipchak tribes of the adjacent plains of southeastern Russia. The Ossetians came as guards to the Forbidden City in Beijing, and the Kipchak to fight Qaidu Khan, becoming an army of frontier occupation in western Mongolia and parts of Siberia. From these sites they repeatedly raided the forces of Qaidu Khan but never eliminated the threat from the independent tribes.

Although never commonplace, through the centuries, stories about women warriors appeared regularly enough in Asian and European steppe history not to be considered as novelty. Their deeds were usually explained as arising from unusually dire circumstances or in some cases from exceptional aptitude. The ability of women to fight successfully in steppe society when they failed to do so in most civilizations derived, however, from the unique confluence of the horse with the bow and arrow. In armies that relied on infantry and heavy weapons such as swords, lances, pikes, or clubs, men enjoyed major physical advantages over women.

Mounted on a horse and armed with a bow and arrows, a trained and experienced woman warrior could hold her own against men. Women fared better in combat based on firepower than in hand-to-hand combat. Although archery requires strength, muscular training and discipline prove to be more important than brute force. An archer, no matter how strong, can never substitute mere might for skill in shooting. By contrast, good swordsmanship requires training and practice, but a sufficiently strong person wielding a sword can inflict lethal damage without prior experience.

Because archery depended so much on training, the ability of women to use arrows effectively in war depended upon their developing their skills as young girls. In the pastoral tribes, all children learned to use the bow and arrow, primarily for hunting and for protecting their herds from predators. Both boys and girls needed this expertise. In a family with an adequate number of both sexes, the boys would take the larger animals, such as camels and cows, farther away to graze, while girls stayed closer to home with the sheep and goats. Since wolves would more likely attack a sheep or goat than a camel or cow, the girls had to be able to defend their animals.

Muslim and Christian sources repeatedly described women warriors among the Mongols. The first such mention came in letters from a Dominican friar and an archbishop between 1234 and 1238, reporting on the Mongol threat to Christendom. Like flashing news bulletins from the war front, the letters described, in a mixture of minute detail and fantasy, reports brought into the Russian cities by refugees fleeing the Mongol onslaught. They reported that a Mongol princess led the army and that she not only fought but acted like a man.

The supposed Mongol princess attacked a neighboring prince and looted his province. In a quest for revenge, he captured, raped, and killed her and, in a final act of retribution, mutilated her corpse and chopped off her head. A similar account of the killing of a khan's sister appears in the manuscript of Thomas of Spalato, which describes the Mongol invasion of Dalmatia and the siege of Split in 1242. He adds that many women fought in the Mongol army and were braver and wilder than the men, but the account seems based solely on hearsay, with no reliable specifics.

Although both Muslim and Christian chroniclers described fighting Mongol princesses, their reports do not overlap in place or time, and therefore make it difficult to judge their accuracy. By contrast, both wrote about Khutulun, and she survived in oral folk traditions as well.

As accustomed as the Mongols were to seeing women on horses and shooting arrows from bows, no one had seen a woman who could wrestle as well as Khutulun could. According to Marco Polo, the independent princess refused to marry unless a man could first defeat her in wrestling. Many men came forward to try, but none succeeded. In order to wrestle her, each opponent had to wager ten horses on a bout, and thus she substantially increased the size of her herds. Her parents became anxious for her to marry, and so, around 1280, when a particularly desirable bachelor prince presented himself, her parents tried to persuade her to let him win. He was "young and handsome, fearless and strong in every way, insomuch that not a man anywhere in his father's realm could vie with him." He brought with him a thousand horses to bet on his victory.

A crowd gathered for the match that was held in front of Khutulun's parents' court. It seems that with the hope of pleasing the parents whom she loved so much, Khutulun wanted to let the prince win. That resolve melted, however, in the rush of excitement when the match began. "When both had taken post in the middle of the hall they grappled each other by the arms and wrestled this way and that, but for a long time neither could get the better of the other. At last, however, the damsel threw him right valiantly on the palace pavement. And when he found himself thus thrown, and her standing over him, great indeed was his shame and discomfiture." She not only defeated but humiliated him, and he disappeared, leaving behind the additional thousand horses for her herd.

Gossip and rumors swirled around Khutulun. Leading such a colorful and unusual life without a husband, she became the object of constant interest in her actions and speculation about her motives. Numerous reports maintain that she considered marrying Il-khan Ghazan, one of her cousins, who ruled Persia and Mesopotamia, and that they had an exchange of correspondence and envoys. But she showed no inclination to leave the steppe and live the life of a proper Muslim lady. Because of her reluctance to marry, her detractors alleged that she had entered into an incestuous relationship with her father and thus would take no other man while he lived. In the wake of the salacious accusations against her and her father, she married Abtakul of the Choros clan. He was described as "a lively, tall, good-looking man," and the chronicles state clearly: "She chose him herself for her husband."

The marriage only increased the gossip about Khutulun and her lifestyle. According to one contorted story, she married Abtakul after he supposedly came to court on a mission to murder her father, Qaidu Khan. When he was captured, his mother offered herself for punishment instead of him, but Abtakul refused his mother's aid. Supposedly, Qaidu Khan so respected the mother for trying to save the son and respected the son for trying to save the mother, that he took him into his service and commissioned him as an army officer. Later, when Abtakul was wounded in a battle with Khubilai Khan's army, he returned to the royal camp to recuperate. At that point, Khutulun met him for the first time and fell in love with him.

Despite her marriage, Khutulun continued to campaign with her father. In 1301, Qaidu Khan moved deeper into Mongolia from the southwest, headed for the capital at Karakorum. According to the chronicler Ghiyasuddin Khwandamir of Afghanistan and India, Khubilai's Chinese forces outnumbered Qaidu Khan's army by a hundred to one. They met in battle at Qaraqata near the Zavkhan River. The battle raged for three days and nights, and, on the fourth, Qaidu Khan was wounded and nearly captured.

Qaidu Khan decided to try a ruse that had once worked for Genghis Khan in a battle against the Naiman not far from this area. On the fourth night, "he ordered all his warriors to light fires in several places." When the Mongol generals leading the Chinese army "saw the flames of so many fires, they thought that assistance had reached Qaidu Khan from some source." Instead of staying to fight, however, Qaidu Khan left the fires burning while his men "decamped and withdrew." The enemy suspected a deception, but they were not sure what kind. "Imagining that Qaidu Khan was trying to trick them into drawing closer" and would then ambush them, Khubilai Khan's forces fled despite having been on the threshold of victory over Qaidu Khan's army. As they fled, they set fire to the grass on the steppe behind them to prevent Qaidu Khan's army from pursuing them and to deny their animals pasture if they did.

Following his complete but unexpected victory, Qaidu Khan's wounds worsened. "After this victory Qaidu Khan fell ill with dyspepsia," according to Khwandamir. "Some of the ignorant" attendants "who called themselves physicians gave him twenty-five pills, and the pills turned the illness into dysentery." After a month of treatment, Qaidu Khan died in February 1301. He was buried between the Ili River and the Chu River in a place called Shongkorlog, and Khutulun looked after his tomb for the rest of her life.

According to some accounts, her father respected her so much that before his death he attempted to name her to be the next khan, despite the lack of support within the family for this succession. However, she apparently preferred to continue as head of the military more than to become khan. She made clear that she was "desirous of leading the military and running affairs." Toward this end, "she wanted her brother Orus to take her father's place" as khan and leave her in charge of the army.

The Persian chronicler, who condescendingly disapproved of her involvement in politics, reported with approval that the other contenders for the office objected strenuously and insultingly. "You should mind your scissors and needles!" one of them yelled in angry derision. "What have you to do with kingship and chieftainship?" demanded the other.

Her words were not recorded, but her actions showed what she thought of their objections. She continued in her struggle, "stirring up sedition and strife," in the words of her critics. Yet she maintained the support of her brother Orus. The record is sketchy about her precise actions after her father's death, but in 1306 she followed him into death. Some reports claim that she died fighting in battle, others that she was assassinated. These speculations only heighten the mystery of this unusual woman.

Khutulun, the All White Princess, returned into the fog of history. If today only Marco Polo's account of her had survived, we might well imagine that she was merely a mythical figure, a product of travelers' tales and the fervid imagination. In addition to the works of Marco Polo and the Persian chroniclers, however, part of the story of Khutulun appears in the account of the fourteenth-century Arab traveler Ibn

Battuta. Similarly some elements of Khutulun's life appeared in a Ming Dynasty novel published in the fifteenth century. Yet both the European traveler and the Persian chroniclers recorded stories about her with different details, in different languages, and from different perspectives without contradiction.

With the death of Khutulun in 1306, the Borijin men had won. The queens had been defeated, their lands had been appropriated and distributed among their brothers' sons, and the last defiant rebel princess had passed from the scene. The men of the family had managed to deny the women control over the Silk Route, but they failed to assert their own control. Trade and communication began to unravel as rival warlords quarreled over oases and trading centers like dogs snarling over goat entrails. The Silk Route had been the core of the Mongol Empire, and without it there was no empire.

As the role of women in public life in the Mongol Empire continued to recede over the next century, the elite Mongol men fell into a life of debauched pleasure in their Chinese parks, Persian gardens, and Russian palaces. No heroes came to recharge the energy of the sapped nation. No new allies came to join them. No armies set out to expand the decaying Mongol rule over China. Throughout the fourteenth century, the Mongol leadership, especially the Borijin clan, deteriorated. Each generation proved less competent and knowledgeable, as well as more isolated and corrupt, than the last.

A noxious fog of ignorance and greed engulfed the family, and the khans stumbled blindly in search of physical pleasure and mindless amusements until they were killed by some corrupt official and replaced by another. In the Mongol chronicles as well as in the oral history and folk memory of the people, this debauchery, more than any other factor, brought about the fall of the empire and the fratricidal turmoil that followed.

Khutulun was the last of the wild Mongol women. In Russia, Persia, and China, they began to disappear into the ranks of civilized women, who lived according to the standards of the local culture. They never became quite as domesticated as other women in those countries, but they played roles more similar to those normally allocated to women in powerful dynasties. They operated behind the scenes, making alliances, promoting heirs, fighting with co-wives and mothers-in-law, and pursuing the life of court ladies, who seemed so important to the political life of the moment but had minimal lasting significance on the rise and fall of empires.

One of the few places where Mongol women continued to exercise an important role was in Korea, known to the Mongols as the Rainbow Land of the Son-in-Law Nation. The invasion of Korea began during the reign of Ogodei, but the country was not completely under Mongol control until the reign of Khubilai Khan. The Mongols arranged numerous marriage exchanges with the Korean royal family, and sometimes Korean princes came to the Mongol court to learn the language and customs of the Mongols. Five Korean kings received Borijin daughters as wives for approximately seventy years. Like the other son-in-law states, Korea maintained its traditional laws, administrative structure, and tax system. Unlike the *guregen* of Genghis Khan's time, the Korean sons-in-law were not sent off to distant wars; thus, the Mongol queens of Korea lacked the power to rule that their aunts such as Alaqai Beki had held. It had been the last of the foreign countries taken as a son-in-law ally, but it retained this position until the end of the Yuan Dynasty in 1368.

According to the *Korean Veritable Records* for the year 1442, one Mongol khan looking back on the relations between the two allies wrote: "When our great ancestor Genghis Khan governed all the eight directions . . . there was none under heaven who would not obey. Korea among others was friendlier with us than any other nation, being as close as true brothers might be."

With their mastery of the Mongolian language, their numerous Mongolian relatives, their long time spent at the Mongol court, and even their Mongolian names, the Korean kings appeared largely Mongolian to their overlords. Yet, speaking Korean, with numerous

Korean relatives and Korean names, they still seemed Korean to their subjects. This ability to play both sides benefited Korea greatly, but in the end the schizophrenic life of the kings came at great personal cost to them and their families.

With her own Mongol detachment of guards close at hand and the mighty Mongol army never too far from Korea, the Mongol queen had an independent source of power that curtailed the options of her husband. Yet, as a foreign queen in a sometimes hostile environment, her powers had very definite limits and rarely reached far beyond the range of her own eyesight.

Mongol-Korean relations in the late thirteenth and early fourteenth centuries centered on these queens, and the era is filled with colorful stories of arguments over seating and rituals, angry domestic fights, murders and mysterious deaths, unfaithful kings who preferred Korean women over their Mongol spouses, mothers-in-law placing curses on their daughters-in-law, and wanton Mongol queens who brazenly promoted with impunity a succession of handsome guards, ministers, and attendants as lovers. Secret letters and coded messages dashed back and forth between the Korean Mongol capitals. Envoys of the royals came and went, checking on rival accusations or to plead for mercy, and occasionally Mongol military units moved menacingly in an effort to quell another flare-up. Despite the drama, romance, and intrigue, Mongols and Koreans continued to live their awkward but mutually beneficial alliance; that relationship, however, had ended by the time the Mongol queen Noguk died during childbirth in 1365, during the reign of her anti-Yuan husband, King Gongmin. Soon both the Goreyo Dynasty of Korea and the Yuan Dynasty of China had run their historical course and were replaced by more vibrant ones.

Harmony between the male sky and the female earth continued to fall out of balance as the descendants of Genghis Khan violated virtually every important rule, law, and custom that he had given them. As the Yuan Dynasty deteriorated through the fourteenth century, the court recognized that its officials had abandoned much of their former way of life, including the equilibrium of male and female principles rooted in Mongolian culture and central to the spirituality taught by Genghis Khan.

The Mongol court sought to restore the needed balance through public rituals from a variety of religions. But with the removal of women from the government structure established by Genghis Khan, it was hard for the Mongols to synchronize the necessary male and female components. The last emperor became convinced of a novel way to redress the imbalance. He could imbibe female vitality into his body, making himself the right blend of masculine and feminine essences. If the emperor was perfectly balanced, then his government would be in harmony and the world would be set right.

The way to absorb the needed womanly qualities was through sexual relations performed in a variety of ritually specific ways. With help from loyal retainers, the emperor arranged to recruit a variety of young girls, mostly from the families of commoners, who were specially trained for his service in this urgent spiritual quest to rescue the empire. In 1354, as a way to improve the ritual quality of these diverse girls, sixteen were selected for a special troupe named the Divine Demon Dancing Girls.

The emperor selected ten of his male relatives to assist in these pressing matters of state. Just as Genghis Khan had used ten as the main unit of military organization, with ten squads of ten men each forming a company of one hundred, each of the emperor's specially chosen men was instructed to perform ten times a night in the ritually prescribed sequence of acts. To assist in their work, the emperor had special rooms constructed to perform the rituals, each with appropriate instructive artwork to teach the occupants more precisely their duties and to encourage them in the performance.

The monks, either on their own or with the permission of the emperor, convinced some women of the royal household that they, too, needed an infusion of male essence by being initiated as nuns into the secret practices. A Ming Dynasty investigation later asserted: "The wives and concubines and other women in the palace committed adultery with outside ministers, or allowed monks to stay in the palace to be initiated into nunhood." Their actions turned the Forbidden City into a "place full of obscenity."

All the efforts were in vain; the Yuan Dynasty of the Mongols collapsed in 1368, the Year of the Monkey.

The Mongol royal family, however, did not assume any responsibility for the collapse of Khubilai Khan's dynasty. Instead the Borijin survivors blamed the fall completely on a deceitful trick by the Chinese. According to the mythical account recorded in the *Erdeni-yin Tobci*, the expulsion of the Mongols from China began when a caravan of Kazakh carts appeared at the walls of the Forbidden City. The caravan leader handed a note to the guard stating that he was bringing tribute for the khan, but the sentry would not allow the carts to enter until the caravan leader made him "happy with jewels."

Once through the massive gates and inside the Forbidden City, the merchants quickly set to unloading their immense tribute under the watchful eye of the Mongol guards. The first three sets of carts carried jewels and other valuable gifts. The next vehicles contained armor and weapons that they laid out as though intended for presentation as tribute. From the final carts, the visitors hauled out three large and mysterious objects coated in wax. The merchants explained to the watching guards that these objects were giant candles, and to prove their claim, they lit the wick on each of them. As the wax burned down, it melted the wax off the large metal objects. Once they were free of the wax, it became obvious that the wicks were actually fuses, and each of the large fake candles concealed a cannon. About the time the merchants finished unloading the carts, the fire reached the powder and fired the cannons with resounding noise.

The cannon burst served as a signal to a regiment of rebels concealed in the carts; they sprang out of hiding and rushed to put on the neatly arranged armor and take up the weapons. The boom of the cannon and the mêlée of the rebels woke the emperor, who just managed to escape with the royal jade seal hidden in the flowing sleeves of his imperial robe.

He did not have time to gather his Divine Demon Dancers, and thus the harmony of male and female in the Mongol Empire was abandoned.

The Rabbit Demon's Revenge

EVEN AS THE EMPIRE OF GENGHIS KHAN COLLAPSED, MOST of the Mongols did not want to return home to Mongolia. Members of the Borijin clan in Russia and Persia intermarried with local elites, changed their religion and language as readily as their clothes, and forgot that they were Mongols in order to blend into the new social order.

Of the three major branches of the Borijin family ruling abroad, only the Chinese branch attempted to flee home when their rule collapsed, but most of their Mongol subjects stayed in China. According to the Mongol accounts, a dispersed population of 400,000 Mongols lived across China in 1368. Yet, only 60,000 managed to escape or were willing to flee with the court. The Borijin rulers, now neither Chinese nor Mongol, had so alienated their Mongol subjects and soldiers that at their final moment of expulsion from China by the newly rising and natively authentic Ming Dynasty, the majority of the Mongol commoners chose to stay in China. They preferred to serve China rather than return to Mongolia with the Borijin clan and its corrupt horde of foreign advisors, sexually permissive monks, alien guards, pampered astrologers, and nondenominational spiritual quacks.

Not knowing where to go in Mongolia, the royal refugees headed back to the Kherlen River, to the source of their myths at the foot of Mount Burkhan Khaldun. The caravan stretched back across many miles, and it took many weeks before all the people and animals arrived. One cluster after another limped back. The camels carried large leather trunks and folded tents of colored silk and damask.

Although on horseback, the women wore their heavy Mongol-style jewelry, their flowing gowns of embroidered gold lined with cashmere, and their coats of tiger and leopard skin trimmed with sable. The children rode on carts pulled by lumbering oxen and yaks. The men wore their silk sashes tied extra tight against the hunger and the constant bouncing on horseback. The people and all they carried arrived coated with a thick layer of Gobi dust. The armor was bent, the lances twisted, the flags tattered, the horses thin.

The many Mongols who stayed behind in China or near the border during the Ming Dynasty continued to be a part of the Chinese historical record. Those who returned to the Mongolian Plateau, however, largely passed out of the recorded history of their neighbors. But the Mongols were now literate and relied upon their own written documents and chronicles to supplement their oral stories. Today we would know almost nothing of Mongolia during this era if it were not for two Mongolian texts written in the seventeenth century. The *Altan Tobci*, meaning the "Golden Summary," was recorded around 1651 in a jumble of names, stories, and genealogies; about a decade later, it was followed by the *Erdeni-yin Tobči*, meaning the "Bejeweled Summary" or sometimes translated as the "Precious Summary." The accounts were recorded separately, long after the events contained within them occurred, and the details, particularly dates, vary between the two versions. Yet they agree in the overall narrative of events and in the identity and actions of the major players.

The exodus from China was significant, but many of the refugee soldiers streaming into Mongolia were not even Mongol. They belonged to the European Ossetian and Turkic Kipchak soldiers originally brought as imperial guards for Khubilai Khan, who had feared his own Mongol warriors as well as the Chinese.

The Mongol herders, following their traditional way of life on the steppe, did not welcome these strange Mongols gladly. During their seven generations away from home, the royal family had not become Chinese; however, they no longer lived as Mongols. They had all the confidence and bravado of the original Mongols of Genghis Khan, but they had none of the skills, strengths, or stamina. They seemed to have abandoned the virtue of Mongol life and ignored the virtue of Chinese civilization, preferring instead to combine the worst of both. The only occupation they had learned was ruling, and after the death of Genghis Khan, they had not done that well. Once back in Mongolia, they found themselves marooned in a vast sea of grass with little knowledge of their own nomadic culture.

The returning refugees hardly recognized their fellow Mongols who had remained north of the Gobi and continued to follow the traditionally rugged and independent life of nomadic herders. Throughout the sojourn of the royal family and their retinue in China from 1211 until 1368, these Mongols never completely submitted to the rule of their Mongol relatives from the Chinese capital. These Mongol traditionalists remained loyal to the spirit of Genghis Khan by following leaders such as Arik Boke, Qaidu Khan, and Khutulun, but they rejected, or at least remained suspicious of, the Yuan Dynasty established by Khubilai Khan and operated to the exclusive benefit of his descendants for nearly a century.

The Mongols who had dismounted in China and lived there for more than a century had lost their ability to survive in the harsh conditions of Mongolia. For them, hunting was an elaborately ritualized sport, not a survival skill; it was best done with transport elephants, dancing girls for the long evenings, trained warriors to pursue the animals, beaters to drive the animals to where the royals waited with their bowmen at their side, and a cadre of chefs to concoct exotic delicacies from the game.

They did not know how to stalk a wild animal, much less skin the animals or tan the hides. They did not know how to shear the sheep or make clothes from the wool, because they had grown accustomed to wearing silk woven by anonymous workers in the far corners of their erstwhile empire. Each Mongol aristocrat in China had his own private herd, but they were for show and glory, like the ten thousand white horses of the Great Khan. Their century and a half in China had not acculturated them to any new skills; it had merely deprived them of their old ones from lack of use.

The returned Mongols and their foreign guard began eating up everything they could find without regard to season or weather. They slaughtered the animals indiscriminately, and they grazed them without concern for the survival of the pasture for another year. They chopped down the forests and fouled the landscape. They still had their passionate love of horses and tried to maintain their large herds even if sheep, goats, cows, and yaks proved more efficient at converting grass into meat.

Within only a few years, the returning Mongols ate up their homeland, destroyed the pasture, and burned the wood. To survive, they had to move ever farther north into the Siberian forests, west on the mountains and plains around the Altai, or back toward the south, to China from whence they came. The north was colder, harsher, and held fewer resources. The west was still inhabited by the steppe tribes that had not settled in China, and they maintained all the vigor and hostility of the old Mongols.

Though the Ming had chased them from the capital city, the Mongols did not consider themselves to have been overthrown. They had merely lost some territory. The newly emerging Ming Dynasty now controlled the agricultural parts of China, essentially the areas occupied by the dominant Han ethnic group. In victory they changed the name of the Mongol capital to Peiping, meaning "the North Is Pacified," but many areas still lay beyond their reach. The Ming forces did not take Sichuan until 1371 and Yunnan until 1382. Other areas such as Mongolia, Manchuria, Korea, eastern Turkestan, and Tibet remained permanently beyond the effective control of the Ming, leaving them with a far smaller China than the Mongols had held. Backed by the loyalty of many of these other areas, the Mongols still considered themselves to be the legitimate, though temporarily exiled, rulers of all China. They controlled vast but empty territories, with few subjects, no cities, and only minor trade routes connecting China with the forest tribes of Siberia.

Even when the Ming soldiers hunted down the Mongol khans and killed the last ruling descendant of Khubilai Khan in 1388, the Mongols found other members of the Borijin clan to claim the office. Because of the continuing respect for the memory of Arik Boke Khan as the defender of Mongol values against the Chinese administration of his brother Khubilai, some of Arik Boke's descendants now came to the fore to claim the office. In thirteenth century, Arik Boke had wanted to keep the imperial capital in Mongolia, and now his distant heirs resurrected that possibility. They no longer had the option of locating their capital in another country, since they had lost all the territory that Genghis Khan's army had conquered, from the Pacific to the Mediterranean and from the Arctic to the Indian Ocean. Now 150 years after the founding of the nation in 1206, they found themselves right back on the high, dry, cold Mongolian Plateau where Genghis Khan had started, and they were about to lose that. More precisely, they were about to lose their power over their ancestral territory and to become prisoners in their own homeland.

The Mongol Empire ended abruptly on a snowy day in 1399 when the sex-crazed spirit of a rabbit jumped on Elbeg Khan and captured his soul. Some observers may point to a more gradual decline of the empire from other causes, such as the outbreak of plague earlier in the century or the triumph of the Ming rebels in 1368, but the Buddhist chroniclers clearly saw the role of the rabbit as an intimate but secret protector of Genghis Khan's clan.

The rise of the Borijin family stemmed from another snowy day two centuries earlier, around the year 1159, the Year of the Earth Rabbit. Genghis Khan's father was out hunting a rabbit, and the rabbit lured the hunter on a path past a patch of freshly deposited urine. The yellow splash pattern of the urine in the fresh snow indicated that it had been made by a woman. The hunter decided to let the rabbit survive and turned instead to hunt the woman; he found her, kidnapped her, and with her produced Genghis Khan and the Mongol royal family.

Normally the rabbit stood as a symbol of cowardice within the animal kingdom since it is so easily frightened, but having had its life spared, the rabbit became a secret guardian of the family through its rise to power. Genghis Khan founded the Mongol Empire in the Fire Rabbit Year of 1206, and in the animal cycle of years, the rabbit returned every twelve years. Each time it brought some special encounter with the Mongol khans.

Hunting always carried a close association with marriage and sexuality, and generally only men hunted. A boy's first kill symbolized his marriage to a daughter of the forest, and to mark this loss of virginity, older men smeared fat from the animal onto the boy's flesh. Genghis Khan personally performed the ceremony on his grandsons Khubilai and Mongke after their first kill in 1224 near the Ili River on the frontier between the Naiman and the Uighur territory. The boys were eleven and nine years old, respectively, and had killed a rabbit and an antelope. In keeping with the theme of hunting as marriage, men had to refrain from sexual relations with their wives prior to embarking on a hunt.

Somewhere along the way, the Borijin clan forgot about its relationship with the rabbit and the debt owed to the animal as the source of the family's power. When the Yellow (Earth) Rabbit Year returned in 1399, the Mongol ruler, Elbeg Khan, again met the rabbit at the edge of the forest, but this time the encounter produced a much more gruesome result. Elbeg Khan had had no luck that day and was anxious not to return to camp without some game. Although the white rabbit was in the white snow, Elbeg Khan saw it. He carefully pulled an arrow from his quiver, fixed it in his bow, aimed, and shot the rabbit.

As Elbeg Khan approached the rabbit, he could see it dying atop the freshly fallen snow. A single arrow had pierced its body, but with an ever-weakening pulse, its heart squirted a spray of blood that collected in small red pools in the snow. The sight of the red blood on the white snow created a hypnotic effect over the Great Khan. He seemingly entered into a trance and stared transfixed at the peaceful face of the rabbit and at the marked contrast of the two colors of red blood on white show—each so beautiful and yet so dramatically different.

It was at this moment that the soul, the *shimnus,* of the rabbit abandoned its dying body and entered into Elbeg Khan. The *shimnus* could not bear to leave the sight of its old body, and thus, through the eyes of its new body in Elbeg Khan, it stared back at its former self, the dead rabbit.

Finally, the *shimnus*-possessed Elbeg Khan spoke to his hunting companion in a pleading voice. "If only there were a woman this beautiful—with a face as white as snow and cheeks as red as blood."

Rather than helping the Great Khan escape from the trance, his hunting companion, Dayuu, who was also being pulled inextricably into the horror about to unfold, encouraged the delusional desire. "But there is, my khan, such a woman," responded Dayuu, but then he seemed to taunt the mesmerized khan. "But you may not see her," he added.

"Who is she?" demanded the anxious and bewildered khan.

"She is the wife of your son," answered Dayuu. "She is splendid like this," he said pointing to the exquisite color on the white snow.

A strict taboo forbade a man from entering the *ger* belonging to the wife of either his son or his younger brothers, all of whom were collectively referred to as sons. While younger men had friendly access to senior women married into the family and might themselves one day marry one of them, a senior man had almost no interaction with the wives of his junior relatives and certainly could never marry one. Even to bring milk or food to her *ger,* he had to stand outside and pass it to her through an opening in the *ger* wall without seeing her or entering the dwelling.

Upon hearing that the beauty of his son's wife was as great as the rabbit blood on the white snow, Elbeg Khan felt an irresistible urge to see her with his own eyes despite the law against doing so. His trance-like daydream suddenly acquired a focus and a goal that took his sight and attention away from the dead rabbit.

Genghis Khan once said that "when a khan behaves like a commoner, he will destroy his Mongol subjects." Elbeg Khan was about to commit a crime that would nearly destroy the precious little that remained of the dwindling Mongol nation. The diabolical tangle of transgressions began as Elbeg Khan returned from hunting to his main camp determined to see this young woman.

"Show me what I have not yet seen," he ordered his assistant, showing that he clearly understood the forbidden nature of his request. "You who bring together what is distant; you who satisfy my desires, my Dayuu, go!"

Dayuu slyly watched and waited for the appropriate opportunity to arrange a tryst between the khan and his daughter-in-law. After seeing the khan's son leave to go hunting, Dayuu cautiously approached the beautiful young wife. "The khan commands you to let him come and visit you to see how beautiful you are," he informed her.

Fully understanding the meaning of the proposal and its impropriety, she adamantly refused. "Are the heavens and earth no longer separate and it has now become acceptable for a great khan to see his daughter-in-law?" she demanded of the messenger. "Or has my husband now died?" she asked, "and the khan comes to tell me of it?" Suspecting an even deeper supernatural change, she perceptively asked, "Or has the khan turned into a black dog?"

The messenger returned to Elbeg Khan with the harsh words of rejection from his son's wife. In his wrathful envy of his own son and in his fixation on seeing the woman with a face as beautiful as blood on fresh snow, Elbeg Khan mounted his horse and went out hunting his son. His sexual obsession had grown so strong that nothing could prevent his fulfilling that desire. The khan found his son and killed him.

Elbeg Khan rode back to the camp to rape his dead son's widow. Rather than satisfying the khan's desire, however, the attack only increased it. As his obsession with the young woman grew, he made her his wife. When she became the new *khatun*, Elbeg Khan made Dayuu the *taishi*, an office generally equivalent to prime minister and the highest position allowed to any man outside the Borijin Clan.

The curse of the rabbit spirit now began to spread, like a vicious plague of the soul. The beautiful young woman, the innocent victim who had lost her husband and was forced into a new marriage, became infected herself with the same wicked obsession of red on white, but in her the spell found a different focus. She needed to see her new husband's red blood on the white skin of the friend who helped him to kill her first husband and violate her. Just as the khan lusted after sex, she lusted for revenge, and she would use sex to avenge herself on both of them.

The unwilling queen watched and waited around her new imperial *ger* in the royal camp. Her opportunity for revenge came when, once again, the Great Khan left to hunt with his falcon. Dayuu arrived at the royal tent. Because the Great Khan was not there, he waited outside the door.

The aggrieved queen saw the man and sent a servant out to him. "Why wait out on the cold steppe?" asked the servant, "when you can come into the royal home where it is warm?"

Dayuu accepted the invitation and approached the royal *ger* of the newly installed young queen. When he entered, she greeted him not with anger but welcomed him into the tent with exaggerated honor and lavish hospitality. She served him a platter of prized foods, including butter dainties and dried dairy dishes. She also offered him a drink of twice-distilled mare's milk, the potent "black drink" of the steppe tribes. As the minister quickly showed signs of inebriation, she told him, with deceptive humility and feigned appreciation, what a great debt she owed him "for making my poor person important, for making my insignificant person great, for making me a queen."

In appreciation, she said that she wished to give him her personal silver bowl. According to steppe etiquette, he had to drink the contents of the offered bowl to show his acceptance of the gift. But when he did so, he immediately fell unconscious.

The queen moved quickly toward her prey. She dragged his drugged, limp body onto her bed. She then tore out clumps of her own hair, ripped her clothes, and clawed herself all over her body. She tore at the fabric lining the walls, and then she began to scream for help. Servants and guards came running to her aid, and she showed them the wounds of red blood on her white flesh that, she said, came from fighting off a sexual attack from Dayuu, her husband's friend and councillor.

The queen sent out her servant again, this time to find her husband, the khan, and summon him home to deal with the crime against her and against his honor and the prestige of the family. When the khan returned, she emotionally explained that she had summoned his councillor to thank him for making it possible for her to marry the khan. Then, when she gave him her bowl in gratitude and he drank its contents, "he wanted to become intimate with me," she explained. "When I refused, he attacked me."

Slowly regaining consciousness, the councillor heard the voices around him repeating the accusations against him. He panicked, and his fear gave him a new burst of energy with which he managed to jump up and flee from the tent. He grabbed the reins of the first horse he found, jumped on it, and raced away from the royal camp.

With the assumption that the flight proved his friend's guilt, the khan called his men together, and they set out in pursuit. Just as he had hunted down the white rabbit, the khan now hunted down the friend who had helped him. When the khan caught up with the councillor, a fierce fight ensued between the two men. As the khan approached, Dayuu fired an arrow and struck Elbeg Khan in the hand, slicing off his little finger.

In retaliation, the khan shot his former friend and let him lie moaning in agony before finally killing him. Now the enraged khan skinned the body of his friend precisely as he had skinned the rabbit. The khan brought the flesh from the dead man's backside to his young queen as a gift of revenge against her accused attacker.

For the aggrieved queen, however, the punishment of only one of the two men who had wronged her failed to quell her anger at the murder of her first husband. In the words of the chronicles, "She lay on her bed without satisfaction." But when her husband approached her with the man's skin dangling from his wounded hand, she reached out and took the khan's wounded hand. She brought it up to her lips to kiss it, and she lovingly licked the blood from the stump of his missing finger. At the same time, she gently took the gift of the freshly flayed skin of her husband's dead friend and also brought it to her lips.

The khan now saw what his obsession for a woman as beautiful as the red blood on white snow had brought him—only now it was red human blood, his own blood, dripping onto the snow white fat of his former friend. She gently licked the skin in the same way that she had licked her husband's bleeding finger, and then she swallowed the grease of the skin together with the blood of her husband.

"Although I am a woman," she proclaimed to her husband. "I have avenged the vengeance of my husband. When I die, there will be no regret."

Only now did the khan fully comprehend the evil of his own deeds, and on account of his evil sins, his family would pay dearly. The queen had avenged the crime against her, but that act proved to be no more than the opening of the rabbit's curse on the royal family and the Mongol nation. They would now fight among themselves, one Mongol tribe against another, clan against clan, sister against brother, mother against son, husband against wife, and daughter against father.

The sordid tale of Elbeg Khan summarizes, as well as any other explanation, the degenerate state of the Borijin clan. Their Mongol nation seemed to be gasping through a protracted death. The Mongol power appeared to have at last entered its final phase. On the fertile steppe where millions of animals once roamed, now hunger stalked the few surviving animals and threatened the nomads who depended on them. The clans and tribes moved in scattered groups across a once beautiful landscape now ravaged by war and overgrazing and through forests decimated by the returning royal court. Animals starved amid the environmental degradation, and roving gangs of thugs seized the animals that survived. The returning invaders abided by neither Mongol custom nor law. It was not yet the end of time, but surely the end could not be far away. A constant stream of Mongols made their way across the Gobi to surrender to the Ming Dynasty and seek jobs as soldiers or border administrators.

Gangs of former foreign guards and their Mongol allies of the moment seized rival Borijin boys to proclaim them khan or to mock them and degrade them as objects of derision, exploitation, and torture. They tossed the title of Great Khan back and forth from one member of the Borijin clan to another the way that horsemen tossed around the carcass of a goat in a game of tribal polo. Men who once would have laid down their lives for their Borijin leader now made and replaced the Great Khans on any whim.

The daughters of queens who once set out from Mongolia to rule the world now served as nothing more than tools of amusement and instruments of competition among the basest of men. Like looters of the treasury playing with jewels as though they were dice, the powerful men of the moment seized Borijin girls to trade among one another as little more than sexual toys. After all, if the Great Khan was not above raping his son's wife, then why should any man refrain from whatever lust might strike his heart?

The Mongol nation and the once glorious Golden Family sank so low and suffered so much abuse that it would possibly have been a blessing for the whole family to have died and the name of the nation to have disappeared into the wind like the cold ashes of an abandoned camp. So many nomadic nations had risen, fallen, and disappeared in the thousands of years since humans first learned to herd animals and turn the sea of grass into sustenance. The torn and neglected banner of the nation was tattered and scattered like clumps of wool stuck in the brown grass. Even the horses seemed too exhausted to raise a cloud of dust. In the pages of history, the passing of yet one more such nation, even one once as powerful and important as the Mongols, hardly would have seemed surprising.

Yet amid all the depravity and defeat, one woman held her ground, kept her focus, and looked forward to a day when the nation might be reassembled, the flags raised again, and dignity restored to the royal clan. Like a small thread on which the fate of the Mongol nation fluttered, she alone sustained its spirit. She was Samur, the daughter of Elbeg Khan by birth, but the true daughter of Genghis Khan in spirit, strength, and sheer stubbornness.

She was born in the 1380s, in the first Borijin generation to be reared back in Mongolia after the expulsion from China. Samur carried the Chinese-derived title *gunj,* which the Mongols had adopted during their stay in China and substituted for the older Mongolian title of *beki* previously used for princesses. Samur Gunj began life as a victim of all the corruption and chaos engulfing the Mongol nation and her Golden Family. Her debut into world history came in the midst of the sordid affair of her father with his daughter-in-law.

After her father, Elbeg Khan, killed his ally and councillor Dayuu, he realized what a tactical error it had been, even though he believed it was morally justified. In a desperate effort to maintain his office of khan and avoid being killed in revenge for what he had done, Elbeg gave his young daughter Samur to the dead man's son as a peace offering and compensation for the killing. By receiving Princess Samur as a wife, Dayuu's son also received his dead father's title and command of the Oirat in western Mongolia.

Elbeg Khan's most dangerous enemy, however, was not among outside rivals and former allies; it was within his own family. Samur's mother was Elbeg's senior wife, Kobeguntai. She had become deeply resentful when her husband took his new young wife, and now he took her daughter from her to pay off the political debts incurred by his sins. She found a supporter of her own, killed Elbeg Khan, married her co-conspirator, and left the nation adrift without a khan. The turmoil resulting from the Great Khan's terrible deeds would last for nearly a century.

At no moment in this long ordeal of the coming decades would Samur hold supreme power anywhere; yet throughout it, she held the survival of the nation in her hands. Her actions determined its fate as she faced crisis after crisis. For more than half a century, Samur fought unsuccessfully to reunite the Mongol nation and to free her male relatives in the Borijin clan from their captivity by their own guards, who perpetually fought among themselves for the meager riches left in the country. Her husband held the office of *taishi* of the Oirat, and when he died in the struggle to liberate the Mongols, her son stepped forward to take the title and resume the battle.

From roughly 1400 until 1450, while the so-called Great Khans were held prisoner of various strongmen, she formed a powerful force based in the Oirat tribes in western Mongolia and constantly, if vainly, attempted to resuscitate the Mongol royal family and liberate them from their captivity. She encouraged her husband to mount repeated campaigns to rescue the nominal Great Khan from his captors, and when her husband was killed in this effort, she encouraged her son in the same pursuit until he too was killed.

The Golden Clan established by Genghis Khan had completely lost control of the reins of state, and they were held captive by an unusual assortment of men. Their captors had Mongolian names, spoke the Mongol language, wore Mongol clothes, sometimes had Mongol wives, and in general, had become an intimate part of Mongol society. Yet they remained quite different from the Mongols. These men derived from an odd mixture of captives whom the Mongols had brought back from Ossetia, Russia, Ukraine, and other parts of Europe to be their imperial guards, but who, over time, had taken control of the royal family.

The type of strongman who ruled Mongolia in the fifteenth century was typified by one who carried the nickname Arugtai, meaning "the One with the Dung Basket," in reference to the job he performed in the court of Elbeg Khan. Despite his lowly status, like all dung collectors he had the ability to roam freely throughout the day in search of dried dung. This freedom also gave him the opportunity to talk with many people, and he thereby became a source of information for members of the household. From this position, he slowly gained power and moved into the political vacuum left by Elbeg Khan's death. He made his hostile attitude toward the Borijin clan clear. "It is dangerous to let the offspring of a savage beast roam freely," he said. "You should not indulge the son of your enemy." On the basis of this policy, Arugtai hunted the Borijins down to kill them or keep them captive for future schemes.

After the death of Samur's husband and then her son, she encouraged her grandson Esen to become *taishi* and to continue her struggle against the strongmen who controlled her male relatives and to reunite the Oirat and Mongol tribes. Following the failures of his father and grandfather, Esen quickly and easily began assembling the Mongol tribes—some through conquest, but many through persuasion. The Mongols seemed suddenly invigorated and ready once again to follow their conquering leader to the ends of the earth.

In order to recapture control of the Silk Route, Esen began to raid the Muslim oases under the rule of Ways Khan, yet another descendent of Genghis Khan. Esen defeated the Muslims repeatedly: "It is told that the [Muslim] khan fought twenty-one battles" against the Mongols. "Once he was victorious . . . [but] in all the rest he was routed." Esen captured him three times but released him. With almost a sigh for the incompetence of Ways Khan, the Muslim chronicler concluded the statement with "God knows best."

During a campaign in 1443–45, Esen quickly took control of the oasis of Hami, along the Silk Route west of the Gansu Corridor, and then conquered the Three Guards, the Mongol units whom the Ming employed to guard their borders. He rallied Mongol unity and called upon them to remember their identity. Mocking the titles given the Three Guards and other Mongol leaders by the Ming, Esen reminded them that, unlike himself, who had no titles directly from Genghis Khan, they held important titles granted by him to their forefathers and that they should honor them above Ming titles. After the defeat of the Three Guards, the Jurched (Manchu) voluntarily submitted to Esen. Officials on the Ming court lacked the ability to take strong military action against their former allies who were now deserting them, and they mistakenly calculated that merely suspending trade with the rebels would soon return them to Ming authority.

Esen reunited not only the Mongolian Plateau but also most of the Silk Route—modern Inner Mongolia (south of the Gobi), part of Manchuria, and some territory south of the Yellow River near the Gansu Corridor. In 1449 he achieved his most important victory over the Chinese and captured the Ming emperor. For the first time in nearly a century since the fall of the Yuan Dynasty, the Mongols posed a real threat to China. From their last effort to rule China, the Mongols understood that it was far easier to conquer China than to control it, and this time they made no effort to occupy or run the country. Esen used the emperor by taking him on raids of Chinese cities in order to persuade them to surrender or at least create fear of fighting the Mongols and thereby possibly injuring their emperor. This tactic did not work for long, and eventually Esen released the bedraggled and discredited emperor, knowing that his return to Beijing would keep the Ming officials busy fighting one another and leave the Mongols in peace for a while.

Esen had united the Mongols and defeated the Muslim ruler and the Ming emperor, but in the most important confrontation of his career, he could not overcome the determined will of his grandmother. Samur supported her grandson throughout his conquests and as he drove out the warlords and the old guards. Early in his career as *taishi*, he seemed to share her desire to reunite the Oirat and Mongol people under Borijin rule. He had been successful in liberating the Borijin family and the Mongols from foreign rule, but they continued to quarrel among themselves. In hopes of uniting the people, Esen sought to further integrate the ruling families of the two tribes with a marriage between his sister and the new khan.

The plan seemed to work, and Esen's sister produced a son. With a Borijin Mongol father and a Choros Oirat mother, the infant son seemed the perfect heir, but in a miscalculated move, the khan decided to name another son his heir. As the khan became increasingly independent, Esen grew bitter and ever more skeptical that his grandmother's Borijin clan had the wherewithal to rule, even when given the opportunity. Esen struck him down and replaced him with another Borijin as his puppet. Again, Esen sought to unite the two families and their respective tribes. This time, he arranged a marriage between his daughter and the son of the new puppet khan. If she could produce a son, he would be a Borijin and be Esen's grandson.

Suddenly, for some unexplained reason, the strategy fell apart; Esen turned violently against his grandmother's clan and all the members. They had failed him too many times and turned against him even when he tried to save them. He decided that Mongolia would be better off without the royal family. Instead of returning the Borijin family to power, he decided to exterminate it.

To initiate the plan to rid himself of all the descendants of Genghis Khan, Esen erected two large adjoining *gers* under the pretext of sponsoring a feast and celebration. Under one of the *gers,* his men dug a deep hole and covered it over with a felt carpet. In the other, Esen waited to greet each of the nobles of the royal family. On the clever pretext of offering maximum respect to each guest, Esen ordered that they be brought into the feast one at a time beginning with the lowest-ranking individual and escorted by two members of Esen's entourage. As each man entered, Esen stepped forward with a bowl to offer him a drink. At this moment all of Esen's men began to sing very loudly in honor of the man while his two escorts strangled him, dragged his body into the adjoining tent, and threw it into the pit beneath the felt carpet.

The awaiting dignitaries outside the tent suspected nothing since the loud singing drowned out any screams or cries of the victims. The khan and most of his court met their death that night. Only the khan's son, who was also Esen's son-in-law, managed to avoid the trap when his servant warned him that he saw blood seeping from beneath the tent walls. Although he escaped a dramatic chase by Esen's men, someone killed him soon thereafter. From this gathering and the accompanying campaign, it is said that, by 1452, Esen had killed forty-four nobles, thirty-three lesser nobles, and sixty-one military officers from the Borijin clan and its allies. After this bloody campaign a new saying arose that "nobles die when gathering, dogs die during drought," and was often repeated as either a threat or a warning to the powerful.

Samur's whole life had been devoted to restoring the Borijin monarchy, and now she and her grandson were divided. Although already an ancient lady, she prepared for one more battle before she could die, and this time her enemy was her grandson. He had killed nearly every male relative she had and almost destroyed the chance of restoring her clan to power. The struggle between grandmother and grandson came down to a fight to save the one last infant boy born to the Borijin clan.

Esen's young and recently widowed daughter was about to give birth. If the baby turned out to be a boy, he would be Samur's final hope of having a Borijin descendant who might possibly grow up to be khan. A son, Samur's great-great-grandchild, could hold a direct claim to the throne as the legitimate descendant of Genghis Khan and the heir to his father and grandfather. It was a thin thread of hope, but Samur had successfully prevailed in equally desperate circumstances in the past.

Samur and the child's mother, though many years apart in age, shared a common experience of becoming a young widow trapped in a set of political machinations over which each had little control. More than anyone else at the time, the two women seemed to keep clearly in mind the good of the larger nation rather than just their own careers or that of any individual person. Acting together across those generations, they not only saved the baby, they set in motion a long series of events by which women would play the dominant role for most of the coming half century; these women would eventually put the nation back on the proper path of unity and cooperation. But that journey would be a long and harsh one.

Inevitably, Esen learned of the pregnancy, and he moved quickly. He planned to force his daughter into a new marriage, after which her Borijin baby would be killed at birth. Samur helped her great-granddaughter escape and hide, and the young widow successfully gave birth to a boy. She named her baby Bayan Mongke, meaning "Prosperous Eternity."

Esen, the boy's grandfather, sent out a party of men to find his daughter and her infant to see what sex it was. He issued harsh orders to the men. "If it is a girl, comb her hair," he instructed them. "If it is a boy, comb his throat."

The mother recognized the execution party as it approached, and immediately discerned its purpose. Knowing that the men would first examine the boy's genitals, the mother showed no fear and held the baby out in front of her in the customary Mongol way of holding a child to urinate. With her fingers hidden inside his clothes, she pulled back his testicles and held back his penis in a way that obscured the male genitals while he urinated. After watching the child urinate, the leader of the assassination party felt satisfied without the need for a more direct examination. "It is a girl," the leader reported back to Esen.

Esen remained suspicious of his grandmother and his daughter. Knowing that the boy remained in danger, Samur had the baby brought to her own *ger*. She was still a queen, the daughter of a Great Khan, the descendant of Genghis Khan, and the wife and mother of khans. Even her own grandson would not violate the sanctity of her *ger*.

In place of the boy, they substituted the infant daughter of a serving woman. This time, when the inspector returned to the mother's *ger* and opened the baby's clothing, he carefully examined the genitalia to make sure that there could be no deception or mistake. Again, he reported back to Esen that his grandchild was definitely a girl.

Such a trick may have temporarily preserved the boy's life, but word of the deception quickly spread across the steppe, and in fulfillment of his worst suspicions, Esen learned the truth. Samur might be able to shelter and protect the boy for a while, but at her age she could not personally stand guard over him every moment of every day. Esen repeatedly tried to locate the boy and kidnap him through trickery without harming Samur.

Esen wrote to his grandmother and pleaded with her to surrender the baby to his men. She mocked her grandson for being afraid of an infant, his own grandson. "Do you already begin to fear," she angrily wrote back to Esen, "that the boy when he grows up will take vengeance on you?"

On one occasion, she hid him inside an overturned pot over which she heaped dried dung. The intended fate of the heir became clear when the soldiers found another baby boy that they thought might be the child they wanted. After stripping him naked to ensure that this child was truly male, they wrapped a cord around his neck in order to strangle him without spilling any blood. At the last moment, the soldiers realized he was not Bayan Mongke and spared him but continued their hunt.

After three years of struggle and deceit, Samur knew that such defiance and clever ruses could not continue successfully for long, and now, probably somewhere in her eighties, she might, at any moment, be incapacitated or die, thereby leaving the child to face a nearly certain death. She also realized that her grandson Esen had become increasingly desperate and unpredictable in the bitter rage that he felt toward her clan. He had already broken so many ancient laws in the last few years and killed so many descendants of Genghis Khan that he might even strike directly at her.

In her final act of service to her nation and clan, Samur decided to send the three-year-old baby far away from the area controlled by her grandson and entrust him to loyal Mongols for safekeeping. Such a plan posed grave danger. Even if the child survived the escape and the long journey, who could be certain what fate might await him on the other side of the Mongol nation?

A group of men loyal to the family of Genghis Khan, or at least seeing a route to future honor and riches, agreed to spirit away the boy under the leadership of a commander who had entered Esen's service at age thirteen but felt unappreciated for his many military achievements.

After hearing of the flight, Esen became angry but sensed the excellent opportunity to finally capture the child. He sent out a new squad, and soon the pursuers overtook the men fleeing with the infant. In a free-for-all skirmish over control of Bayan Mongke, the two sides began shooting at one another. In an effort to protect the baby or to confuse the pursuers, the men carrying him tied him tightly in his cradle and hid him.

For whoever captured him, the infant heir constituted a valuable trophy for which many different factions would pay dearly. Esen's men surmised precisely what had happened, and they began scouring the area for the hidden child. Realizing that the pursuers were closing in on the hiding place, one of Samur's men raced his horse directly at the spot. Esen's men saw him and also headed in the same direction. They were too close for the rescuer to dismount and pick up the infant. He had only one chance to swoop by the hiding place, bend down without stopping, and hook the child with the end of his bow. The bow caught on the cradle, and with one powerful lunge of his arm, he tossed the cradle high into the air, above and out in front of the horse. As the cradle fell back toward the earth, the man caught it perfectly and securely. Without breaking speed, he managed to outrun Esen's men.

The escapees traveled for weeks, deep into Mongol territory. There they entrusted the boy to the care of a sympathetic family loyal to Samur and her family, but the hearth of the Borijin clan would not be relit quickly. Esen still held power, but somehow his grandmother's public defeat of him had turned the tide of an increasingly frustrated nation of followers, and they rose up in revolt in 1454.

In the ensuing battle, Esen's enemies seized his family and herds while he fled virtually without supporters. Thousands of his followers hungered for revenge against him for killing some beloved member of the family. The opportunity for that retribution fell by chance to Bagho, a man whose father Esen had murdered.

Bagho caught up with the khan, killed him, and dragged his body up into a tree on Kugei Khan Mountain. Here he left it for the world to see. The hanging body replicated in grisly detail the origin myth of Esen's Choros clan that states they descended from a mythical boy found dangling from the Mother Tree of life like a piece of fruit. The clear political statement for those left behind was that legitimate power of the office of Great Khan belonged exclusively to the Borijin clan.

The grandmother Samur and her grandson Esen died about the same time. She ended her days with this one small victory and with the faint possibility that it might grow into something much larger—that maybe her dreams of a united Mongolia under the Borijin clan could be fulfilled after her death. Like all of us at the final moment, Samur had no way to foretell if her life's work would have a permanent effect or simply wash away in the tide of coming events.

Daughter of the Yellow Dragon

ANDUHAI WAS BORN IN 1448, THE STRONGEST AND
most imperial of all the zodiac years, and the only one with
a sign designated for a supernatural being: the Yellow
Dragon. According to some records at the time of her birth, her parents lived well south of the Gobi, possibly near the oasis of Hami in
modern Xinjiang; according to another tradition, she was born on the
Tumed Plain in the vicinity of what later became the city of Hohhot,
the capital of today's Inner Mongolian Autonomous Region. In either
case, she grew up in relatively arid zones of what is now northern
China, and this area and type of environment remained sentimentally
important to her throughout her life.

By the mid-fifteenth century, the clan system created and imposed
by Genghis Khan had totally deteriorated, but a new one had not yet
emerged. The Mongols had returned to the political chaos that preceded their unification in 1206. Clusters of formerly unaffiliated families formed expedient amalgamations that sometimes took an ancient
name or sometimes a new one. An individual's tribal or lineage allegiance might change several times during a lifetime, and even if the
group remained the same, the name could be altered.

Manduhai was a member of one such clan conglomerate, the
Choros, which included members of the defunct Onggud and Kara
Kitai as well as the still surviving Uighurs, Oirat, and Uriyanghai. The
Choros clan had recently ascended to unprecedented power under the

leadership of Esen, and Manduhai was born at the height of his power, just before he launched his campaign to exterminate the Borijin. Soon after Manduhai's birth, around 1451, Esen appointed her father, Chororsbasi-Temur, as *chingsang,* an office somewhat like prime minister, of his newly united Oirat-Mongol nation. Despite this grand title, Chororsbasi-Temur and his family continued to live the pastoral life of Mongol nomads.

The Choros clan occupied part of the former Onggud territory that had been ruled by Alaqai Beki and then annexed by Khubilai Khan's Yuan Dynasty. Soon after the fall of the dynasty in 1368, however, soldiers of the new Ming Dynasty burned the Onggud cities and killed or chased away the people. The Onggud nearly lost their tradition of literacy, and the royal family no longer functioned with enough independent power to make its own marriages. The Onggud returned to the countryside as herders while trying to maintain some meager trade that echoed pathetically the lucrative trading empire they had once commanded along the Silk Route. They had declined from the ranks of an ancient Turkic nation under the queen Alaqai Beki to being just one more of the many poor Mongol tribes struggling to survive in the ruins of a glorious, but lost, empire. It was as though the empire and cities had never even existed.

The Uighur still held a geographic base in the oases of China's western deserts, and although significantly diminished in importance, they survived as an ethnic group. By the time that Manduhai's father assumed responsibility for the region, the Onggud name was no longer used; the people were lumped together under a variety of other ethnic names, including Oirat and Uighur.

Manduhai's clan recognized a special spiritual relationship with their founding Mother Tree common to many of the Turkic tribes; the Choros, like the Uighurs, acknowledged no mythological father. For the Mongols, the primary mythological dyad consisted of the Earth Mother and the Sky Father. For Manduhai's clan, the primary spiritual pair consisted of mother and son, symbolized by the tree and her offspring or the mother wolf who raised an orphan boy.

Manduhai probably had some kinship connection to Samur Gunj, but its importance would be difficult to calculate. Manduhai was only six years old when her father, although he had been appointed by Esen, joined the resistance to Esen and particularly to the policy of exterminating the Borijin. It is not possible to determine if her father and Samur Gunj were actually allied conspirators in their opposition or merely found themselves as common enemies of Esen.

By the time Manduhai was old enough to be aware of what was happening around her, the momentary unity and vitality of the Esen era had ended. Despite her father's role in overthrowing Esen, neither her father nor any of the other rebels could maintain control of the miniature empire Esen had assembled. Without Esen, the system collapsed back into near anarchy on the steppe.

Even the Mongol chroniclers could not keep up with the comings and goings of episodic claimants to the office of khan. For some years, no khan was mentioned, and then two young boys in succession appeared as khans with the backing of their respective mothers and other unknown players. Both boys, and apparently their mothers as well, were soon killed by rival factions. As with horses lost in a race, there was much dust and hectic movement, but no clear winner. Moreover, it did not matter who held the office because there was no united nation to rule.

During this period of renewed disintegration, fresh predators stalked the outer fringes of the steppe tribe. Just as wolves hunt the old, young, and weak, the foreign predators began circling the wounded Mongols. The new warlords created a base in the oases of the Silk Route to the west of the Gansu Corridor. These warlords bore Muslim names such as Ibrahim, Issama, and Ismayil or Ismail, but such names may have been adopted merely for commercial convenience in dealing with merchants from Muslim countries. Even Esen had once agreed to a nominal conversion to Islam in order to marry the Muslim khan's sister and had given two sons Muslim names, but Esen never practiced the faith. The significance of the names remains unclear.

The warlords and their warriors included many of the former imperial guards, particularly the Kipchak, but also some of the Asud of Ossetia. Having lost their stronghold on the Mongolian Plateau during the campaigns of Samur's husband, son, and grandson Esen, they fled south into the more remote areas of the Gobi and into the deserts of northern China. The warlords' coalitions included large mixtures of a more mysterious group known alternately as Mekrit, Megrin, and Begrin, who appear only fleetingly but at important moments in the chronicles.

This new threat originated in the oases of Turfan and Hami. These two cities operated as trade centers for long-distance caravans along the thin line of oases connecting China with the Middle East and Europe, but in these days, only a trickle of the former trade flowed through. The cities now served as desert hideaways for rebels and bandits rather than crucial chains in a commercial network. Nevertheless, the oases supported a sufficient agricultural population to accommodate a small military force, and the desert around them offered protection from the Ming army or other enemies.

From a base in Turfan, a new warlord named Beg-Arslan sought to move into the vacuum of Mongol politics, replace Esen, and set up a puppet khan. He planned to make his daughter Yeke Qabar-tu into the *khatun* of the Mongols by finding a Borijin heir to make khan, and then marrying her to him. This move would effectively allow Beg-Arslan to run the country as the imperial father-in-law. One obstacle to that plan was Yeke Qabar-tu's reputation as an unattractive woman. Her name meant "Big Nose," and for the Mongols, who often referred to themselves with pride as the "No-Nose Mongols," the prospect of siring a child with Big Nose lacked appeal. Mongols associated such noses with Westerners, mostly Europeans and Muslims, rather than with East Asians. If nothing else, her Mongol name clearly indicated that Yeke Qabar-tu's origin, and that of her father, lay beyond the Mongol world.

The male descendants of Genghis Khan had dwindled to just a few, primarily ineffective old men, but also a few young boys whose mothers or other relatives claimed that they had been fathered by

Borijin men who had subsequently died. From the contenders, Beg-Arslan selected a modest but tractable man named Manduul, made him Great Khan, and married him to Yeke Qabar-tu sometime between 1463 and 1465.

Despite the ability of warlords to make and unmake the khans and their marriages, they lacked the power to force consummation. The khan did not like Yeke Qabar-tu. He "stayed absent from" her and "did not co-habit with her." Not surprisingly, Big Nose produced no children. Some chronicles mention that Manduul was sick in the time that he knew her and that was the reason he did not cohabit with her. Although she continued at court as queen, apparently she and the khan avoided each other as much as was practical.

Of seemingly far less importance, around the year 1464, Manduul married Manduhai, who was about sixteen, nearly twenty-five years his junior. There is nothing surprising about the match, since she came from a political family, but what mixture of political and personal preferences underlay the marriage is not clear. Perhaps she was beautiful and appealed to the khan; perhaps he simply wanted a wife who was not a foreigner.

Some chronicles refer to her by the title *khatun,* or "queen," at this point, but others refer to her merely as a princess, indicating some possible contention or confusion on her initial status at court. Eventually there would be no question about her rank, but it remained ambiguous for her first several years as a wife. She entered quietly. Nothing is mentioned of how she came to be Manduul's wife, and nothing about her seemed worthy of much attention at the moment. For almost a decade she would have no apparent role to play in political life, but when the moment came, she would seize it and become the most powerful queen in Mongolian history. This child bride would one day lead armies and command a nation, but for now young Manduhai silently watched and learned from everyone around her.

No physical description of Manduhai survives, but as the more beloved wife, Manduhai presumably met some of the simple but precise standards by which Mongols of her era judged beauty. Because the body was so hidden by heavy layers of clothes, the traits of feminine beauty stressed specific facial qualities. Mongols favored a round face with relatively small features; the ideal beauty had a face shaped like the moon, with very pale skin except for bright red cheeks: the redder, the better.

Manduhai did not find the lavish royal tents waiting for her as they had been for the wives of the Great Khans of the earlier Mongol Empire. These luxurious *gers* of old had been known to accommodate a thousand people, boasting walls lined with silk and fur and furnishings of gold and silver. When those early queens went out on campaigns with their husbands, they traveled in special *gers* permanently erected on large mobile platforms, pulled across the landscape by several dozen oxen. All of these amenities had disappeared with the end of the imperial era, and at the Mongol royal court, Manduhai probably lived a modest but comfortable life comparable to that of her childhood.

Manduhai's name meant "Rising" or "Ascending" in the sense of the sun rising in the morning, a flag or banner being raised up overhead, or a queen or king being enthroned; in more recent times it has come to mean economic or technological progress. In all senses, it has carried a powerful, awesome, and decidedly sacred connotation. The names Manduul and Manduhai derived from the same root word for ascension, and the similarity of the two could not have been ignored. The marriage match could have been made on the basis of the similarity of names, which may have been interpreted as a sign of their nuptial destiny, or Manduul could have changed or modified his queen's name to make it more similar to his when they married. Whether merely coincidental or artificially contrived, the similarity would have been viewed as seemly.

Manduul held the title of Great Khan of the Mongol Empire. This title represented a claim to be not merely the ruler of the Mongols, but also the legitimate ruler of China, Korea, Manchuria, and Central Asia, albeit in exile—though in truth he did not even rule his own house-hold. Beg-Arslan had taken the lesser title of *taishi*, but he operated mostly south of the Gobi, where he could better exploit the richer resources there.

Manduul remained north of the Gobi, although it is not clear if this was his choice of refuge or if Beg-Arslan sent him there to limit his influence. So long as he controlled the trade in and out of Mongolia and maintained access to conscript Mongolian boys as needed for his raids, Beg-Arslan seemed unconcerned with where Manduul stayed, so long as it was out of the way.

In a nomadic society, a herder's campsite reveals much about that individual's character and temperament. Choices about fall, winter, spring, and summer camps demonstrate a pattern and a way of think-ing. Does the herder care most about what is good for the horses or the cows? Is he inclined to take risks or seek security? Does he prefer the solitude of the Gobi or the fertility of the steppe? Is the herder a loner far from others or a convivial person who wants neighbors?

Although a khan needs to worry about the welfare of the people more than his own herd of animals, his choice of location still reveals his spirit and ambitions. Manduul and Manduhai made their capital camp far away from the centers of action in China and along the Silk Route. They set up their mobile court in an area called Mongke Bulag, a tributary of the Old Orkhon River. The name Mongke Bulag meant "Perpetual Spring" or "Eternal Source," indicating a constant flow of water throughout the year. The small canyon-valleys with permanent springs offered the basic requirements for a comfortable winter camp, and the surrounding steppe had ample grass in the summer, but also enough wind to keep away mosquitoes. It was good for camels, goats, and cows—especially for horses and sheep—but lacked the elevation necessary to support yaks.

The landscape evoked a pleasant intimate feeling of almost iso-lated tranquility, and its same small scale indicates that it lacked suffi-cient grazing for the number of animals needed to support a large army or even a large court of retainers. The location indicates that

Manduul did not have a large army, and he was not trying to assemble one.

Only a few days' horse ride downstream to the northwest, the much wider pastures of the old imperial area of Karakorum would have offered far more extensive grazing for the horses of a more ambitious khan. By contrast, Mongke Bulag resembled a defensive retreat or possibly a place of forced exile and confinement, providing Manduul with little opportunity to influence trade or diplomacy.

According to most texts, Manduul had no children, and he possibly did not reside in the same *ger* with either Manduhai or Yeke Qabartu. Yet occasionally two women, Borogchin and Esige, are mentioned as daughters of Manduhai. Since they were too old to have been born to Manduhai during her marriage to Manduul, they appear to have been close female relatives of Manduul, possibly daughters from a prior marriage of Manduul, or more likely each was a niece or younger sister who lived with him as a daughter. Soon after the arrival of Manduhai, Borogchin married either Beg-Arslan or his son and went to live with her husband in the south.

The old khan certainly had no sons, but he had two distant male relatives. Each was a rival heir-in-waiting, and each tried to cultivate a close relationship with the old khan in the hope of succeeding him. Just as important, each of the potential heirs needed a close relationship with the queen in order for her to accept him as her next husband in the event of Manduul's death.

The strongest rival was clearly Une-Bolod, an accomplished warrior and a member of the Borijin clan, albeit through descent from Genghis Khan's brother Khasar rather than directly from Genghis Khan himself. Such men, however, had held the office in the past. His genealogy may not have been ideal, but it clearly qualified him for the position. Regarding his heritage, he was quoted as saying that what mattered most was that all the members of the family descended from Hoelun's womb, thereby making his ancestor Khasar and Genghis Khan equal. His most compelling advantage as a potential heir derived from his record of military accomplishments in a time when the Mongols seemed woefully lacking in the skills for which they had once been so renowned. During the time of Esen's rule, Une-Bolod had taken refuge on the Onon River out of loyalty to his Borijin clan.

The other rival was still more an unproven boy than a man. He had no record of accomplishing anything, but he was almost precisely Manduhai's age and came from a similar background to hers. He was the young boy Bayan Mongke, whom Samur Gunj had rescued from Esen's murderous rampage.

In the years after Esen's death, when there were long stretches without a khan, Une-Bolod served as the head of the family from the traditional homeland of Genghis Khan on the Onon River. When Samur sent the infant Bayan Mongke to safety among the Mongols, it was to Une-Bolod's territory in eastern Mongolia that he fled. Despite Une-Bolod's seniority by a decade or more, he recognized the infant as his "elder brother," meaning from the lineage of the elder brother Genghis Khan, and therefore having priority in the line of succession to become Great Khan. Une-Bolod placed the infant with a herding family, possibly with the expectation that he might be lost or forgotten over time. The family lived in a remote and isolated section of the South Gobi, where a very sparse but mixed population of Mongols and former Tangut eked out a meager subsistence.

Because of the way that they grew up, Bayan Mongke and Manduhai had more in common with each other than they had with either Manduul or Une-Bolod. Although reared on opposite sides of the Gobi, both Manduhai and Bayan Mongke experienced a similar life in nomadic *gers* and subsisted from the same kind of traditional steppe herding. They resided far from the bizarre combination of stifling constriction and wanton privilege that marked court life. Although Genghis Khan had lived nearly three hundred years earlier, in many ways the childhoods of Manduhai and Bayan Mongke, possibly more than any other descendants', resembled his. Like him, they had been raised on the margins rather in the center of the territory.

As herders, rather, they learned to wrestle animals into control, to always keep camels separated from horses because of their natural antipathy for one another, and to recognize where the cows could graze undisturbed by goats and sheep. They learned how to disassemble the *ger,* load the entire household onto only five camels in a precisely ordered fashion, move to a new camp, and rebuild the home. They knew when to bring the animals to shelter before a storm or how to track them afterward.

A child of the steppe was trained for survival and for constantly making vital decisions. Every morning, the herder steps out of the *ger,* looks around, and chooses today's path according to the results of last week's rain, yesterday's wind, today's temperature, or where the animals need to be next week. The quest for pasture is the same each day, but the way to find it varies. If the rains do not come, the herder must find them; if the grass does not grow here, the herder must find where it does. The herder cannot remain in one place, be still, and do nothing. The herder is forced to choose a path every day, time and time again.

While the farmer follows the same path to the same fields every day, the herder looks across a landscape of perpetual possibility. No fences or walls bar the way, but neither are there roads to guide or bridges to cross. The steppe is infinite opportunity. The options depend on the ability of the person who sees them and can find how to utilize them to meet today's needs. The mountain becomes what the herder makes of it: a barrier to the herd's migration or a refuge from the harsh blizzards and fierce sandstorms of spring and fall. A stone can be a hammer or something to throw at a lurking wolf, or it may mark the place to make a new hearth for today's camp.

In such a world, children such as Manduhai and Bayan Mongke had to learn to think to survive. The child should learn from the parents but always be able to act alone and not merely follow orders. Wrong choices inflict terrific pain. A movement in the wrong direction can lead the animals on a death march of slow starvation and thirst. A box canyon may serve as a protected winter camp, but if the grass is insufficient for the animals, they will weaken and the wolves will slowly pick them off one by one. The child of the steppe learns to correct these wrong choices quickly or else die. The rigors of the nomadic life make a child into a self-reliant, hardy, and independent adult.

Both Manduhai and Bayan Mongke also knew the experience of being suddenly plucked from this pastoral life and taken to the royal court of an elderly relative. The new life not only freed them from the unending chores of daily herding life but also offered enticing opportunities for adventure.

After surviving the repeated attempts to kill him in infancy, Bayan Mongke reached sexual maturity, if not adulthood, early. At age fourteen he became a father and at fifteen became an unwilling contender for the title of Great Khan, an office that he did not yet want and was destined never to achieve.

He fathered a baby boy with Siker, the daughter of the Uriyanghai commoner family with whom he found refuge near the modern border of Mongolia and China. Her father seemed anxious to raise the family status by acquiring a Borijin son-in-law and grandchild, and rather than adopting Bayan Mongke as a son, he treated him as resident son-in-law performing bride service. Siker was probably a few years older than he, since girls of that era normally did not become reproductive before age sixteen and were rarely allowed to marry before that age. The chronicles describe their relationship as a marriage, but the evidence suggests that neither Siker nor Bayan Mongke developed a liking for the other, nor for the baby they shared.

Bayan Mongke was the grandson of Esen on his mother's side and of Manduul Khan's elder half brother on his father's side. In addition to this bone bond, both the elder and the younger man had Oirat mothers. Manduul saw in the young boy a much less threatening heir than the warrior Une-Bolod. As a rival to Une-Bolod's hope to become khan, Bayan Mongke helped to insulate the old khan from possible assassination or overthrow.

About the same time that Manduhai came to live as the wife of Manduul Khan, the old khan brought Bayan Mongke to court.

Manduul apparently saw in Bayan Mongke the son he never had, plus the prospect of revitalizing the long-moribund court life. Whether for political or emotional reasons, the old uncle and his young nephew formed an unusual partnership. Each seemed to energize the other, and both perceived a benefit from the novel union.

At the court, Bayan Mongke made a dashing appearance, which he knew how to use to his advantage. He was young and handsome, with a flair of his own. He wore a brocade *deel* embroidered with gold and lined with squirrel fur, and he had a strong preference for riding chestnut horses. As a sign of his rank, he wore a golden belt, an object of majestic symbolism to the Mongols of that era. The Idiqut of the Uighurs had referred to the golden belt when he said to Genghis Khan: "If I receive but a ring from your golden belt, I will become your fifth son and will serve you."

Manduul Khan bestowed on Bayan Mongke the title of *jinong*, meaning "Golden Prince" but signifying that he was now the heir and therefore the crown prince of the Mongols. After *khan*, the title of *jinong* had the highest prestige in the country. The importance of the office was evident in a Mongol saying: "In the blue sky above, there are the sun and the moon. And on the earth below, there are the Khan and the Jinong."

Bayan Mongke's promotion also meant a demotion for Une-Bolod to the third most important member of the clan. As the new *jinong*, Bayan Mongke assumed formal responsibility for the *ger* shrine to Genghis Khan, and he acquired possession of the black *sulde* from General Une-Bolod, who had been in control of the land and shrines, and who had been, at least unofficially, the presumed heir to the throne.

Despite all the attached ritual duties and ceremonial authority, the office of *jinong* lacked genuine authority over anything. Neither khan nor *jinong* exercised the real power since it was in the hands of foreign warlords; Beg-Arslan held the lower-ranking title of *taishi*, but actually exercised control of the comings and goings of people and goods in and out of Mongolian territory.

Sometime between 1463 and 1465, Manduul also changed Bayan Mongke's name to Bolkhu, meaning "Rising Up" or "Coming Up," which carried similar connotations to his own and to Manduhai's "Rising." The chronicles make it appear that Manduul installed his nephew not merely as his heir, but as a complete co-ruler. The uncle and nephew lived together "in peace and harmony," and together they "brought the nation under control with strength and power." The language used reflected the same organizational techniques used by Genghis Khan in his metaphor of the two shafts on the cart of state.

The chronicles do not describe the ceremony of installation for the Golden Prince, but based upon the golden belt, horse, and *deel* that he received, the ceremony seemed similar to the one during which Genghis Khan and his childhood friend and eventual ally Jamuka exchanged vows of brotherhood before a "leafy tree" in the Khorkhonag Valley, agreeing to become two shafts of one cart. In that ceremony, each of the men put a golden belt around the waist of the other, and they exchanged horses. "They declared themselves sworn friends and loved each other," according to the *Secret History*. Afterward, "they enjoyed themselves reveling and feasting, and at night they slept together, the two of them alone under their blanket."

Bayan Mongke was close in age to Manduhai, and their youthful presence brought a renewed vigor to the staid Mongol court. However, they seemed more rivals than potential partners. He was admired and became the center of court attention, while she seemed ignored by her husband and everyone else, except for General Une-Bolod.

Compared with her aging husband, Une-Bolod was a vigorous man. Compared with the inexperienced crown prince, he was a mature man. While her husband had led an undistinguished life on the margins and the crown prince was much too young to have any accomplishments, Une-Bolod was a traditional Mongol man, a proven warrior. From the start, he seemed aware of Manduhai's future importance, knowing that the man who had her favor after her husband's death would become the new khan.

The young crown prince had none of this sophistication. He had won the total support of his uncle, and now his interest was not so much in wooing the attention of a future queen as in striking out for new adventures. He was ready to raid, take to the battlefield, and make his mark in the world.

Without any major accomplishments of his own, Manduul Khan seemed eager to support Bayan Mongke's aspiration. Manduul's first effort was to gain control of the local area. The khan and the prince set out to impose their authority on the tribes in central Mongolia. They used the excuse of avenging the murder of Manduul's predecessor, the boy Molon Khan, but through a series of campaigns they seemed to be establishing control over their base in order to mount a challenge to Beg-Arslan, or whoever came to power in the south. Mounted on his pale chestnut horse, Bayan Mongke led the army and brought the surrounding tribes back into submission under Manduul, who accompanied his heir but did not participate in the fighting.

Conquering other Mongols and raiding small camps may have been gratifying to a young man on his first escapade and to an old man whose life had lacked adventure, but it produced little material or political result. One tribe was about as poor as the next. For real raiding and plunder, they had to look south of the Gobi to the Silk Route or to the Chinese cities. Just at this fortuitous moment, a message arrived informing the Mongol court that the Ming emperor had died in Beijing some months earlier in 1464.

Bayan Mongke had not only a claim on China by virtue of his descent from his ancestors Genghis and Khubilai Khan, who had conquered the country, he had an even more immediate connection to the dead emperor. This was the same emperor whom Bayan Mongke's grandfather Esen had once captured and held prisoner in 1449.

The crown prince longed for action, and he wanted to break away from the tranquil isolation of the Mongol royal family. He did not seem sure of what he specifically sought to achieve, but he wanted something spectacular. It would not suffice to conquer neighboring clans and fight the endless Mongol feuds. He aspired to follow the heroic tradition of his ancestor Genghis Khan, to conquer whole kingdoms and assemble an empire. The route to fame and glory ran to the south, across the Gobi to the oases of the Silk Route or the cities of China, and now with the death of the old Ming emperor, fate seemed to have opened an opportunity for him in China.

The preoccupation of the Ming court with the rituals and the internecine struggles accompanying the death of the old emperor and the transition to a new emperor provided young Bayan Mongke his opportunity to strike out toward the south and prove himself as a would-be conqueror and future khan of the Mongols. Even if he could not persuade his aged great-uncle to make the journey, he could do it himself. Manduul allowed his nephew to go accompanied by Une-Bolod, the Mongol's most experienced military leader.

To reach China from the Mongol court, Bayan Mongke and his small party of soldiers had to travel six to eight weeks from the Old Orkhon down the Ongi River, which they followed south into the Gobi until the river dried out in the desert. Moving across routes leading from one spring to another, the army would need to cross the desert, interspersed with several small clumps of mountains, and then finally descend from the Mongolian Plateau into Inner Mongolia.

The small Mongol force lacked the ability to conquer even a single Chinese city, but the Mongols devised a strategy of following the example of Genghis Khan, who acquired a beachhead south of the Gobi by making an alliance with the Onggud prior to his invasion of China. Now these same lands were occupied by Mongols allied to the Ming but performing the same old Onggud function of guarding China from assault by the tribes of the north. Bayan Mongke and Manduul sought to use their ethnic ties and shared heritage to reunite the Mongols north of the Gobi with the ones living under Chinese control. Many more Mongols lived in China under Ming rule than in Mongolia, and perhaps if unity could be reasserted between the two groups, they might be able to overcome the Chinese once again and restore the empire.

Only a teenager could have had such a dream, and only an inexperienced old man could have encouraged him in it. Bayan Mongke headed off on his first major assignment. He rode into the border zone to lure the Mongols away from the Ming and to negotiate a pan-Mongol alliance. He found a receptive audience among the Mongols, who had grown weary of the Ming rule and the unfulfilled promises and obligations of the court. As a youthful soldier, apparently destined to one day become the Great Khan of the Mongol nation, Bayan Mongke excited their pride and ambition. For those prone toward imperial nostalgia and visions of Mongol glory, the dream rose again of uniting the tribes and restoring Mongol rule over China. For those who wished more material rewards, Bayan Mongke stimulated greed for the days when the Mongols controlled all the productive wealth of China and the mercantile traffic of the Silk Road.

Both the Mongols and the Ming court maintained false and often silly perceptions of themselves and each other. Every society produces its own cultural conceits, a set of lies and delusions about itself that thrives in the face of all contrary evidence. The Mongols believed that they could not be completely defeated. Even after being driven back north of the Gobi, they still pretended to be the rightful rulers of China and much of the rest of the world. The Mongol royal court was just waiting for a shift in the will of heaven that would propel them back to their rightful place as rulers of the most extensive empire on earth. To fill in the gaps between their beliefs and reality, they sat around the fire telling of clever Mongol concubines, morally lax Chinese queens, oversexed Mongol soldiers, impotent Chinese emperors, and secret pregnancies. All the tales ended with the deception of Chinese court officials and the conclusion that through some form of clever deceit, the Ming emperor was really a Mongol. Thus, the Mongols had never been truly defeated or chased out of China, merely replaced by some of their Mongol kinsmen in another guise. The men chuckled over the stories and then headed out to hunt another marmot and gather some dried cow dung to build a fire.

These stories also served as justification for any type of raid or military expedition. They had a story that while the Ming emperor had been held captive by the Mongols, he fathered a son with a Mongol girl. Thus, if needed, they had yet one more claim to be the legitimate rulers of China and even to have the legitimate heir of the dead Ming emperor. In the intervening years, the identity of the girl and her son had been lost, but they could certainly be found if needed. The justification, however, did not matter until the Mongols had a sufficiently strong military force to rival the Ming. The story of the secret heir might be useful as a propaganda tool for legitimizing their rule if they conquered China, but it had little use in rallying Mongols to fight.

The Mongols undermined the truth of their defeats with sexual intrigue; the Ming courtiers undermined the truth of their failures by renaming and redefining it. The Chinese believed that they had never really been conquered at all. By assigning Chinese names to each of the foreign conquerors, they almost obliterated the unpleasant memory of alien domination. Periodically, the eunuchs of the court invited in a Mongol horse trader, dressed him in elegant new clothes, gave him a letter glorifying the Ming emperor, and ushered him into the court, which accepted his goods as foreign tribute and gave him lavish gifts in return. Later the eunuchs could laugh over the filthy fingers and crude manners of the barbarians as they slurped bowls of hot noodles, and then return to drawing pornographic pictures to give to the next foreign delegation.

After one hundred years in power, the Ming Dynasty had spent its initial vigor and matured into a protracted middle age. Prior to Esen's capture of the Ming emperor, the dynasty had its confidence, even if it lacked youthful energy. After the capture, the nation suffered from a lack of both, and their traditionally exaggerated fears of the Mongols began to haunt the Chinese once again. The nervous fear clouded every diplomatic discussion and prevented the court from uniting behind a single comprehensive policy of how to deal with the barbarian threat.

As the Ming weakened and the turmoil among the Mongols continued, renegade Mongols began making deeper and more frequent raids into Chinese territory. The renewed raiding seemed closely tied to Bayan Mongke's coming of age and his expanding prominence at court as *jinong*, and Chinese chroniclers showed an increasing fear of him and other Mongol raiding parties.

In plotting to attack the Chinese cities, young Bayan Mongke faced an unusual foe headed by a teenage emperor of almost the same age. The Ming heir became emperor in approximately the same year that Bayan Mongke became crown prince. Their lives were marked by similar experiences of near death, years in hiding, and then sudden elevation to power at the center of a powerful court. Esen's campaigns against their families had been the source of the early suffering for both of them.

But in addition to these odd similarities, there were marked differences as well. The power behind Bayan Mongke was his older uncle; the power behind the Chinese emperor Chenghua was his older nursemaid, Lady Wan, whom he loved.

The new emperor had been born in 1447 just before Esen captured his father. During his father's captivity, the little crown prince Chenghua lost his position, had his name changed, was shunted aside, and lived in constant danger of being killed. The harsh uncertainty of his perilous childhood left him a nervous and introverted child, made all the worse by a severe stutter when trying to pronounce words beginning with *s, zh, ch,* and *sh* sounds. Within the closed world of his nursery, Wan nourished and entertained the shy, vulnerable boy. She dressed herself and him in military uniforms, played elaborate games, and staged colorful and exciting military charades with real soldiers.

In 1464, at age seventeen, the emperor ascended the throne when

Lady Wan was thirty-two years old. For as long as he could remember, she had been his most intimate companion and his protector, and at the appropriate time she had initiated him into sex. Although it was common for the servant women to meet an emperor's sexual needs when required, such women came and went with little more notice than the changing flowers in a vase; but this young emperor seemed inordinately attached to his nurse.

When he became emperor, he married an appropriately aristocratic lady in order to have an official empress. She quickly learned of his attachment to Wan, and she bitterly resented it. Within weeks of being installed in her new status as the highest-ranking woman in the empire, Empress Wu claimed that the nursemaid had been discourteous to her and ordered that she be flogged in a clear show of rank and resentment. Outraged, the teenage emperor stripped his wife of her title of empress after only a month and a day in office, banishing her to a remote palace within the Imperial City, where she lived out the next forty-five years until her death.

Chenghua could not make a servant into an empress, even one as beloved as Wan, but he continued to live openly with her. Two years later, when the emperor was nineteen and Lady Wan was thirty-six, she gave birth to a son, who soon died. After the death, officials began writing memoranda to the emperor, asking him to seek relations with other women in his household in order to produce an heir and, as an intended but not stated consequence, to decrease the power of Lady Wan, her family, and her entourage. The emperor obliged by having a son with one of his wives, but the child died suddenly just after being declared the heir. Suspicion naturally fell on Lady Wan, but the emperor stood fast by her.

Following the loss of their son, the emperor showed no lessening of his commitment to Lady Wan, despite her inability to get pregnant again. Although she could not appear in court as the official empress in the gowns and clothes that accompanied the title, Lady Wan chose her own individual way of marking her identity: She often chose to wear men's military clothes. As the only woman at court dressed as a general, she flaunted her unique position.

The Chinese sources report that Bayan Mongke of the Mongols came into Chinese territory and met with the local Mongol leaders; they blamed the young prince for instigating the troubles that followed. Soon after the suspicious visit, Mongols on the border revolted against their Ming overlords. They rose up in 1468, exactly one hundred years after the Ming expelled the Mongol khans of the Yuan Dynasty.

Bayan Mongke was not Esen. He stirred up some mild enthusiasm with the border Mongols, stoked the ashes of past glory, and tempted their appetites for adventure and plunder. During this time, the Ming border guards, disguised as Mongol bandits, raided the goods being sent to the loyal Mongols who were helping the Ming protect the border. This system of theft had frequently been used by the underpaid and underappreciated Chinese soldiers to supplement their difficult life in a forsaken post. The local commanders, who benefited from the corruption, wrote back reports blaming all such raids on outlaw Mongols. In addition, when the Mongols loyal to the Ming attempted to send tribute to the emperor, Chinese soldiers robbed them as well, and again blamed it on other, savage Mongols living in the wild. The local Mongols lost their goods and got the blame for the robbery.

The misconduct of these Ming soldiers probably had more to do with causing the border tensions than the arrival of the ineffectively young crown prince of the Mongols. Fearful of the discontent brewing along the border, and fully aware of the danger Bayan Mongke's visit might spark among these tentatively loyal Mongols, the Ming court sent out an expedition to capture the provocateur and reinforce its authority. If they could capture the heir to the title of Great Khan of the Yuan, they might have their ultimate triumph over the old dynasty, which still had not surrendered. By luck, the first Ming force sent to capture Bayan Mongke failed in the summer of 1468, but in the following year, a stronger force arrived and, by cutting off the supply of food to the border Mongols, quickly starved them out by early 1469. Bayan Mongke managed to escape back north into the Gobi and on home, but the Ming forces captured the local Mongol leader and hailed the feat as another great victory over the barbarians.

The records of this time remain silent on what happened at the Mongol court during the absence of Bayan Mongke. Yet events would soon unfold to show that Manduhai, unseen and unheard, had been making her own alliances. As the aging khan weakened and the young khan dashed about on the Chinese frontier, Manduhai solidified her position, made a few allies, and prepared as best she could for the uncertain fate ahead. For her, everything up until then had been a training period in which she watched, learned, and waited. Soon she would have the opportunity to test her skills.

For the moment, she had two rivals, both about her same age and at the start of their careers. Her immediate rival for power at court and within Mongolia was Bayan Mongke. In the longer term, however, she and the Ming emperor, using intermediaries and proxies, would become involved in an indirect but lifelong struggle for control over the borderlands, while living lives that would have uncanny, and probably not coincidental, similarities.

The Falling Prince
and the Rising Queen

SEXUAL POLITICS DESTROYED THE COURT OF MANDUUL Khan. The Tibetan chronicle states that the horrendous charges and countercharges about the incidents were too dreadful to repeat, but of course the author teases the reader with a hazy sketch of events displayed to tantalize more than inform. The Mongolian chroniclers more eagerly described specific details of some events while obscuring others, depending on the genealogical connections and political allegiances of the writer. Each chronicler had some personal connection to the people in the story and often wanted to protect a particular person's reputation while placing the blame firmly on another.

Sex is always political, and in politics every relationship is potentially sexual, or at least is open to accusations of being so. Usually the sex remains just a little hidden in the domain of speculation, gossip, and rumor, but in the breakup of Manduul Khan's court, almost every person was accused of an inappropriate relationship with someone, or several people, in the group.

Bayan Mongke came to court for sexual purposes, at least some of which were clearly stated. He had already proved his ability to father a son, and now he would be expected to do so again to carry forth the Borijin clan. As the heir, the young prince Bolkhu Jinong would also marry the wives of the old khan when he died. This custom reached far back into steppe history and set them clearly apart from their Chinese and Muslim neighbors, who disapproved highly of this practice. As a Confucian scholar wrote of them, "They marry by succession their stepmothers, the wives of their deceased younger paternal uncles, and the wives of their deceased elder brothers." He further described the Mongols as facing the ridicule of future generations, stating that only through "civilization and law" could the Mongols abolish these incestuous, barbaric traditions.

By installing Bayan Mongke and giving him the title Bolkhu Jinong, Manduul made this expectation clear. As the khan bragged about the nephew when presenting him, "He will be a fruitful branch from the noble Borijin family tree." The khan used a metaphor understood by every Mongol. He compared the young prince to the fermented mare's milk saved at the end of the horse milking season for next year's fermentation. Manduul Khan called his nephew the *khorongo* for the Borijin lineage.

According to Mongol tradition, the heir would wait until the father died before taking one of his wives. Yet sometimes among the tribes from Siberia to Tibet, when one man failed to father a son, another member of his lineage, or bone, might help to do so. In Tibet, such relations had official standing for two or more brothers married to the same wife, but in Mongolia, such marriages had no historical validity. Still, any child born of a married woman became the child of her husband. Genghis Khan made this rule clear in acknowledging his wife's first-born child as his own son, despite his wife's capture and brief marriage to another man. As Genghis Khan declared, if he himself claimed to be the father, what right did any other person have to dispute it?

Ahmad Ibn Arabshah, an Arab writer who lived and traveled extensively in the Mongol world at the opening of the fifteenth century, carefully observed and recorded the habits and customs of the Mongols. He noted two aspects of their conjugal life that surprised him. Women retained control and all rights over their dowry after marriage, and women commonly had sexual relations with other men in their husband's family, though they would never do so with any man outside of it. This also seemed in keeping with Genghis Khan's dictum separating family issues from communal issues, whereby he decreed that affairs of the *ger* should be settled in the *ger* and affairs of the steppe on the steppe.

The European historian Edward Gibbon, who evidenced little respect for any of the steppe tribes, described the Mongol homes and their habits with ostentatious contempt. "The houses of the Tartars are no more than small tents, of an oval form, which afford a cold and dirty habitation for the promiscuous youth of both sexes."

The sexual and political dynamics of Manduul's court produced much confused commentary and speculation. Initially the senior khan seemed infatuated with his young heir and refused to see anything wrong in what he did. Bayan Mongke seemed eager to please the khan and keep his support. As a child whose survival often depended on ingratiating himself to more powerful people around him, Bayan Mongke understood the importance of this role.

Bayan Mongke may have been inexperienced in warfare and international diplomacy with the Chinese court, but he understood the dynamics of the Mongol court. His hold on power in the short term derived from pleasing his uncle, but in the long term it depended on the favor of Manduhai or Yeke Qabar-tu, since as the heir he had to marry one of them, preferably the senior wife, to become khan after his uncle died. It behooved him to cultivate favor with one of them now, but it was a dangerous path in controlling precisely how far the relationship should go while the old khan still lived.

Manduhai had no reason to like or trust the young prince. He had essentially replaced her at court. Her husband confided in the prince, not in her. Her husband lavished gifts and power on him and had made the young prince co-ruler, a position that should have gone to the younger and heretofore favored wife. The dashing prince in his golden robes and belt on his chestnut horse attracted everyone's attention, and those around her pushed her toward an amicable relationship with him in the hope that she might eventually marry him and produce heirs with him.

Manduhai's misgivings about the young prince were shared by General Une-Bolod. The prince had replaced Une-Bolod as the heir. A political alliance can be made on a mutual attraction, but it can just as easily be made on a shared antipathy. Because the young prince's presence threatened both of them, Manduhai and Une-Bolod had a natural alliance in their dislike of him. Soon, gossip linked the two romantically as well.

General Une-Bolod was a descendant of Genghis Khan's younger brother Khasar. The lineage of Genghis Khan and the lineage of Khasar had perpetuated the sibling rivalries of the two brothers. The two branches of the family usually worked closely and amicably together, but occasionally the relationships ruptured out of antagonism into hostility. The descendants of Khasar never forgot that he was a better marksman with a bow and arrow, and they repeatedly complained about the lack of credit and material reward for their ancestor's role in creating the empire and for the family's continuing contribution to the nation through the rise and fall of the centuries.

Manduul's unwillingness to trust Une-Bolod completely was based in a two-hundred-year-old dysfunctional relationship between the two lineages within the Borijin clan. Genghis Khan and his descendants frequently suspected Khasar's line of plotting against them and of being so envious that they might betray them and try to seize the office of Great Khan. Aside from the direct competition between Genghis Khan and Khasar, rumors of amorous rivalry and adulterous betrayal also plagued them. Genghis Khan heard repeated reports of an affair between his main wife, Borte, and his brother Khasar. She certainly knew him well, and as a young bride she had lived in the *ger* with Khasar and the rest of Genghis Khan's family. Though never confirmed, the suspicions constantly plagued their relationship and continued to intrigue their followers long after all the parties had died.

Yeke Qabar-tu, Manduul's first but unloved wife, sided with the Golden Prince. Manduhai was her rival for power as well as his. Soon rumors circulated through the royal encampment about the relationship between the senior queen and the young prince. Someone provoked a servant of the prince to report their relationship to the khan. The servant told the khan that the Golden Prince was plotting to do evil to his uncle and that he was attempting to "rob" the khan of his wife, but he did not state specifically that they were already engaged in a sexual union.

For a boy to have sexual relations with the wife of his uncle did not constitute a crime. So long as the female in-law had a senior position to him, as both Manduhai and Yeke Qabar-tu did in regard to Bayan Mongke, no taboo was broken. The adultery would not be an issue unless it represented a possible conspiracy by the older woman and young prince to replace the khan. The implicit politics far surpassed the sex act in significance and potential impact.

When summoned to answer the charge, instead of flatly denying it, the Golden Prince objected to the khan that he would not listen to slander from a servant. Under Mongol law, his accusation, even if true, constituted a capital crime of betrayal. Several times in history, Genghis Khan had executed people for similar offenses of betraying their master, even when the betrayal was done with the purpose of aiding Genghis Khan himself.

The khan sided, once again, with his nephew. He turned his wrath on the servant and accused him of seeking to create "trouble between two brothers and to divide them." The khan ordered his guards to slice off the accuser's lips and nose for having made the statement. After this punishment, they killed him.

The khan's response to the first accuser demonstrated clearly where his affection and trust lay. The Golden Prince came first. No one else in the court dared to raise an objection or voice a criticism of the khan's favorite.

The plotters against the Golden Prince had been deterred, but not defeated. They needed to find a person outside the court, someone who was not a vassal. They also needed an eyewitness to offer direct testimony of sexual infidelity. Simply trying to "rob" the khan of his wife had not been sufficient.

Events in the south kept Beg-Arslan preoccupied expanding his control of the Silk Route ever eastward toward the Chinese border at the Gansu Corridor. Too busy to personally manage the affairs of the Mongol tribes in the north, he sent his young protégé Issama, called Ismayil in the Mongol chronicles, to Manduul's court to maintain his influence over the royal family.

Beg-Arslan had been *taishi*, the overlord of the Mongols, but now Ismayil assumed the office. Ismayil immediately took command of the Mongol army. Une-Bolod, who had been the former commander, retired from court life and returned to his own home area. With Une-Bolod out of the way, Ismayil now needed to rid himself of the other contender for power, the Golden Prince.

Ismayil was a young warlord on the rise, and soon he was looking for ways to increase his own power independently of Beg-Arslan. He devised a plan against the young prince, but one that also could cause a rupture in Manduul's relationship to Beg-Arslan by implicating Yeke Qabar-tu, the senior queen and Beg-Arslan's daughter, in a plot to overthrow Manduul.

First, Ismayil confronted the Great Khan privately with direct evidence, which he claimed he had seen with his own eyes. He insisted that the charges made by the servant against the prince were true. "Out in an isolated place," he informed the khan, "the Golden Prince and your wife met in conjugal embrace." Ismayil wanted to give the khan time to reflect on the charges, and he did not attempt to push the khan into any type of decision or action. Having successfully injected the poison of doubt into the khan's mind, Ismayil left him to fret alone.

Then Ismayil, posing as a friend and ally to both sides that he was working to turn against each other, approached the prince to warn him that he had lost favor with his uncle the khan. Ismayil reported to the prince that his uncle Manduul had learned the truth about the charges made by the dead servant; he knew that the prince was having an affair with his uncle's wife. Not only had the khan turned against the boy, according to Ismayil, but he intended "to do evil" to the Golden Prince to prevent him from forcefully removing the old man.

The prince refused to believe Ismayil's warning that his uncle could turn against him. Ismayil advised the prince to be cautious and to be watchful because someone was about to trick him. He told the gullible prince that "the proof" of his uncle's anger would soon be on its way to him when a messenger would arrive from the khan. He said that the khan would send someone to question the boy's loyalty and to trick him into saying something that could be used against him.

The allegations against the Golden Prince weighed heavily in the old khan's mind. It seemed not to matter to him that his wife Yeke Qabar-tu may have betrayed him, but it deeply bothered him that the boy, whom he loved so much and whom he had made his heir, might have rebelled. "This is the second time that I have heard the charges," he was quoted as saying. He began to reconsider the earlier statements made by the now dead servant against his "younger brother."

"I myself am not in good health," he reasoned. "I am without male descendants, and after I am dead, my queens and people will be his." The charges, rumors, and conjecture churned in the khan's mind. "Maybe they are true," he speculated to those around him. The khan wondered if the boy was rushing too quickly ahead, as though he had already replaced the khan and need not respect him any longer. "It is bad that, starting now, he should have such excessive desires."

Wavering in his opinions, the khan sent another person to talk to the young prince, to tell him that a second set of allegations had been made against him. The khan wanted his young heir to defend himself, reaffirm his loyalty, and remove the stain of the charges against him.

"The khan asks," said the envoy, "what reasons do you have to be against me?"

The prince immediately remembered the warning of Ismayil that a messenger would come to trick him. The prince became highly tense and agitated, but in his confusion he did not know how to answer. Having always depended on his charisma and good luck to solve his problems and propel his interests, he had no education and no words with which to devise a strategy or argue his own case. The prince merely stared nervously at the messenger and said nothing.

The envoy reported back to the khan about the prince's frantic state and that the prince refused to answer the chargers.

The khan accepted the silence as guilt, and he now convinced himself that he had been betrayed by the young prince. "It is like this, it is true that he has evil intentions towards me," he said. The khan openly deliberated on the plight of the Mongol nation and the most appropriate action to preserve it. The khan considered the painful consequences for the nation if it had no khan. Yet, perhaps in confusing his own emotions toward the prince with the needs of the state, he concluded: "The people do not need a ruler like him." The boy had strayed too far, too fast. "So saying, the khan became enraged."

Since the days of his infancy when his great-great-grandmother Samur had saved him from the wrath of his grandfather Esen, flight had been the only response that the prince had learned in the face of grave danger. The Golden Prince heard about the khan's anger, and without trying to explain his case or clarify his actions, he impulsively fled the royal camp in fear.

Ismayil waited, and then the khan came to him with his decision. He told Ismayil to gather the army and go after the prince. Once again, the Mongol nation headed into civil war. People had to choose sides between the old, but still ruling, khan and the upstart prince, who had so enthralled the khan, the court, and the people, but who was now labeled a traitor and rebel. Few people came to the prince's side.

Perhaps the khan remembered that after Genghis Khan's gift of a golden belt to Jamuka, the two men, who had sworn eternal friendship three times, only stayed together for a year and a half. The khan and his nephew were parting in much the same way that Jamuka lamented his parting from Genghis Khan. "Together we ate food that is not to be digested," Jamuka said. "To each other we spoke words that are not to be forgotten." Then the words of outsiders drove them apart. "We parted for good saying . . . that we had exchanged weighty words, the skin of my black face peeled off in shame." But he deeply regretted the separation. "And so I have been living unable to come near you, unable to see the friendly face of my sworn friend the Khan. Saying to myself that we had exchanged unforgettable words, the skin of my red face came off in shame." In the separation from one another, Jamuka concluded, each of them had to live "with a long memory."

The prince had few options open to him, and he had no one to whom he could turn. He suddenly concocted a strange plan to flee to Manduul's and Ismayil's nemesis: the father of the queen with whom he was accused of having the affair. Perhaps with Beg-Arslan's approval they might together remove the old khan, and then the prince would marry Yeke Qabar-tu, produce an heir with her, and thereby make Beg-Arlsan the grandfather of the next khan.

Fearful of arriving unannounced in Beg-Arslan's camp and confronting him alone, the prince sought out Borogchin, a Borijin woman described as Bayan Mongke's sister and as Manduul and Manduhai's daughter. She was most likely a niece of Manduul and thus, under the Mongol system of kinship, would be equivalent to a sister for Bayan Mongke and a daughter to Manduhai. She had been married to Beg-Arslan or his son. The prince found the camp, which consisted of several *gers* for different wives and relatives. Borogchin received him warmly, but she and her two sons immediately moved to hide him in their *ger*.

She did not think that his plan for redemption would succeed.

Beg-Arslan would not be so easily turned against Manduul and Ismayil, two underlings who, as far as Beg-Arslan knew, had always followed his leadership in the past. The prince would not find protection from Beg-Arslan, who much preferred having an easily controlled old man as khan rather than this impetuous, and apparently easily frightened, youth.

The nature of Borogchin's relationship to the young prince is not clear, but someone recognized the beautiful chestnut horse of the prince hobbled nearby to graze. As soon as Beg-Arslan heard, he came looking for the rider.

When Beg-Arslan could not find the prince, he confronted Borogchin, demanding to know where the young man was hiding. Fearful of lying to him, but unwilling to expose the prince, she replied with a question. "If he comes around me should I hand him over to you?" she asked Beg-Arslan.

"If I see him near you," Beg-Arslan responded in boastful anger, "I shall eat his flesh and drink his blood." He rubbed his hands across his face and hair; it was recorded that he became so agitated that his nose began running. He smeared the yellow mucus across the tip of his nose and stormed away.

Later, in a ruse to lure the prince out of hiding, Beg-Arslan left to go hunting. Borogchin used his absence to encourage the prince to flee, and Beg-Arslan's spies failed to see the prince leave. When they could not find his horse, they knew he had escaped and they sent word to Beg-Arslan.

The warlord sent a messenger back to camp demanding to know where the chestnut horse had gone. Borogchin insolently responded that she had already sent the prince safely home, and she demanded to know why Beg-Arslan wanted to harm her relatives when she never did anything to harm his. "Have I enmity towards your kin?" She claimed that the prince was only a clan brother of hers. "Have I jealousy towards friendly relatives?" she defiantly asked.

By so defying as powerful a man as Beg-Arslan, she knew that her life and the lives of her sons might be in danger. To protect them,

Borogchin then sent her sons away; however, she decided to stay behind to face Beg-Arslan's wrath. "I myself will die," she explained to the boys as she bade them farewell. After that encounter, no further mention of Borogchin occurs in the chronicles.

Having failed to find refuge with Beg-Arslan, the Golden Prince fled this time out into the Gobi in search of sanctuary with his wife, Siker, and their son. The Gobi, however, does not keep secrets. Word soon reached the Mongol royal camp that the prince had returned to his former home, and Ismayil set out in pursuit of the young prince. Always fortunate enough to hear when someone came after him, the prince again abandoned his wife and son and fled farther east into the Gobi.

Ismayil found the camp of the prince's family and seized it, all the animals and everyone there. He even claimed Siker, the prince's wife, for himself. Somehow in the mêlée, the baby boy born to Siker and the prince disappeared.

For the moment, Ismayil's work seemed done. He had rid the Mongol court of both General Une-Bolod and the young prince. With the prince's wife as his own, he now returned south, where the Mongols were having some renewed success raiding the Chinese, and where Beg-Arslan, still his overlord, was planning a full assault on the Chinese in the Gansu Corridor and the territory of Ningxia.

Ismayil departed, but his allies now occupied most of the Gobi, and it would not be long before they would find the Golden Prince.

The political scene at the Mongol court changed dramatically and permanently: Manduul Khan was dead. The senior queen, Yeke Qabar-tu, disappeared, never to be heard from again. How these events transpired, and in what order, remains unknown, but around the same time, the exiled Golden Prince also met his final fate.

Chinese and some Mongolian sources record that at this point the prince began to style himself as the Great Khan and actually tried to raise an army of supporters. No matter what title he used at this moment, the Golden Prince seems to have been wandering alone in the immense Gobi. Having deserted his family and fled from the royal camp, the prince who had so recently dazzled the court now had only a few loyal companions remaining. He still had his beautiful clothes, his handsome horse, and dreams to rule as Great Khan of the Mongol nation.

It was 1470, the Year of the Tiger. Without allies in Mongolia, he seemed to have the idea that he might escape back to China, where he had been received with some enthusiasm in his failed effort to challenge the Ming court. Perhaps he could enlist the help of the Chinese and return to enforce his claim as Great Khan, or perhaps the Ming emperor might receive him and be willing to help put him in command of their distant enemy.

He followed a remote trail southward with one attendant who knew the area. To reach China, he had to cross the territory of the Yungshiyebu, the allies of Ismayil. He ran out of food and water somewhere near the modern Mongolian-Chinese border, in the area where today the Beijing-Moscow train crosses. Since his companion came from the area, he sent the man to seek out his family and possibly secure assistance from them. The companion found his family, but rather than offering help for the prince, they convinced the man to stay at home and abandon the prince in the desert.

The Gobi has occasional springs and wells, but there are so few that there is almost always someone camped around each one. The prince knew that in order to reach water, he had to pass through the encampment and certainly would be seen. Nearly dying of thirst, he took a chance and went anonymously into a small camp, where he obtained some *airag* from a young girl. Although he did not reveal his identity to her, he rode a fine white and chestnut horse, and was dressed in his brocade *deel* lined with squirrel fur and tied with a golden belt. He looked an unusual sight in the middle of the desert.

After the prince hurriedly refreshed himself, he headed back out into the desert. The young girl found several young men and told them about the wealthily clad young man, and five of them saddled their horses and raced off after the unusual visitor.

Although the prince and his horse had water, the horse was slow and worn. The men easily overtook him. When they reached him, one shouted at him, "What sort of man are you?"

"A traveler," the prince responded, trying not to reveal his identity to them.

"Give us your belt," the attackers demanded.

The prince refused. The belt was an emblem of manhood, and being of gold made it both a precious object but also a higher symbol of his royal rank. To rob a man of his clothes, particularly his belt, constituted one of the gravest insults, as well as a financial loss. The very word "beltless" stood as a synonym for "woman." It was almost all that the prince had left in this world.

One of the men grabbed the bridle of the prince's beloved horse while the others pulled him from the saddle and killed him.

Because a man's *deel* is next to his skin, it absorbs not only his sweat and odor but a part of his soul and his fate. No matter how beautiful and costly his *deel,* the assailants dared not put it on and possibly assume the fate of this Golden Prince. Instead, they seized his gold belt, took his beautiful chestnut horse, and left him.

Many dreams ended there in the Year of the Tiger. The beautiful prince, whose mother hid his genitals to save his life, who crouched in an iron pot under a mound of dung, who was tossed in the air at the tip of a bow and rescued by a man racing on horseback, who grew up in obscure poverty but briefly reigned beside a khan who dressed him with gold and silk and told him that he could conquer the world, was dead at age nineteen. Bayan Mongke Bolkhu Jinong, the Eternally Rich Rising Golden Prince of the Mongols, lay stretched out on the Gobi rocks, beltless and lifeless in a silk *deel* embroidered with threads of gold and lined with squirrel fur.

No one mourned him, and as his body rotted in the desert, the survivors of his drama had to go on living. With all the important actors now dead, the twenty-three-year-old Manduhai stood alone on an empty stage. Her fate seemed hardly more auspicious than that of the dead prince. Her first husband was dead and so was his heir. The widowed queen was only a junior wife from a distant place. She had been given in marriage by her family, but now the clan to which she had been given was empty. Everyone was gone.

Death had taken away every role Manduhai knew; life had taken away her fate. The dead khan left no male heir to marry her. Manduhai was still queen of the Mongols with every right to continue ruling, but for the first time since Genghis Khan created the nation, it appeared that he had no descendant to be khan.

Life had not prepared Manduhai for this moment. She did not yet know of what she might be capable. She had no man to fight for her, no woman to advise her. The road before her had no destination and no markers. There were no myths or stories to instruct her, no sayings to guide her. Even if the young queen had learned to read, she had no scripture to inspire her and no priest to counsel her.

There was no time to learn. An unprotected widowed queen was the target for any ambitious man who wanted to become khan. With the khan and crown prince both dead and no other heir around, marrying the dead khan's wife was the only legitimate path to power. She was the target and trophy for any ambitious man on the steppe. It was a unique moment when the office of khan was completely open to whoever could claim and occupy it. Whatever warlord or general powerful enough to seize the queen would prove that he had the blessing of the Eternal Blue Sky to become khan.

It was better for her to choose among the contenders rather than wait for one of them to take her by force. Who would be her new husband? Une-Bolod, the accomplished warrior whom it was supposed she loved, would be the safest and most traditional Mongol choice. As a descendant of Khasar, he was a member of the Borijin clan, even if he did not belong to the lineage of Genghis Khan. With him, her life might be the closest to what she had known in the past.

But the ambitious warlord Ismayil was already the *taishi* of the

Mongols, and he had cleverly manipulated the downfall of the prince. With his connections to the trade caravans, he offered exotic trinkets and other delights, and she could return to live in the warmer climate among the southern oases of the Silk Route. She would drink grape wine from glass goblets made in Italy and enjoy luscious melons cooled in underground irrigation chambers. Throughout the winter she could nibble delicacies sweetened with raisins, and the men around her would wear gleaming white turbans and carry swords of sparkling Damascus steel.

The tempting luxuries of the Muslim warlords paled, however, in comparison with those offered to Manduhai by the Ming court of China. If she would but follow the choice of the slain prince and flee to the Chinese border and request refuge, the officers of the Ming court would almost certainly provide her with a good life, in return for which she need only swear loyalty to them. As the widow of the Great Khan, she would be a starring addition to their menagerie of captive barbarians. She would live as a coddled symbol of the final acknowledgment by the Mongol royal family, and thereby the Mongol nation, of the power of the Ming Dynasty and the superiority of Chinese civilization.

Under Chinese cultural protocols, a new dynasty demonstrated legitimacy and heavenly favor not only by seizing the government and taking control of the country but also by receiving the formal surrender of the defeated dynasty. Nothing short of this official surrender could mark a legal and final conclusion of the Yuan Dynasty. If Manduhai would only perform this public ritual and kowtow to the Ming emperor in a lavishly staged ceremony, she would be guaranteed a life of luxurious ease. She might even be admitted into the emperor's harem as a concubine and have her every need catered to by a phalanx of eunuchs. If she sought to live alone, they would provide a pampered widowhood for her, with a household of servants and retainers. She could even take a husband if she pleased. Comfortably within the cocoon of the Chinese elite, she would never have to endure another worry or responsibility so long as she lived.

She had to choose quickly: the handsome Mongol noble, a fierce Muslim warlord, or a pampered Chinese widowhood.

Une-Bolod certainly presented the most compelling case. "I will light your fire for you," he said in his proposal of marriage sent by messenger to Manduhai. "I will point out your pastures," he promised. The reference to the fire meant that he would give her sons by which to start a new dynasty. For a woman with no male heir, the offer must have seemed tempting, but she showed no hesitation in emphatically rejecting his offer.

"You have a tent-flap I must not raise," she responded to Une-Bolod. "You have a threshold I must not step over." To make sure that he did not think she was merely being coy, she added firmly, "I will not go to you."

The people around Manduhai in the Mongol court knew of the proposal, and they knew of precedent by which she should marry the popular, dashing general. Manduhai asked the people for their advice to her.

"It would be much better for all of us," the first person answered, presenting a simple and practical reason that the nation needed a fully grown man. It will be better for the nation "if you would accept the proposal of Une-Bolod."

The second speaker disagreed, with a longer and more profound explanation. For Manduhai to marry outside the lineage of Genghis Khan, even if it were to a descendant of his brother, "your path will grow dark." With such a marriage, she would no longer be the queen. "You will divide yourself from the people, and you will lose your honored and respected title of *khatun*." If Manduhai would devote her life to the Mongol people without thinking of personal comfort or benefit, she was told, she would follow the white road of enlightenment for herself and her nation.

Manduhai thought about the responses for a moment, and then she turned to the one who recommended that she accept Une-Bolod's proposal. "You disagree with me just because Une-Bolod is a man and I am only a widow," she charged. Growing angrier as she spoke, she said, "Just because" I am only a woman, "you really think that you have the right to speak to me this way."

Queen Manduhai raised a bowl of hot tea and flung it at the head of the supporter of this marriage. Manduhai had made the first independent decision of her life. She had decided not to marry any of her suitors. She was the Mongol queen, and she would make her own path.

It was the Year of the Tiger.

PART III

Wolf Mother
1470–1509

Queen Manduhai the Wise, recalling the vengeance of
the former khans,

set out on campaign.

She set in motion her foot soldiers and oxen-troops, and

after three days and nights she set out with her cavalry.

Queen Manduhai the Wise, putting on her quiver
elegantly,

and composing her disordered hair,

put Dayan Khan in a box and set out.

ALTAN TOBCI § 101

Family of Manduhai Khatun
and Batu Mongke Dayan Khan

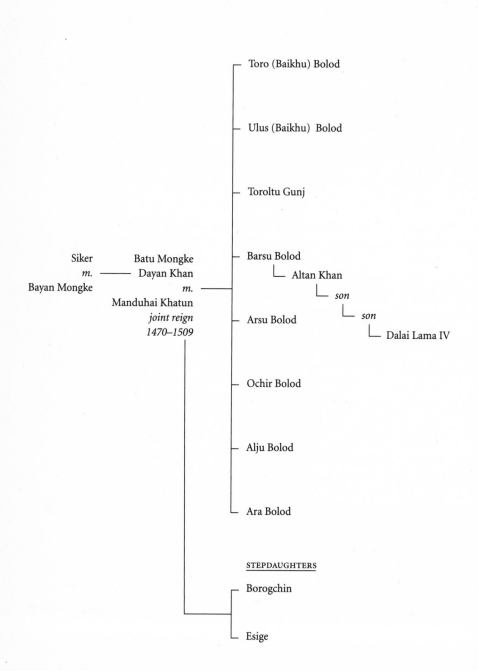

Toro (Baikhu) Bolod

Ulus (Baikhu) Bolod

Toroltu Gunj

Siker
m.
Bayan Mongke

Batu Mongke
Dayan Khan
m.
Manduhai Khatun
*joint reign
1470–1509*

Barsu Bolod
└ Altan Khan
  └ *son*
    └ *son*
      └ Dalai Lama IV

Arsu Bolod

Ochir Bolod

Alju Bolod

Ara Bolod

<u>STEPDAUGHTERS</u>

Borogchin

Esige

The White Road of the
Warrior Widow

MANDUHAI WISHED TO RULE, BUT NOT ONLY DID SHE have no experience, she had no army. All the soldiers were loyal either to their respected general Une-Bolod or to Ismayil Taishi, the highest ranking official in the government.

Yet Manduhai had one thing they did not have—a baby boy. This was not her own child; he was the abandoned infant of the Golden Prince. He was the only living male descendant of the bone of Genghis Khan, the son of the *jinong* and the heir of the Great Khan.

The boy's name was Batu Mongke, son of Bayan Mongke and Siker. The child was born in the South Gobi—one of the most sparsely settled areas of the Mongols', with broad expanses of rocky steppe essentially void of vegetation except sparse clusters of grass. The harsh area, however, was not hostile to herding. With easy movement, the herders could take their animals from a place with no grass into one where the rain fell.

A thin ribbon of mountains, known as the Three Beauties (Gurvan Saikhan Nuruu), slices through this part of the Gobi. The mountains form the tail end and the most southeastern extension of the larger Altai range. Here they gradually disappear into the gravel and sand of the Gobi. On an otherwise flat terrain, their relatively modest-sized peaks seem lofty and dramatic; they climb high enough to snag some of the moisture passing overhead in the winter. These snows melt in the summer and run into ravines and small brooks that make this area an ideal place for herding animals. Mountain springs provide water during the summer, and the canyon walls block the Arctic winds in winter. The ravines and canyons form a labyrinth that offers quick protection to the local residents from intruders or passing armies. A network of goat tracks across the mountains connects the larger canyons with one another.

Although sparsely inhabited, trade routes crisscross the area, keeping it from being truly isolated. The vast open area of the Gobi connects the northern part of the fertile Mongolian steppe with the southern part of the plateau in China's Inner Mongolia. Similarly, the mountains moving toward the northwest connect the area into the more fertile expanses of western Mongolia.

With his father murdered and his mother kidnapped, Batu Mongke passed from hand to hand. His mother, Siker, now the wife of Ismayil, in time had children and created a new family with her husband, seemingly without regret for the husband or the child she had lost.

At first, Batu Mongke apparently lived alone with an otherwise unknown old woman referred to as Bachai of the Balaktschin. In her extreme poverty, she seemed barely able to survive by herself and proved either unable or unwilling to care for the infant. In an exceptionally harsh and sparsely populated environment such as the Gobi, a child is more dependent on its mother or other caretakers than children growing up in a benign climate surrounded by people.

The temperature drops so low at night that, even under blankets, children cannot generate enough warmth to survive. They must sleep next to larger adults or at least clumped together with several other children. During the day, the child must be carefully monitored with frequent rubbing of the hands, feet, and exposed parts of the body to prevent frostbite. In a milder climate, a urine-soaked child might develop painful skin irritations with the potential for longer-term problems, but in the Gobi, the urine can quickly freeze and threaten the life of the child immediately. Even a simple fall outside can quickly lead to death if the child is too slow to get up again. In the fall and spring dust storms, a child can become lost within only a few feet of the *ger* and gradually be buried and suffocated in the dust.

Children typically nurse for several years, and supplement this with the rich dairy products available in the fall, but when winter sets in, the child must eat meat or very hard forms of dried and cured dairy products. To survive on the meat and harsh foods of the Gobi, the child must have the food partially chewed by an adult or much larger child in order to swallow and digest it.

Bachai did not provide the intensive care the boy needed, and after three years of neglect, Batu Mongke was still alive, but just barely. As one chronicle states, he was "suffering from a sickness of the stomach." Another reported that he acquired "hunchback-like growth." Manduhai learned of the child's existence and his perilous situation, and she arranged for allies to rescue him and place him with another family. Had the existence or location of the only male descendant of Genghis Khan become generally known, it was nearly certain that one faction or another would have tried to kidnap him or kill him in pursuit of some nefarious plan.

A woman named Saichai and her husband, Temur Khadag, who is sometimes credited along with his six brothers with being the child's rescuer, became the new foster parents for the boy, and set about trying to restore his health and rehabilitate his body. His new mother instituted a long treatment in the traditional Mongolian art of therapeutic massage or bone setting known as *bariach*. Gentle massage and light bone adjustment still forms a regular part of child rearing among the Mongols and is viewed as essential to the child's body growing in a properly erect and aesthetically pleasing manner. Older people in particular, such as grandparents, sit around the *ger* in the idle hours, rubbing the child's muscles and tugging at the bones and joints.

Saichai rubbed the child's wounds with the milk of a camel that had recently given birth for the first time. The milk was prepared in a shallow wooden bowl with a veneer of silver over the wood. Both the milk and the silver had medicinal properties important to Mongol medicine. The treatment required persistent massage by rubbing the milk onto the damaged parts of the boy's body and rubbing the warm silver bowl itself against the afflicted area. By this persistent massage of his damaged, but still growing, body, the bone setter gradually adjusted the boy's bones and gently pushed them back into proper alignment. In the words of one chronicle, she wore through three silver bowls trying to repair Batu Mongke's broken body. As is so often the case with suffering, the physical damages proved easier to treat than the emotional ones.

After the good care of the foster family, Manduhai sent for Batu Mongke when he was about five years old. His foster father set out with him on a horse to escort him across the Gobi to the royal court, but while crossing a stream, the boy fell from the horse and nearly drowned before the father could jump from his horse and rescue him. Since the streams of the Gobi are quite small and only rarely have water in them, it seems strange that the boy would have had so much difficulty getting up and remounting his horse unless he was already badly injured or was severely hurt in the fall. For whichever reason, he arrived at the camp of Manduhai in quite bad physical condition, and his survival remained in doubt for some time.

Manduhai's first challenge was to install him as Great Khan in a way that people would view as legitimate. Genghis Khan left precise laws in place prescribing that the Great Khan must be elected at a *khuriltai*. If the candidate, and there was only one at a time, did not attract representatives of an overwhelming majority of the tribes and clans, then anyone not attending could always deny the legitimacy of the election. Genghis Khan's descendants had violated the spirit of the law from the start. Khubilai Khan made a mockery of the *khuriltai*, and Khubilai's descendants abandoned it entirely. Subsequently, a khan sought legitimacy by being installed in office before the *sulde*, the horsehair banner of Genghis Khan that usually remained in the area of Burkhan Khaldun. But in the turmoil of Manduul and Bayan

Mongke's battles, it temporarily disappeared or was under the control of someone not sympathetic to Manduhai's quest.

Without the legitimizing process of the *khuriltai* or control of the *sulde* of Genghis Khan, Manduhai had to find another way to make the installation of a new Great Khan both legal and known to everyone. Manduhai needed the support of the people, and to achieve this, she also knew that she herself needed some semblance of spiritual or religious support for what she wished to undertake. Every time Genghis Khan wanted to rally his people to a cause that he thought might be difficult for them to support, he made a very public pilgrimage up the sacred mountain and prayed there until he felt that he had been granted the support.

Manduhai chose to install Batu Mongke at the hitherto seemingly unknown Shrine of Eshi Khatun, the "First Queen." The shrine, like many others, was little more than a tattered felt tent mounted on a cart and pulled by an ox or camel from one Mongol camp to another and from one sacred site to another. The importance of a nomadic shrine to the people on the steppe far exceeded its humble and worn appearance.

Mongols worshipped male spirits on mountains or rocks piled up like a miniature mountain, called an *ovoo;* rocks, mountains, and cliffs constituted the bones, and therefore the male element, of the earth. Female spirits were worshipped near bodies of water, which formed the life-giving female parts of the earth, or else in caves, which were the wombs of Mother Earth. In contrast to the stationary *ovoo,* the *ger* became a sort of portable cave that allowed worshippers to honor the female spirit wherever she was taken.

Both the male *sulde* and the female *ger* had a home territory, but as befitted the needs of a nomadic society, each could be easily transported anywhere it might be needed. When the *sulde* needed to be moved, a mounted warrior carried it by hand. The *ger* was always transported on a special ceremonial cart similar to the one normally owned and driven by women. When the tribe moved into a new homeland, their shrine led the way and sanctified the land as the people followed behind.

Some elements of the shrine derived from ancient female Earth Mother worship in Inner Asia, but it also contained elements and possibly relics of Mongolian women such as Alan Goa, from whom all Mongol clans traced descent, and Hoelun, the mother of Genghis Khan. The Shrine of the First Queen may have been one or several of the Eight White Gers erected in honor of Genghis Khan's queens at Avarga. Between the confiscation of women's *gers* by Khubilai Khan and the repression of female shrines by a later form of Buddhism, little information survives about them. Had it not been for the importance of Manduhai's visit to the Shrine of the First Queen, we would not know that it had existed.

In choosing for the first time to install the Great Khan in the shrine dedicated to a female, Manduhai was not merely seeking to restore the dynasty of Genghis Khan. She also sought to restore the male and female spiritual balance that had been so important to the success of Genghis Khan, but so persistently ignored by his heirs. While the Eternal Blue Sky offered inspiration, only the Mother Earth could offer success and fulfillment of the endeavor. Manduhai already had the inspiration of the Eternal Blue Sky; now she needed the support of the Earth Mother to bring her plan to reality.

Before a small crowd of her apprehensive supporters, in the fall of 1470, still the Year of the Tiger, Manduhai dismounted from her horse at a respectful distance away from the shrine. Some of her retainers gathered behind her in support, others remained on their horses and watched from a distance, clearly as spectators rather than participants. She approached the final distance toward the shrine on foot as a humble petitioner approaching a sacred cave. When she came close to the front of the cart, she stopped and performed the *tsatsal* ritual, tossing fermented mare's milk into the air as an offering to the spirits.

Although her words would be addressed to the shrine and she would face away from the crowd, there could be no question that, in addition to being the spiritual outcry of a pilgrim, these words constituted a desperate plea of a queen to her people. This would be the most important political speech of her life. She had to make it clear to her people not only which choice she wished to make, but why she wanted them to follow it and accept her.

Everyone knew the danger, both supernatural and bodily, that hung over these appearances of a national leader before a sacred shrine. Only a few decades earlier, the son of Samur Gunj had appeared at one of the shrines dedicated to Genghis Khan as a supplicant to take the office of Great Khan, but he had been killed. Whether one believed the popular explanation that the arrow had been fired supernaturally by the spirit, or one accepted a more mundane source for the killing, by the end of the ceremony, the supplicant lay dead on the ground in front of the tent.

Despite the ritual precision of the ceremony and the real dangers lurking within it, Manduhai called out at the door of the tent. She began her emotional plea with a statement of deep personal desperation and confusion. In language reminiscent of religious hymns and sacred scriptures, she described her own life as wandering senselessly in a place "where black cannot be distinguished from white." Her world was so dark, she lamented, that she could not distinguish the different colors on a multicolored horse.

She addressed the spirit of the First Queen as the source from which emanated light and wisdom. Manduhai pleaded for wisdom to pass out from the divine gates of the First Queen's world into the visible world of humans. Still standing in the open air outside the tent after this emotionally strained and somewhat frightened plea for help, Manduhai began to present her case in a formal, legalistic manner, calling upon the dynastic and cultural traditions of the Mongol state. She was laying out her case before the people, and she obviously had already made a choice of husband that she wished them all to accept.

First, she stated the problem confronting the Mongol nation

because the royal family had no men to serve as Great Khan. "The Borijin clan is under the threat of extinction," she explained. The Mongols were living in a time of discord and violence. As articulated clearly by one of her descendants, "there was suffering," and the state of the world was not stable. The Mongols did not resolutely distinguish between "khans and commoners" nor between "good and evil." As the chronicler summarized the situation, "At that time the Borijin Golden Clan deteriorated."

After expounding on the dire condition of the Mongol people, Manduhai presented her own personal predicament. As though pleading for mercy before a judge, she lodged her complaint that she was being forced into marriage by another man and by the public support that he had.

Speaking about Une-Bolod, the favored candidate to take her in marriage and become Great Khan, she acknowledged his power and popularity. "Because he is big and powerful," she explained, he "wants to take me for his wife." She made clear her unwillingness to marry the popular candidate, and to make her rejection of him unambiguous and irrevocable, she closed the door on him forever with a special oath and request of the First Queen. If she should ever yield to him, she placed a curse upon herself: "If I do it, I beg you First Queen, punish me harshly."

For the people gathered at the shrine, it must have been disappointing and perplexing as they sought to understand what the queen wanted. If she ruled out so steadfastly the most popular of the Mongol generals, then would she choose one of the Muslim warlords or an already arranged deal through the Ming court? Was their queen about to deliver her nation into the hands of foreigners? Was she about to betray them and the office she had served?

Knowing the suspicious questions and fear in the minds of those around her, and possibly remembering the killing of the previous royal pilgrim, Manduhai quickly dispelled all these options and reasserted her loyalty. "If I desert you and your descendants," she proclaimed to the First Queen and to the Mongol people in the simple imagery that every herder would immediately comprehend, "then take your long horse snare and lasso me."

She continued, in the strongest and most vivid form of oath that a Mongol could make, asking that if she brought any harm to her people or failed to protect them, "then may you break and rip apart my body." For the Mongols, execution through mutilation constituted the least noble and most feared way of dying because it allowed all the soul-bearing liquids, especially the blood, to flow out onto the earth. Such a death not only kills the body but destroys the soul and pollutes the earth. Manduhai made it clear to everyone that if she failed in her duty and promises, she was requesting precisely such an ignominious death for herself. She added the wish that in killing her, the First Queen or the Mongol people should separate "my shoulders from my thighs." In tearing apart the body, the oath breaker would surrender all connection to everyone, since the dismemberment would break the bones symbolizing the father and rip apart the flesh symbolizing the mother.

The graphic oath made reference to one often employed by men going to war and swearing loyalty to one another in the face of all enemies; it was an explicitly male form of oath taking. Traditionally as part of the oath, the men killed three male animals—a stallion, a ram, and a dog—by cutting them in half. They separated the halves of the three animals and, standing between them, they made their vow: "O God! O Sky! O Earth! Hear that we swear such an oath. Here are the males of these animals. If we do not keep our oath and break our word, let us be as these animals are." For Mongols, this vow before the Sky and the Earth constituted the highest oath possible. A lesser version of the oath was to hold out an arrow, break it into two pieces, and then hold the two pieces stretched far apart to show that the oath taker expected to be broken and pulled equally far apart for breaking the vow.

After thus vowing never to desert her people, Manduhai invoked the protection of the First Queen. "I act as a daughter-in-law," she said to the First Queen, emphasizing her loyalty to the Borijin clan.

Manduhai's plea made it clear that in rejecting Une-Bolod, she rejected all the options presented and had not considered the Muslim or the Ming alliances. Instead of the three options, Manduhai was seeking a new path unknown and unexpected. She would surrender her power to no man.

With a sense of public drama and experience in how to build popular support, Manduhai called forth her choice to present to the First Queen and to her subjects. The figure who stepped forward from the crowd was not even a real man at all, but an awkward child only six or seven years old, dressed in big boots. Despite the extra height provided by the triple-soled boots that he wore for the occasion, he could scarcely control his own body, much less guide a nation. At an age when he had barely learned to command a horse, how could he command the armies needed to protect his office and his people?

Manduhai introduced the boy to the spirit of the First Queen and to the assembled crowd as the grand-nephew of her late husband. "By coming to your tent," she said very clearly to the spirit of the First Queen, "I wish to make your descendant Great Khan even though he is still a young boy."

Even if he trembled in fear in his oversized boots, merely by standing before the shrine of the First Queen and the assembly of Mongol nomads, Batu Mongke showed both tremendous bravery and total reliance on Manduhai, who guided him. Twice before in the previous generation, boys of his age had been proclaimed Great Khan, only to be murdered by their rivals before they could reach full maturity. Other fully grown men who bore the title were also ignominiously struck down and killed by the Muslim warlords who tried to control them. Any one of the new boy khan's rivals for power might descend upon the unorthodox inauguration to seize Manduhai, but now that she had publicly proclaimed him Great Khan, any usurper would have to kill the young boy to make his own claim supportable.

Batu Mongke stood at the Shrine of the First Queen before the people who were supposed to be his subjects, and was acclaimed by Manduhai as the new Great Khan, but his battered body still bore the signs of ill treatment. Fortunately for him, the heavy Mongol boots of manhood not only increased his stature, but the thick, stiff hide that came all the way up to the knee formed an inflexible brace that served to hold him erect even if his knees weakened and began to buckle during the long public ceremony.

In his short but miserable life, he had cultivated a keen ability to discern other people's motives and an intuitive recognition of their strategies in what they sought from him. In this life of betrayal and suffering, he had one attachment to one ally and guide, to whom he showed unswerving trust. Batu Mongke's willingness to stand bravely and tall before all these dangers showed an extraordinary confidence in the judgment and guidance of the one person who had orchestrated this event.

He had little choice about relying on Manduhai, but he soon learned that, in her, he had found not only a savior but also a guardian and mentor. She would be the one person who remained loyal to him and protective of his safety and his political interests until the day she died. Though no one else in the mounted throng may have had the confidence in her ability to protect him and to unite the nation, he showed no sign of doubt in her on that, or any other, day in his life.

She perceived something in him that escaped the notice of others, and he found in her something that no one else could see. They had an understanding and faith in each other that seemed to surpass the limited views of those around them. Over the next thirty years, the two of them, like Qaidu Khan and Khutulun two centuries earlier, formed an indivisible if unlikely team, united by a bond that transcended generation and gender and which allowed them to achieve together what neither could have done alone.

Manduhai and young Batu Mongke shared something important. They were both totally alone in the world. Both had been taken from their places of birth by circumstances beyond their control, and both had to live without the vast kinship network so important in tribal society. In Mongol society, a person depended almost totally on kin to provide all the supports needed in life. No religious, market, or fraternal organizations existed outside of the kinship network. The most dreaded misfortune in life was to be without family. The tragic figure in Mongol mythology was always the orphan. Many songs and poems bemoaned the sad fate and the empty future of such a person. The second most tragic figure was the widow whose husband left no male relative to marry her.

Queen Manduhai and Batu Mongke formed a strange dyad of precisely these two outcasts. They had no parents, siblings, aunts, uncles, nieces, nephews, or even cousins. Everyone had either died or disappeared to some unknown place and fate. In a sense, both had been abandoned by life. Yet, through some tortured sequence of events and unusual circumstances, they had found each other and made an odd emotional alliance and political union. The orphan and the widow could scarcely be expected to survive alone, but they were not alone. They had each other.

In officially making him Great Khan, Manduhai was also formally marrying the boy. While the office of Great Khan was conferred until death, the marriage would be considered a temporary formality until the boy was grown. At that time the two of them would negotiate whether to continue it or for him to take another wife. In the meantime, she was still the Mongol *khatun* and would rule alone in her own name as well as in his. For now, an inexperienced young queen who was barely more than a girl herself stood united with a crippled little boy of seven. Nothing about them appeared encouraging or inspiring. It scarcely seemed plausible that such an unlikely pair could survive the coming winter, much less conquer the quarrelsome Mongol tribes and take on foreign enemies.

Throughout their reign, as on this awkward inaugural day, they frequently benefited from the underestimation of their abilities by those who struggled against them. In the world where physical strength and mastery of the horse and bow seemed to be all that really mattered, no one seemed to anticipate the advantages of patient intelligence, careful planning, and consistency of action. Neither Manduhai nor Batu Mongke possessed the physical strength of even a lowly soldier in their army, and yet they had some form of charisma that must have come as a direct gift from the sky.

Henceforth the chronicles no longer referred to Manduhai as Manduhai Gunj or Lady Manduhai; instead she was clearly the queen, Manduhai Khatun.

She proclaimed this unlikely candidate as the Great Khan of the Yeke Monghol Ulus, the twenty-seventh successor to Genghis Khan, and the ruler of all the lands and peoples within the world ocean. In keeping with Mongol imperial tradition, she had already picked out an auspicious title that resonated with meaning on many symbolic levels. She bestowed upon Batu Mongke the title Dayan Khan. Believing in the power that sounds have to make ideas and wishes into reality, she had chosen a name with deep meanings for both the Mongols and the Chinese. When heard with the Mongolian ear, the name meant the "Whole Khan," or the "Khan of the Whole," a title that stressed unity, the most elusive yet necessary of goals for survival of the steppe tribes. Her choice of title clearly asserted her goal to overcome the divisions by clan and locality. She would unite them, and he would be the khan of all Mongols. In particular, the title showed her rejection of the taishi's claim to rule over the Oirat of western Mongolia. Dayan Khan would rule the north and the south, the east and the west. He was the Whole Khan.

As if the Mongol claim was not sufficiently presumptuous or excessively ambitious, the same sounds of the Dayan Khan title carried a more ominous meaning when heard with a Chinese ear. To them it meant the "Great Yuan," reasserting loudly and clearly the Mongol claim to be recognized as the rightful rulers of China and the loyal heirs of the old Yuan Dynasty.

His new title could easily provoke the highly sensitive and insecure Ming court to send out an army to avenge the affront to its honor and inflict some horrifying form of public execution. For a less serious offense, the earlier Jin Dynasty had seized one of Dayan Khan's ancestors in the twelfth century and nailed him onto a wooden contraption in order to force his submission, a goal that he denied them throughout the agonizing crucifixion. If the Chinese captured the new young khan, they could easily do far worse to force him to give up his title, resign his office, and surrender all control of his dynasty to the Ming emperor.

Manduhai's arrogance at giving him the title Dayan irritated the Ming officials, but they could only respond with symbols since they lacked the resources to impose their will militarily. The Ming chose to fight words with words and titles with titles. They refused the words Dayan Khan, and instead they conferred upon the boy a far lesser status in their own records. They ignored both his barbarian name and his presumptuous title and mockingly referred to him as *Xiao wang zi (Hsiao-wang-tzu)*, the "Little King" or "Little Prince." Chinese chroniclers had occasionally used that title in earlier records, particularly when an underage boy sat on the throne, but for Dayan Khan, they used the title throughout his reign. This contention over the khan's title plagued Mongol-Ming relations through the reign of Dayan Khan.

Despite giving the young boy the title that staked a claim to rule all of China for the Mongols, Manduhai pursued a specific policy that showed no plan to invade or conquer China, much less to rule it. She seems to have learned from the earlier experiences of the steppe tribe, mostly notably of Genghis Khan, that the strategy of fighting, conquering, and then administering so large an empire cost the Mongols far more than they gained.

The failed efforts of her predecessors, such as Esen, her husband's great-grandfather, had shown that the Mongols lacked the military strength to conquer the massive armies and fortified cities of China. Although Genghis Khan had used firepower very effectively in his time, the advancement in firearms had negated the Mongols' most important asset, their ability to use bows and arrows very effectively from horseback. No matter how well trained and extensively prac-

ticed, a warrior with a bow and arrow could not compete with cannons and firearms. Ultimately, gunpowder favored the sedentary civilizations over the nomadic.

Rather than conquering the Chinese, Manduhai seemed clear in
her actions that she wanted to utilize Chinese production to the benefit of her people. She sought to trade with the Chinese where possible,
but to raid them when trade failed. Either through trading or raiding,
she showed clear determination to get what she needed.

Among the Mongols, not everyone accepted the khan, newly proclaimed at the Shrine of the First Queen. Some thought such an act
should be taken at the Shrine of Genghis Khan, who had founded the
dynasty and the nation. With so many irregularities accompanying the
ordination of this young man as khan, anyone who wanted to find a
reason not to support him could certainly do so.

After the installation of Dayan Khan, Manduhai returned with the boy
to her royal camp. Like all Mongol capitals, hers moved constantly
throughout her life according to the seasons, the changing weather,
and the needs of the time. Her summer camp moved around the fertile
steppes and returned frequently to the Kherlen River, but as important
as that area was for the history of the Mongols and the Borijin clan, it
was not her home. Manduhai Khatun and Dayan Khan were ultimately people of the drier steppe. The softly rolling hills, vast stretches
of green pasture, and above all the trees of the northern steppe
remained alien to her.

She was a woman of the open land, where the eye would never be
blocked by mountain or tree and where nature yielded a more sparing
but highly appreciated life than in the luxuriant extravagance of the
green steppe. Her home was a rocky but firm soil. The pebbles, sand,
and gravel might shift underfoot, but they provided a secure base on
which to stand or build a *ger*. The ground never rotted, and even in
winter the soil was too dry to freeze as it did in the steppes and forests
of the north.

For people of the Gobi the sight of standing water in a lake or flowing water in a river seemed unusual and slightly unnatural. Water belonged in the clouds above, and when it fell to earth, it immediately made its way down into the sand, where it waited to be dug out when needed. Just as the grassy steppe of the north had more grass than the animals could eat at once, the rivers and lakes had more water than they could drink.

In the winter, Manduhai moved her capital down the Ongi River into the edge of the Gobi. The Ongi was the only river that flowed south into the Gobi, and it had long been a major route connecting Karakorum with the old empire in China. The Ongi had water for only a few months of the year, in the summer when the snow in the mountains melted and the spring rains combined to create this small river. Occasionally, it carried enough water to make a small lake called Ulaan Nuur, but usually the empty lake bed and the river stood dry.

Of course, even when the water ceased to flow aboveground, moisture still seeped below the surface. It occasionally bubbled up to form a spring, or one could dig a short way into the light soil and quickly find water. The backdrop of mountains on the northern side offered some protection from the winds blowing directly from the Arctic. The drier conditions prevented blizzards except in the most exceptional of years.

In changing her capital camp from the more isolated place she had inhabited with Manduul Khan, Manduhai made a break with the past. Whether intentionally signaling her plans or merely following her own preferences, the move south and out into an open area closer to a trade route indicated a new engagement with the world. She herself probably did not yet know the precise nature of the new policies she would pursue, but she certainly knew that they would be different from the past. Perhaps she would expand Mongol commercial participation in the Silk Route; she might confront the Muslim warlords or even the Ming Court. Or, she might do all of those things.

Manduhai Khatun and Dayan Khan went to their new camp to enjoy it for a short while and to give the boy a little time to adjust to her and the new people around him. He needed to become comfortable with them because she was about to take him to war. As a khan, even as a little boy, war would be his profession, and it could never be too soon to begin learning it.

With a Great Khan at her side, her newly found firmness and strength, Manduhai was ready to set out on her white road of life.

☘

Winning the War and
Raising a Husband

VOWS, PRAYERS, AND RITUALS BEFORE A SHRINE ADDED much needed sacred legitimacy to Dayan Khan's rule, but without force of arms, they amounted to empty gestures and wasted breath. Only after demonstrating that she had the skill to win, as well as the supernatural blessing to do so, could Manduhai hope to rule the Mongols. She had enemies on every side, and she needed to choose her first battle carefully. She had to confront each enemy, but she had to confront each in its own due time. Manduhai needed to manage the flow of conflicts by deciding when and where to fight and not allowing others to force her into a war for which she was not prepared or stood little chance of winning.

The enemies she faced after proclaiming Batu Mongke as Dayan Khan were the same who had vied for control over her before she made the proclamation. The Ming Dynasty to the southeast, although weakening, still presented a major threat to the Mongols and claimed the right to rule over them. The Muslim warlords of the Silk Route, fractious and quarrelsome as ever, continued to grow in power in the southwest and still sought to control the Mongols by controlling their khans.

Throughout their history, the steppe tribes had periodically experienced population and military pressure from both China and the Turks, but for thousands of years, the way west remained open as the escape valve. The Slavic people had never been able to close that valve or resist the Asian tribes' thrust toward Europe. In the fifteenth century, however, for the first time, Ivan III managed to close it and even reverse the pressure by pushing some of the Mongols back toward their homeland. By 1470 when Manduhai installed Dayan Khan in office, Mongolia had effectively been sealed shut. The Siberian Arctic to the north prevented movement in that direction, and the Chinese Ming, the Muslim states of Central Asia, and the Slavic Russians of the West sealed off the Mongolian Plateau on every side.

Manduhai's first, and possibly most strategically important, victory came without a battle. She managed to prevent a failed suitor from becoming an enemy. Une-Bolod, the descendant of Khasar and the general under her husband Manduul, remained loyal. She had rejected his marriage proposal, but he recognized the legitimacy of her insistence that all Mongols should rally behind the boy khan.

By remaining loyal to her, and thereby to the descendant of Genghis Khan, he stood next in line to inherit the office of Great Khan and to marry her if anything should happen to the sickly child. Considering Dayan Khan's condition, caused by his mistreatment as an infant and then the injuries from the fall into the stream while being brought to Manduhai, such an untimely death must have seemed quite possible.

Manduhai had pressed a legalistic case for installing the boy on the throne, but the same logic and adherence to Genghis Khan's law would force her to accept Une-Bolod next. In the absence of the boy, all the same arguments would support him, and by remaining loyal to her and the boy now, he prepared the way for a legal succession in the future.

Similarly, if Manduhai should be killed in battle or be incapacitated in any way, Une-Bolod stood as next in line to become regent for the boy. By remaining loyal to both Manduhai and Dayan Khan, Une-Bolod would already be well positioned in the middle of the camp, and if anything happened to either the queen or the khan, he would assume power. He would not need to rally an army and descend on the royal camp; he and his warriors would already be in place.

Manduhai's power base was in the central Mongolian steppe, a well-watered land good for animals and easily traversed. By having Une-Bolod's loyalty, she had no worry about the immediate eastern area, since he controlled it. The Siberian tribes to the north had never posed much of a threat to the steppe people. The western tribes offered her the least support, but her most dreaded enemies lay to the south, across the Gobi—the Ming in the southeast and the warlords in the southwest.

Manduhai decided to confront her enemies at home first, before looking south, by strengthening her western flank. After consolidating her rule over the Mongols and attaining a firm grip on the whole of the Mongolian Plateau, she might consider leaving home to confront her southern rivals, but she could not do so with the possibility of resistance or revolt at her back.

Western Mongolia was home to a variety of tribes, independent clans, and factions in shifting alliances. They were Mongols with a mixture of Turkic steppe tribes as well as Siberian forest tribes in a constantly changing array of ethnic, clan, and geographic names. Groups could be referred to by the name of their individual clans, lineages, or tribes. Or they could be referred to by the name of a dominant group in their area, as well as by a geographic feature of the area. As the people moved from one area to another or as one lineage rose and fell in local prominence, the identification might change.

A more diverse assortment of tribes lived in the west than in the more homogenous east. The topography and microenvironments of the Altai Mountains and adjacent steppes offered sustenance for a larger variety of animals than eastern Mongolia. Camel herders lived in the southern deserts. Herders of goats, sheep, cows, and yaks occupied the mountain areas, and reindeer herders lived in the north. All the herders kept horses if the animals could survive, but if not, they rode camels, yaks, oxen, and reindeer.

Through the centuries, the area attracted a variety of ethnic groups from other places as well. When Islam first spread into Central Asia, many Christian tribes sought refuge here, as well as some Buddhists and Manicheans. Later, Muslims joined them, sometimes as traders, but often fleeing from their own political and schismatic struggles.

Stretching back more than a thousand years, to the time of the Huns and then to the eighth-century Turkic empires, the Mongol state always had its base in the center between the Tuul and Orkhon rivers. The Mongols had strengthened their hold on this area, in part by moving other steppe tribes into the west along the Altai Mountains to serve as a buffer against the unknown but threatening forces of Muslim Central Asia, the Europeans, and the Mongols' steppe neighbors.

Through the centuries, the Oirat, called Kalmyk by the Muslims and Russians, had spread out of their original forest home in Siberia; by the time of Manduhai's reign, their name had expanded into a generic term encompassing all the western Mongol and Turkic tribes around the Altai Mountains. Since the time of Genghis Khan's daughter Checheyigen, the Oirat, as a son-in-law nation, usually had a female of the Borijin clan come to marry their leader. Over time, the leader of the Oirat came to be known as the *taishi*, while the title *khan* was reserved primarily for the Borijin leaders. For a while, the joint titles and the marriage alliance kept the two parts of the Mongol nation closely connected.

When the Mongols weakened in the time of Elbeg Khan, both the Ming court and the Silk Route warlords tried to separate the eastern and western Mongols and play them off each other. Both foreign powers sought to promote the Oirat as a separate nation, apart from the Mongols in the east, with equal leaders deserving of their own titles.

As the Ming Dynasty declined in vigor and the ties with western Mongolia became harder to maintain, the warlords of the Silk Route began pursuing the same strategy of dividing eastern and western Mongols, and they had more success. Until the time of Esen, the *taishi* was a western Mongol and lived among the people over whom he ruled. After Esen's assassination, the Turkic warlords such as Beg-Arslan and Ismayil claimed the title and the right to rule the Oirat, although they preferred to stay close to their trade oasis cities along the Silk Route and to control the Oirat indirectly from a distance. As long as the *taishi* kept trade goods coming into the Oirat territory, no one seemed to mind.

Manduhai had to retake control of the Oirat, unite the Mongols, and thereby deprive Ismayil, and the future warlords, of the title or power to rule over the Oirat. She did not yet have an army large enough to cross the desert and conquer the oases of the Silk Route where the warlords held their power base and where large segments of the Oirat lived. But she was ready to challenge Beg-Arslan and Ismayil for command over the Oirat living north of the Gobi. Even if she could not conquer them completely, she needed to neutralize the warlords' ability to use the Oirat against her.

In preparation for the first major campaign, Manduhai sent a train of ox carts laden with equipment and provisions with an infantry escort to guard them. She and the main army would leave later and pass by the infantry and supply carts. The organization of the army showed clearly that Manduhai's plans for making war reached a much higher state of forethought and execution than the usual raids that had characterized much of steppe warfare over the previous two centuries. In an organization uncharacteristic of steppe leaders, she used infantry and cavalry as well as the caravan of supply carts; her army more closely resembled that of a sedentary state than that of a nomadic one.

Three days later, the young queen was ready to depart. The chronicles all agree that she fixed her hair to accommodate her quiver. The hairstyle of noble married women of that era precluded fighting or any other manual endeavor. She removed the headdress of peace and put on her helmet for war.

By taking off her queenly headdress, known as the *boqta,* she removed virtually the only piece of clothing that separated a man from a woman. The *boqta* ranks as one of the most ostentatious headdresses of history, but it had been highly treasured by noble Mongol women since the founding of the empire. The head structure of willow branches, covered with green felt, rose in a narrow column three to four feet high, gradually changing from a round base to a square top. A variety of decorative items such as peacock or mallard feathers adorned the top with a loose attachment that kept them upright but allowed them to flutter high above the woman's head. The higher the rank, the more elaborate the *boqta*, and as queen, Manduhai would have worn a highly elaborate one. She would have worn her hair in a knot underneath a hood that helped to balance the *boqta*. The contraption struck many foreign visitors as odd, but the Mongol Empire had enjoyed such prestige that medieval women as far away as Europe imitated it with the *hennin*, a large cone-shaped headdress that sat toward the back of the head rather than rising straight up from it as among the Mongols. With no good source of peacock feathers, European noblewomen generally substituted gauzy streamers flowing in the wind at the top.

As in many martial cultures, the bow and arrow served not only as a major weapon in war but also as a major political and martial symbol. For the Mongols, hanging up the bow and arrow in the *ger* symbolized peace, and taking them down symbolized war. Even a young boy such as Dayan Khan could have easily taken down the bow and quiver of arrows and strapped them on to symbolically lead the army. By stressing that Manduhai did it, the chronicles show clearly that she personally commanded the army.

As described in the *Altan Tobci*, "Queen Manduhai the Good, like the great khans of former times, set out on campaign."

She did not, however, leave the boy behind. He was the khan, and he would accompany her army whether he was yet capable or not. In the words of the *Altan Tobci*, she put the young khan "in a box and set out." Other sources described the container as a leather case, a woven basket, or a wooden box strapped to a horse.

When moving from camp to camp, Mongol parents often put young children in a specially made box without a top that they tied to the side of a camel's two humps. From this secure place the children could be easily moved and kept out of the way, and they could often be seen with their heads poking out of such boxes as they bounced along on the camel.

By age seven, however, Dayan Khan certainly should have been able to ride a horse with some degree of mastery. Children began riding at age three or four, and by age five, many of them, both boys and girls, were able to engage in grueling races of more than fifteen miles. Particularly since the boy now occupied the highest office in the Mongol world, it seems odd that he would not be riding a horse. At the same time, the chronicles mention that his box was carried by a horse, and not a camel; horses are not used as pack animals, so the choice of animal indicates an unusual situation.

The young khan possibly still suffered from the ailments of his earlier childhood, and perhaps he could not ride. Several times in his life he had accidents falling from a horse, and therefore Manduhai seemed to be taking no chance of having the young khan injured as she went off to battle. Because she led the troops in his name, his presence, in some form or other, was vital to the legitimacy and success of the campaign. For generations, the men who held the title of Great Khan had rarely ventured forth on a real military campaign, but Manduhai was showing that although he might be a crippled boy, he was still the khan and would go with her into battle. Her leadership and his bravery inspired others to follow her as well.

The Mongol armies at the time of Manduhai still utilized the left-right organization of Genghis Khan. Whether in camp or on the battlefield, the leader remained always at the center of the army, surrounded by several concentric circles of protectors. The main detachment then spread out as two large wings from the center. Even when moving across the countryside, the army moved in this spread-out formation rather than in the single-file formation of most battalions. In this way, the Mongol army was constantly in formation to move into battle.

In some armies, the commander rode at the front of the troops. But in the wing formation, with the commander in the center, the two wings moved out somewhat ahead of the leader. From this position at the rear, the commander could see the entire army and be in a much better position to make decisions and give orders. The commander could call for a large number of battle formations to be used in attack, and these could be changed frequently in a cascade of attacks that confused the enemy.

At the beginning of the Mongol Empire, uninformed opponents sometimes mocked even Genghis Khan as a coward for staying behind the front line in battle, but the effectiveness of the Mongol strategy proved itself not only in their consistent victories, but also in the rare loss of life of their commanders. Despite her untraditional approach to organizing her army, Manduhai knew better than to depart from this proven military formation. She took her position at the center of the army.

A herd of horses can move only as quickly as its smallest and youngest members can run. Horses can outrun most dangers, but wolves are swift, nimble, and wily. The wolf pack cannot threaten the strong stallion, who can attack with his hooves and severely injure or kill an adult wolf, but because there is only one such stallion, he poses little threat to the pack as a whole. To protect the vulnerable foals and colts, the females herd them into a tight circle that the mares then surround in a tight fortification, thereby forming a wall of hooves against the attackers. Thus fortified, the mares easily beat off with their hooves any wolf that may nip at them, but the horses remain rigidly in place until the wolves move on toward easier prey. The lone mature stallion circles around almost helplessly as a sentry, lunging ineffectively at the wolves that easily jump out of his range.

From thousands of years together on the steppe, the two animals know each other's threats and each other's defenses. The wolves stand little chance of breaking the mares' defense, but sometimes they can lure out an overconfident and easily provoked young male that lacks the instinct or experience of the females. Such an untested male will strike out against a wolf that then lures him toward the rest of the wolves, which are hiding in ambush. They race out, attack the startled young male, and rip his flesh apart.

Manduhai already knew the lesson of the mares, but now she needed to learn from the wolf. She could already protect and guard, but Manduhai needed to learn to hunt, stalk, retreat, lure, attack, and win. She first sought to lure out her enemies from their protected stronghold and confront them in the place of her choosing.

Manduhai carefully selected the battle zone. She led her army toward the large open area west of the Khangai Mountains and east of the Altai. Whoever controlled this area, now mostly located in the modern Mongolian province of Zavkhan, had the best position for controlling the west. Because the area comprised the large open steppe, it was the best place in the west for horse herds. The numerous small rivers of the area drained the ice that melted from the mountains, and abundant meandering streams provided adequate moisture for what would otherwise be too dry a zone for extensive herding. The places without such moisture became sandy deserts, giving the large area a highly varied landscape, with patches of drifting sand dunes and verdant pastures adjacent to the many streams.

The combination of ample water and extensive grass made for fertile grazing in an otherwise arid west. Whoever controlled this central area would have the largest herds of horses in the area, and thereby food and transportation for the largest army. They would be able to dominate the entire area from central Mongolia to the Kazakh steppes. For these practical reasons, Qaidu Khan and his daughter Khutulun came to the same area for their major confrontation with the armies of their Mongol cousins in the Yuan Dynasty, and it was here that Qaidu Khan died.

Zavkhan lay north across the Gobi from the oasis where Ismayil had his stronghold, and it was difficult for him to cross such a vast, dry expanse with a large army. For him to make a campaign so far away from his base would have attracted the attention of the Ming army along the Chinese frontier, and they might have seized the oases that they claimed, but which he controlled. If he lost control over the oases, he would also have lost control of the Silk Route. He would have been left without a military or a commercial base.

Because he could not send in a large force to protect his claim on the Oirat territory, Ismayil sought to govern the Oirat by controlling their access to Chinese and Middle Eastern trade goods. Manduhai had no such material incentive with which to entice the Oirat. Nevertheless, from the time of Genghis Khan's daughter Checheyigen, the Mongols and the Oirat had maintained close social and marriage ties. Manduhai came from the Choros clan of the Oirat, as did Dayan Khan's great-grandfather Esen. In addition, many of Dayan Khan's female ancestors had been Oirat of different clans.

The chronicles do not explain how Manduhai chose the area or how she came to have the strategic knowledge that she exhibited consistently throughout her military career. Did she know about the battles of Qaidu Khan and Khutulun? Had she learned about the techniques of Genghis Khan? Did she follow the direction of her best general, Une-Bolod? Or did she merely possess some kind of born genius for strategic thinking?

Manduhai's expedition of conquest resulted in a number of moderately sized skirmishes, but few large battles. She found little opposition in the west. She came with the true khan, the descendant of Genghis Khan; even the most ardent supporter of the *taishi* knew that the Great Khan outranked him and that it was to the Great Khan that they owed their ultimate allegiance. Some of the Oirat sided with Manduhai from the start, and others eventually came to her side.

In the midst of one of the battles, Manduhai's helmet slipped. This was her first military campaign, and she may not yet have been accustomed to the battlefield. Since craftsmen usually made helmets to fit men, her helmet likely was large on her head and insecure. The displaced helmet dangled briefly from her neck before falling away completely and landing in the dirt.

For any warrior, much less for a commander, only the loss of the horse would be more dangerous than the loss of the helmet. Without it, her head immediately became an open target for any Oirat who wanted to shoot her or attack her with a sword. But for her or one of her underlings to dismount to retrieve the helmet would be to face the even more dangerous prospect of being trampled under the hooves of either the enemy or her own soldiers.

An Oirat warrior was the first to notice the unfortunate loss. "The Queen has no helmet," he called out. Such a cry almost certainly seemed like an invitation to mob her like wolves on a wounded deer, but instead of taking advantage of her unexpected vulnerability, the Oirat soldier shouted for someone to "bring another." When it appeared obvious that no one had a spare helmet to offer, he removed his own helmet in the midst of the battle and presented it to her. The chronicles do not name the Oirat who, quite probably, saved her life; they only specify his ethnicity. She possibly had a contingent of Oirat fighting with her, or he could have been a chivalrous enemy warrior. No matter whether he had already joined Manduhai's side or fought against her in the skirmish, the record of the incident showed the level of respect she maintained among the Oirat.

Manduhai cleverly managed to turn the loss of her helmet to her advantage. The headgear of a person is so closely associated with the soul and its heavenly protection, since the sky is seen as the hat of the Earth, that Mongols sometimes deliberately discard a hat as a way of changing that fate and striving for a new one. Realizing that the sight of the commander losing her helmet could frighten her followers enough to cause them to flee from the battle, Manduhai dashed forward even more boldly and fiercely, determined to demonstrate that her change of headdress promised certain victory. In the words of the *Altan Tobci,* her enemy reportedly swarmed at her as thick as a cloud of dust, but she fell upon them and "destroyed them entirely, and annihilated them." She took prisoners beyond counting, and she killed their leaders who had been disloyal to her and Dayan Khan.

Victory was often marked by imposition of some relatively unimportant but symbolically meaningful laws on the defeated. The *Yellow Chronicle of the Oirat (Shira Tughuji)* listed several such punitive laws issued by Manduhai after her victory. She limited the crest on the Oirat helmets to a length of two fingers. They could not call any *ger* in their land an *ordon*, the Mongol word for palace; and when in the presence of khans, they had to sit on their knees.

The text also mentions a law that the Oirat could no longer eat with a knife but instead had to gnaw their meat. Such a law probably never existed, but Manduhai may have confiscated their knives as a security measure, thereby temporarily depriving them of knives for eating meat until they were again allowed to acquire them.

Manduhai had reunited the Mongols, and she now controlled the strategic area of Zavkhan, necessary to assert her power over the west. Without that control, she would face the dangers posed by a rebel tribe, foreign warlords, or even the possibility of wealthy merchants luring her followers away. Une-Bolod gave her control of the east, and now she had added control of the west.

In addition to its strategic importance, the western campaign against the Oirat was a notable propaganda victory, demonstrating that Manduhai had the blessing of the Shrine of the First Queen and the Eternal Blue Sky. Manduhai showed that she was in control of her country. The khan may have been a small boy in a box, but her strength and determination inspired confidence. For the first time in more than a century, a united and strong central government had control of Mongolia. Manduhai had succeeded in uniting western and eastern Mongolia under the Borijin clan for the first time since Elbeg Khan's fateful encounter with the rabbit in 1399, nearly a century earlier.

Going to war in a basket box may have been an odd way for the young Dayan Khan to grow up, but after the trauma of his earliest years, Manduhai provided the boy with a stable and secure, albeit unusual, childhood. For much of the prior centuries, the domineering warlords had kept a sequence of boy khans as prisoners, whom they exploited, abused, and humiliated. The warlords certainly showed no interest in educating or preparing these boys for leadership because they would never lead. No one expected any of the boys to live to become a fully functioning adult, much less the ruling khan. At most, a boy might be required to reproduce a male heir before being dispatched, or some other male relatives could be substituted as khan or as progenitor.

From the start, Manduhai's actions made clear that she planned for Dayan Khan to rule. He would be a fully functioning and ruling khan, not a figurehead. Manduhai could easily have left him under the charge of nurses or have built a small, isolated camp for him in one of the many canyons of the Gobi or the Altai Mountains. She could have sent him to live in the remote steppe where she had lived with her first husband, Manduul. Instead, they bore the campaign hardships together. Although we have no quotes from him at this time in his life, he well might have said the same words that Genghis Khan said to one of his most loyal followers: "When it was wet, we bore the wet together, when it was cold, we bore the cold together."

Manduhai seemed determined not to repeat the painful mistake of Genghis Khan, who had been a genius in war, politics, and governing but had failed as a father, particularly to his sons. They grew up fearful of him, but undisciplined. They were rowdy and drunken, more intent on hunting, racing, gambling, and womanizing than on learning how to rule. Genghis Khan's shortcomings as a father, in the end, helped bring down his empire and thus undid his lifetime of work.

Manduhai did not have the luxury or the problems of so many extra sons. She had but this one boy, and she was determined to make him into a leader in war and in peace.

She kept him constantly close to her and guarded and sheltered him without delegating that responsibility to anyone. In the words of the *The Jewel Translucent,* Manduhai "protected her jewel-like son." She sought divine blessings for him, and "she truthfully and strongly prayed" to the Eternal Blue Sky: "Lord Tengri, you must watch out for sinful and evil-thinking people!" Constantly but "fearfully she watched over and kept safe her important son." Through her actions she saved the lineage of Genghis Khan, or in the more ornate phrasing of the Buddhist chroniclers, she facilitated "the spreading of the wish-granting, jewel-like Borijin Golden Clan." In this way, "by protecting the infallible Dayan Khan, she lit the Borijin hearth fire."

Manduhai may have united the Mongols under Dayan Khan, but she had not lessened the threat from the enemies outside Mongolia. The Ming Dynasty in China, to the southeast of Mongolia, and the warlords of the Silk Route to the southwest each claimed the right to rule the Mongols, and each eagerly sought to exercise that right. Whoever controlled the Mongols had access to the richest supply of horses anywhere on Earth. For the merchants of the oases, such a treasure promised infinite riches in trade. For the Ming military, access to the horses would provide them with the basis for a larger and more powerful cavalry.

Manduhai's western campaign captured the attention of both rivals. They welcomed the increased turbulence in the Mongol steppes, but the victory of Manduhai and her success at uniting the fractious eastern and western Mongols created a new source of concern for them. Both the warlords and the Chinese still smarted from the pains inflicted on them and the capture of their leaders when Esen nearly united the Mongols. Both wanted to avoid a repeat of those episodes.

While strengthening military control over the Mongols, Manduhai's victories jeopardized existing commercial links. Mongolia had no need to be united if the result was to be left alone in isolation without trade and commerce. Unlike the first Mongols, who only needed a few trade goods such as metal, Mongols of the fifteenth century required commodities from cloth and incense to tea and medicines. The political turmoil and social upheaval since the fall of the Mongol Empire had done nothing to lessen Mongol appetites for the variety of goods they had learned about during the empire's height.

The only thing that the Mongol steppe could produce in substantial excess was animals. The Mongols produced many times the number of animals that they needed for their own subsistence, but they had no one with whom they could trade except the Chinese. The civilizations of Central Asia and Europe lay much too far away, and this left only the Chinese trade as the way that the Mongols could convert their extensive animal production into any other type of goods.

In response to the new round of potentially threatening behavior from the tribes on the Mongolian Plateau, the Ming court in Beijing tried to cut off, or at least control strictly, trade with the Mongols. The lack of trade created a widespread and persistent scarcity of luxury goods for the Mongols, but for the Chinese it created a small but very specific problem. Chinese farmers devoted almost all arable land to the production of crops and to a few animals, such as pigs and chickens, that could live from the scraps of an agricultural society. In so doing, in order to irrigate and plant the fields, they destroyed the pasturelands where horses might graze.

Most Chinese did not care about the reduction in horses, but for the military it was a crucial issue. To fill the need, the Chinese army sought other suppliers of horses when they could not get them from the Mongols. They sometimes imported horses from incredibly faraway places, including Korea, Japan, and even the distant Ryukyu Islands. But no matter how much the officials in the Forbidden City tried to curtail trade with the Mongols, the Chinese soldiers continued it on the border. To ensure the constant supply of horses, they had to provide a constant flow outward of trade goods coming from all over China.

The instability of the horse trade drove up prices. The presentation of an average horse by a Mongol required the payment of a bolt of high-quality silk, eight bolts of coarse silk, and a cash payment equal to an additional two bolts of coarse silk. At the horse markets maintained along the border, similarly disproportionate terms remained in effect. A good horse required payment of 120 *chin* (132 pounds) of tea, and even a poor horse required payment of 50 *chin* (about 55 pounds) of tea. Not only did the Chinese have to pay for poor-quality horses, as tribute they even had to pay for horses that died on the way to presentation.

By the 1470s, the black-market trade in horses had resumed in a vigorous but unofficial way that benefited private merchants more than the government officials, who were barred from participating. The government officials divided into two camps. Some favored allowing the black market to operate because it prevented the large, armed Mongol convoys from marching on tribute missions to the capital. Others, however, regretted the loss of imperial revenues and control of the horses. By 1479, even the authorities had to recognize the importance of the horse trade, and in an effort to recoup control of the profits from it, the Ming monarch restored its legality as an official matter of policy.

The influential eunuchs in the court struggled to confine the horse trade to the traditional system of allowing barbarians to submit tribute. In the official ideology of the Chinese court, by coming to the court and seeing firsthand the world's most opulent and advanced civilization, the barbarians would naturally become at least semicivilized. True civilization for the Chinese consisted of three primary parts: acceptance of Chinese writing; urban or otherwise sedentary living; and loyalty to the emperor. While barbarians probably would not adopt all three, the closer they came to doing so, the better, in the Chinese view.

To facilitate the spread of these three primary aspects of Chinese civilization during the Han Dynasty in the first century, strategists had recommended five types of bait certain to lure the barbarians, strategies still followed by the Ming Dynasty more than a thousand years later. The lures included luxurious clothes to corrupt their eyes; superior cuisine to corrupt their mouths; beautiful women and music to corrupt their ears; massive buildings, slaves, and granaries to corrupt their appetites; and, finally, wine and feasts to corrupt the minds of their leaders.

The Mongols rejected all three aspects of Chinese civilization; they had their own writing; they were committed nomads; and they would never bow to a foreign ruler. Manduhai needed trade, but she refused to go through any of the ceremonies of submission or the rituals of tribute, and she was not tempted by a single one of the five types of bait. The Chinese struggled to understand it. The rejection posed more than a mere insult; it challenged the fundamental worldview of the Ming authorities and threatened to undermine their power if they could not convince a barbarian queen of their superiority.

When she looked southward beyond the Gobi and below the Mongolian Plateau, Manduhai saw enemies on every side, but she also saw home. She knew this land because she was born and reared there. This knowledge and experience gave her an advantage over Genghis Khan and earlier conquerors. Over millennia, the steppe tribes had focused on raiding and conquering cities because that was where the wealth accumulated. With such minute populations compared with the vastness of China, the steppe tribes could rarely conquer more than a few cities before spreading their armies too sparsely. The most successful conquerors had formed dynasties by leaving behind a thin stratum of the Mongol elite at the top of the local social hierarchy, but rarely did these regimes last for long. The enormous population of China eventually swallowed the barbarians or spit them out again.

Sentiment and nostalgia make poor diplomacy, and even worse military strategy. The emotion behind Manduhai's move remains difficult to ascertain, but she had a clear strategy for specific military and commercial goals. The army that controlled the Silk Route controlled the trade. To maintain the east-west unity of the Mongol people that she had imposed through war, she needed the cooperation of the Mongols south of the Gobi to obtain trade goods. If she could keep the trade goods flowing, whether through military force or by a more peaceful means, she could keep the Mongols united.

Focusing on an external goal and foreign enemies offered a small opportunity to keep the quarrelsome Mongol tribes from directing their hostility toward one another. Manduhai realized that she could protect her government and nation by channeling that aggression toward the Muslims and the Ming armies.

Manduhai proved unwilling merely to sit north of the Gobi, as her first husband had done, and wait for caravans of traders to arrive with whatever goods they happened to have left over, demanding whatever price they could. She needed to control the caravans from their source to determine which goods they carried and in which direction they flowed. She needed to develop a new approach to China. She had learned from the negative example of the Golden Prince how difficult it was to unite the Mongols north of the Gobi with the ones south of the Gobi in a concerted effort. Even if united, she knew that they could not control China.

In contrast to the expansive territorial acquisition favored by prior generations of steppe conquerors, Manduhai pursued a strategy of geographic precision. Better to control the right spot rather than be responsible for conquering, organizing, and running a massive empire of reluctant subjects. Control of the area between the Tuul River and the Orkhon gave her power over central Mongolia; control of Zavkhan gave her power over western Mongolia. Now, rather than trying to conquer and occupy the extensive links of the Silk Route or the vast expanse of China, she sought to conquer just the strategic spot from which to control them.

Facing the Wall

MANDUHAI MAY HAVE BEEN THE *KHATUN* AND BATU Mongke the khan, but by claiming the office of *taishi*, foreigners such as Ismayil and Beg-Arslan still had a stranglehold on Mongolia by controlling the Gobi and thereby all the trade with China. Not yet strong enough to confront them directly, Manduhai consolidated her authority north of the Gobi. Although she steadily increased her power, ever since Genghis Khan's conquests more Mongols actually lived south of the Gobi than north. A majority of the Mongols remained loyal to Beg-Arslan and Ismayil rather than to Dayan Khan and Manduhai.

To make Dayan Khan ruler of the whole people, as promised in his title, Manduhai had to win the loyalty of the southern Mongols. Unable at this juncture to mount a military offensive across the Gobi, she chose a more sensible, but still risky, plan. For now, she would let the massive Chinese army contend with Beg-Arslan and his aggression in the hope that they might crush him. The danger, however, was that if the Chinese could not defeat him, Beg-Arslan might emerge with an even stronger claim to being the right ruler for all the Mongols.

Beg-Arslan and Ismayil turned their attention away from Mongolia because the continued crumbling of the Ming defenses presented them with new raiding opportunities. Under Beg-Arslan's control, the southern Mongol army was gradually nibbling away at the Chinese borders, pushing back the Ming forces. Under its weak and distracted emperor, the Ming Dynasty had become an empire in retreat. Beg-Arslan sensed that he might now make his biggest conquest by challenging the Ming for command of the Gansu Corridor and thereby the doorway into China. To occupy the corridor, he needed to attack the Chinese stronghold at Yinchuan, the main city of modern Ningxia. This was the final place besieged by Genghis Khan back in 1227, and it was near here that he died. Thus, in addition to its tremendous strategic and commercial value for anyone seeking to dominate trade, the whole area had acquired deep symbolic importance in the cultural psyche of the Mongols.

If Beg-Arslan could seize this place so closely associated with the memory of Genghis Khan, he would have all the greater hold on the Mongols serving around him. Manduhai's claim to legitimacy derived from the blood link of Dayan Khan to Genghis Khan, but if Beg-Arslan controlled such an important site, it would show that Genghis Khan and the Eternal Blue Sky supported him. Victory in battle would always surpass any other type of legitimacy. Beg-Arslan could claim the mandate of Mongol history.

Beg-Arslan's strongholds at the Turfan and Hami oases were too far out in the desert to function as supply bases for the conquest of Ningxia and control of the Gansu Corridor. He had moved his troops much closer to his target, into a great loop in the Yellow River. The immense river, known to the Mongols as the Black River, to the Turkic people as the Green River, and to most of the world as the Huang Ho or Yellow River, begins its nearly three-thousand-mile journey toward the sea from the Kunlun Mountains in Tibet, flowing north across the Asian continent. Without an obstacle blocking its course, the river could continue northward across Mongolia and Siberia and out to the Arctic, but the giant Gobi and the massive Mongolian Plateau bar its way. The river forms a large loop before turning eastward and heading to the Pacific instead of the Arctic.

The land enclosed by the Great Loop covers about 83,000 square miles, or an area about the same size as the Korean Peninsula. The river provides for agriculture along its sides if irrigated, but the interior area can only support grazing. The topography consists of a plateau that rises up to an average altitude over three thousand feet.

The landscape offers steppes of dry gravel, salt lakes, and shifting sands that farmers and sedentary people found alien and hostile, but which the Mongols found inviting and comforting to their aesthetic sensibilities and beneficial to their pastoral way of life. In contrast to the incredibly hot deserts of the interior or the wet agricultural lands of the river plains, the inner loop offered land sufficiently fertile for grazing, but not appropriate for extensive agriculture. It formed a miniature Mongolia, only farther south and with a more benign climate; threateningly close to the Gansu Corridor, it was also the ideal strategic outpost for the Mongols, from where they could easily strike at the heart of Chinese civilization and commerce.

In a series of elegant battlefront reports that survive from the Ming commander Wang Yue, a clear picture of the issues emerges. He suggested a novel tactic of using trade to lure in the Mongols and then attacking them. Because it proved difficult for the Chinese soldiers to go out and find the Mongols, Wang Yue proposed that government officials should send out large supply trains whose movements could be easily monitored by the Mongols and which would pose tempting targets for their raids. Thus the Mongols could be lured in close and then attacked by the waiting military. Although the policy would not prevent Mongol raids entirely, it would discourage them "to dare to penetrate deeply." Wang Yue began implementation of his policy with campaigns against the Mongols in the summer of 1470 and again in 1471. Although they produced few casualties, they succeeded in heightening the tensions along the border.

After only seven months on his assignment at the frontier a rival officer, Commander Yu Zijun, opposed Wang's offensive strategy. Yu prepared an alternative report, hoping to prevent the Mongols from raiding the frontier settlement at Yulin by reviving an ancient, but long neglected, approach of building a wall. According to his proposal, the wall should be made stronger and larger than the walls of earlier dynasties by constructing it of earth to a height of about thirty feet. Rather than just enclosing specific populated areas, it should be erected along the top ridges of the mountains to provide maximum visibility for spotting approaching marauders and for the relay of signals from one part to another. The signaling alone allowed the creation of an unprecedented long-distance communication network, permitting information to travel faster than a horse, thereby creating the possibility for the coordination of military action along a lengthy line at a much faster rate than the attacking cavalry could facilitate.

Yu proposed building the wall as a more humane response to the Mongol problem, and, as such, it seemed to him more appropriate for a beneficent, civilized nation such as China. The wall would prevent invasion without harming the barbarians. Then, as the Chinese literati had maintained for hundreds of years, the exposure to the complete superiority of Chinese culture would, inevitably in its own natural way, pacify and civilize the steppe warriors. Thus, unable any longer to wage war on the Chinese, the Mongols would become civilized.

The wall would cut across the base of the Great Loop that the Mongols had called the Ordos; eventually, the wall would begin and end at the Yellow River, thereby protecting the agriculturally productive lands within the loop. Yu saw no reason to allocate men and resources to defend empty land that was not productive.

The senior military officials rejected Yu's plan as too expensive, whereupon, at the end of 1472, he wrote another report offering a cost-benefit analysis that showed how his superiors could, in the long run, save money by building the wall. The financial argument also carried a strongly implied but unstated message. The wall would prevent the soldier-farmers stationed on the border from selling their crops to the Mongols or, worse yet, deserting to the Mongols and farming for them. The desertion rates on the border had risen steadily, and the openness of the border prevented the central authorities from exercising power not merely over the steppe tribes, but also over their own soldiers. The carefully constructed wall would keep the Mongols out and keep the Chinese in. From the wall and its watchtowers, the guards could just as easily keep watch over the farming soldiers as they could the approach of potential enemies from the steppe.

Beg-Arslan's invasion deeper into Chinese territory created a sense of fear that propelled the discussion of alternate strategies toward planning for a necessary and quick response. The immediate question was not whether to build the wall, but whether to attack and fight the Mongols or to retreat and let them have the territory they were invading.

Commander Wang waited along the frontier of the Ordos for the Mongol attack. It would come soon, but he could not predict whether they would hit him with a frontal attack on his forces or try to bypass him and raid one of the cities under his protection. Would they loot his stores in a quiet attack under cover of the frequent dust storms from the desert, or would they focus all their fury directly on him, perhaps in a night effort to kill him and thus cripple his poorly trained and poorly supplied army?

Like the lonely commanders who had guarded this remote spot for more than a thousand years before him, Commander Wang stood at the edge of an immense empire, waiting and watching for the next onslaught. He knew that, in a truly concerted struggle, his embittered and disheartened men could not stop the Mongols. All they could possibly do was send a warning to the cities and then stand their ground and die one by one, in a vain effort to slow the assault by a few days and allow the city residents to flee or to hastily improvise some protective strategy. Commander Wang and his men were no more than guard dogs whose sole function in life was to bark at the right moment and then die.

At age forty-seven, far from the family he loved and the comforts of the life he craved, Commander Wang waited. To fill his time, he wrote poems, letters, and long reports, hoping he could still be a part of civilized life by sending his words and name back to be read by someone in the city. From these words, we can see the kind of man that he was, or at least the kind of man he wished to portray to the desk-bound bureaucrats and the supernumerary courtiers who read his work back in the Forbidden City.

In an empire where military men ranked barely above the barbarians whom they were supposed to fight, Commander Wang stood out as a misplaced mandarin, a man trained to become an official in the government hierarchy, not in the military. His assignment to oversee the military command along the border came, in part, as a result of the constant mistrust that the imperial court had in its own army of misfits, exiles, and criminals sent to guard the country. Unable to depend upon them, the court, from time to time, sent out civilian administrators to bring them into shape and keep them from joining the enemy. Wang was more of a guard over the guards than a real functionary.

Knowing that the path to advancement in the Ming military ranks derived more from their ability to use language than weapons, the officers on the front cultivated a style of literary military writing, substituting words and metaphors for victory. As another officer had written: "I braved the snow storm to attack. . . . I ate dry provisions, drank water found along the route, placed myself under the danger of arrow and rock, and caused myself to suffer. I traveled the desert back and forth for three thousand *li,* and for more than forty days. I went to bed with my armor. At that time I thought that I would not be able to survive." Fortunately for the author of this field report, despite failing in his military mission, he survived, managed to secure imperial favor, and lived out his old age in leisurely and comfortable retirement. After all, what cultivated official back in the comforts of Beijing could resist such a literary battle report?

But Wang liked being seen as a man of action, and he knew the value of a well-placed dramatic gesture. When he first appeared at court in 1463, he could not stand the long sleeves that covered the hands and impaired movement; so in a potentially serious breach of court etiquette, he cut down his sleeves to allow his hands to move.

Fortunately, the emperor approved of his innovative style, thereby saving him from the ever-vigilant eunuchs and their efforts to keep the young mandarins under control.

When he found himself stationed in the Ordos near the border with the Mongols, his tactical abilities and his military talents became more obvious as he found success in repeated skirmishes with the raiding tribes. In due time, the court relieved him of all his administrative civilian duties so that he could concentrate exclusively on the military ones.

By February 1472, Commander Wang controlled approximately 40,000 soldiers and territory covering three hundred miles of border in the Great Loop of the Yellow River. Yet a detachment of Mongols, probably under the command of Beg-Arlsan, attacked in a raid that decisively defeated Wang's poorly trained army. After the defeat, the court in Beijing summoned Commander Wang to the capital for a high-level discussion of how to deal with the Mongol threat in the Great Loop. They wanted the tribes pushed entirely from the Ordos area and forced north of the Yellow River.

At the meeting, Wang became trapped between the demands of his superiors and the reality of the troops and resources at his disposal. Commander Wang knew clearly that to defeat the Mongols, he needed an army of 150,000—at least three and possibly four times the size of the one that he had. Yet it would be difficult to supply such a large army in an inhospitable and infertile frontier zone.

Wang devised a new strategy. He lacked the soldiers to defend the border he had, and he lacked the soldiers to pursue the Mongols, defeat them, and expel them from the Great Loop. It was his tactical ability, however, that his superiors had counted on when they placed him in charge. He could find a way when they had not.

His chance came in the autumn of 1473, when Beg-Arslan launched the surprise attack on Ningxia to the south. Commander Wang knew he could not catch up with the Mongols, since by the time he arrived at one ravaged city, the invaders would already be looting another. However, he had decided that if he could not defeat them on the battlefield, he would strike at their civilian camp, where the raiding warriors had left their families and animals in presumed security. If he could not force the Mongol army out of China, he knew how to make them want to leave.

Commander Wang sent out reconnaissance missions into the deserts of the Great Loop. In October he received word that his spies had located Beg-Arslan's Mongol base camp where the army had left their families near the Red Salt Lake.

From their perceived safety by the lake, the families could wait out the winter while their men raided one settlement after another and sent back the looted goods to the encampment. Late in the winter, while the Yellow River remained firmly frozen, the army would return across the ice into safe territory, where they could graze their animals and tend their flocks during the spring and summer before returning the following fall to resume the cycle of winter raids.

Knowing that the Mongols did not expect him to mount more than a token defense, Commander Wang abandoned the prior policy of waiting passively; he set out after the civilian camp. Wang Yue headed out with ten units of 1,000 cavalrymen in each. They marched some sixty miles in two days and nights, and when they neared the camp, the ten military units divided into two large pincers, surrounding the civilians. An effective strategy used by Ming forces in earlier fights with the Mongols involved trapping them along a river or lake that prevented their fleeing. Unable to swim, the Mongols could either die by drowning or by slaughter at the hands of the attackers.

The camp probably had the protection of a small guard, but Mongols depended less on military strength in such cases than on the ability of women, children, and animals to flee quickly. Normally, the Mongol guard set up stations some distance from the camp, and from this advance position they could see the dust of the approaching army, hear it, or simply feel the vibrations in the ground long before it came into the range of ears or eyes. Once alarmed, one of the sentries took responsibility to race back toward the camp and sound the warning to flee, while the remaining guard then attacked the invaders in a delaying ploy to give the others more time to escape. This October attack by Wang Yue's army, however, came during one of the windiest times of the year. The autumn winds sometimes whip across northern Asia, and as they cross the Gobi, they pick up huge quantities of sand and dust.

Just such a storm formed as the Chinese crossed the desert toward the Red Salt Lake. Initially, the Chinese warriors became distressed and nervous with the bad luck of the storm in a hostile and alien environment they already feared. One of them, however, suggested that they could use the storm as a cover while they continued their advance. Wang Yue rewarded the man for his ingenuity and bravery, and he ordered his army forward.

They struck the Mongol camp without warning from both sides. According to Wang Yue's account, his men killed or captured 350 Mongols, mostly women and children. They looted the camp, herded up the animals, and torched the *gers*. Invigorated by their victory over the civilians, the soldiers sought another opportunity to attack. Wang Yue suspected that the Mongol army would soon receive word of the massacre and race back to find whoever in the camp might have escaped or, if possible, to rescue the captives. He set up an ambush and waited. As suspected, the Mongol soldiers came in pursuit of the Chinese attackers, and Wang Yue's army fell on them, managing to retake much of their loot but with few casualties on either side. Although it was not an important strategic battle, the Mongols suffered a profound emotional loss.

At least in the short term, attacking the civilian camp produced the desired impact on the Mongols. As Wang proudly reported, "When the unfortunate Mongols learned of the massacre of their wives and children they fled with tears in their eyes and for a long time afterwards did not show up in Ho-t'ao."

The few Mongols who managed to escape fled the area, and Beg-Arslan was forced to retreat with his Mongol warriors from the Great Loop; they crossed back across the Yellow River and temporarily disappeared back into the unknown wastes from whence they came. The defeat of the Mongols and the massacre in the Ordos achieved the

Ming court's short-term goal of driving the Mongols back north of the Yellow River, but it did not extinguish the Mongol desire and determination to take and reoccupy their former territory. The retaking of the pasturelands south of Gobi became the primary objective of the Mongols under Beg-Arslan, and control of the Ordos ranked as the most important objective toward that goal. Like a wolf retreating into the brush or finding a cave to lick its wounds, the Mongols had left, but they certainly would return.

In the meantime, Commander Wang had become a hero, and a triumphant excitement surged through the court in the Forbidden City. He had achieved the first Chinese rout of the Mongols since Esen's military capture of the emperor in 1449. Rather than detracting from the conquest, the clever ruse by which Wang had won the victory only added to his credit, since it cost so little money and was accomplished with so few troops. Commander Wang had fulfilled his superiors' hopes for him when they had counted on his tactical cleverness to drive out the Mongols.

The Chinese military reports categorized the Mongol casualties together according to age and sex but gave no names or individual information. By contrast, the Mongol chronicles, as they almost always did with a horrendous or shameful loss, ignored the massacre with no mention at all. The Mongols never record the names of the fallen in cases such as these.

The Ming court lacked the will or the means to follow up on the victory in the desert. The Mongols withdrew, and the Chinese army could have retaken and occupied the entire Ordos. They could have crossed the Yellow River and driven the Mongols back up onto the Mongolian Plateau and north of the Gobi. Instead, the Ming forces abandoned offensive strategies and turned to the older defensive mode of rebuilding the wall.

For Manduhai Khatun, the encouraging news of the Chinese victory offered only limited grounds for optimism. The Ming commander had stopped the advance of Beg-Arslan and Ismayil, but he had not killed them. The civilian massacre at Red Salt Lake forced the Mongol army farther back, but Beg-Arslan had lost few soldiers. In some ways he now posed a greater threat to Manduhai than before the defeat.

Despite the Chinese victory, the Ming court recognized that the expulsion of the Mongols from the Ordos would offer no more than a temporary abatement of the struggle. Knowing the reprieve would probably be brief, the Ming officials needed to make a long-term decision.

Lacking an alternative plan of action for a permanent solution, the central government finally acquiesced to Yu's request to build a wall. Rather than wait for the autumn, both Wang and Yu were ordered to begin building different parts of it simultaneously. Yu began immediately in the spring of 1474 with a building corps of forty thousand men. Despite the uncertainty about the stability of structures erected along the highest ridges, Yu built the wall precisely as he had proposed it, stretching out approximately 600 miles or 1,770 *li*. The total cost exceeded a million taels of silver, more than 1.7 million ounces. The final wall consisted of approximately eight hundred connected units of forts and beacon or sentry towers. It had a tower or other fortification about every three-quarters of a mile along the connecting wall.

Wang built his part of the wall farther to the west, and it stretched 387 *li*, or 125 miles. Together, however, the two walls created an impressive barrier. Although the two commanders saw these fortifications as temporary measures until the Mongols could be pacified and peace imposed, they had initiated a major change in Ming military policy that would take more than a century to unfold. For the time being, however, the long-term effectiveness remained difficult to ascertain.

As the wall neared completion, both men received transfers. In 1474 Wang Yue was called to work in Beijing, and in the following year Yu Zijun received a new assignment and remained in public service almost until his death in 1489. During this time, he continued the building of walls and defensive measures for the empire. He applied his engineering skills to the design of only one offensive creation—a large war chariot that could carry ten armed warriors at once. This forerunner of a tank or an armored personnel carrier proved too expensive and unusual, however, and never played a major role in steppe warfare.

The building of the Great Wall posed a problem for Manduhai's strategy of waiting out the struggle in hopes that the Chinese would crush her rivals. The decision to build it meant that the Ming court had given up hope of chasing down the Mongol warlords. Instead, the court had marked a new defensive line and in effect surrendered everything beyond it to them. The Chinese had defeated Beg-Arslan and driven him away from the border, but Manduhai would have to deal with him without their assistance.

By 1475, when Wang Yue came to serve in the court, the emperor had entered the eleventh year of his reign, and he had not been able to produce a viable heir with Lady Wan or any other woman in his household. He was not yet thirty, but Lady Wan was fifty-five, and it was unlikely she would bear another child.

The court eunuchs working in the palace of the deposed empress, who had flogged Lady Wan in a pique of jealousy ten years earlier, appeared at court with a five-year-old boy. According to the story, as the emperor looked into a mirror one day while a eunuch combed his hair, he sighed in regret that he had no son. The eunuch revealed to the emperor the startling news that he already had a son and that he lived hidden in the palace of his first wife, the disgraced Empress Wu.

Since the emperor apparently had not had conjugal relations with the former empress, the eunuchs claimed that the boy had been born to one of her attendants, a woman captured from the Yao nation in the south in 1467. Despite the unusual circumstances, the emperor needed a successor, and he took the boy to Lady Wan. They accepted the boy and officially installed him as imperial heir. The boy's birth mother then died under unexplained circumstances. Suspicion for the death fell on Lady Wan, but the deed may have just as easily been done by supporters of the old empress, who hoped to control the boy and thus have a return route to influence and power in the court.

Lady Wan and her cadre of eunuchs worked hard to stimulate the sexual interests of the emperor so that he might father more children. The chief eunuch in charge of the central stores scoured the country for stimulants, and in the process he acquired vast amounts of pearls, which were thought to have special reproductive powers. In his capacity as the chief publisher of the empire, he gathered pornography and sexual manuals and had them reproduced in elegant volumes meant to enlighten and motivate the emperor. Lady Wan brought in magicians, Taoist and Buddhist monks, and a diversity of charlatans to perform magical rites to help him. Happily for the court, the emperor fathered seventeen children with five women in a little more than a decade.

He continued to live primarily with Lady Wan, who increasingly spent her time supervising financial issues and managing the office of eunuchs, since they controlled the commerce of the empire. Through them, she oversaw most of the major transactions related to tribute and trade, while ensuring that the imperial monopoly over commodities such as salt was maintained. Just as she served as de facto "wife of the emperor," she also became the virtual chief financial officer of the empire.

Too many immediate issues and scandals distracted the Ming officials for them to focus on the long-term concern of Mongols at the border. The problem seemed taken care of. They had repulsed Beg-Arslan's invasion, and now they were building the wall to keep him out. The expenses posed a problem, but they proved a much less interesting topic than the political and sexual dramas of the court.

Manduhai had not been waiting idly behind the Gobi. She had begun creating alliances with some of the southern Mongols in preparation for her eventual move to unite the two parts of the country. To control the south up to the Great Wall, she needed somehow to dispose of both Beg-Arslan and Ismayil, preferably by killing them, or at least chasing them from the area. Rather than fighting both at once, it would be easier to deal with them one at a time. It is not clear if she managed to lure Ismayil into a temporary alliance or if she merely took advantage of a dispute with Beg-Arslan. No matter what the cause, she prepared to move against Beg-Arslan at a time when Ismayil was conspicuously absent.

One of the largest factions of Mongols living along the Chinese border was the conglomerate of old clans and lineages known as the Three Guards. These were Mongols who stayed behind when the Mongol royal court fled north in 1368, and as implied in their name, they had declared loyalty to the Ming Dynasty and worked as border guards. After eighty years of loyal service, they had rebelled and joined Esen about thirty years earlier, just around the time of Manduhai's birth in 1448. Since Esen's death they had operated as free agents, following first one and then another leader while raiding and extorting the Chinese when they could and temporarily serving them when profitable.

The son of one of the main leaders of the Three Guards married one of the two Borijin women whom Manduhai called daughter and who had been closely related to her first husband, Manduul, possibly as daughters or nieces. The other daughter had married Beg-Arslan, but she disappeared after helping the Golden Prince escape. Regardless of whether Manduhai arranged this marriage tie with the Three Guards or not, she took advantage of the relationship. As Beg-Arslan retreated to the west, he found himself geographically farther away from the Three Guards, who were based in the east. Manduhai made her alliance and prepared to deal with Beg-Arslan.

The Mongol chronicles commonly employed personal stories to summarize large-scale events. Thus, the desertion of the Three Guards from Beg-Arslan was presented in terms of a private grudge rather than in political terms. Beg-Arslan fell because of his cruelty and the vengeance it evoked.

According to the story, the Three Guards' break with Beg-Arslan occurred after a visit from their leader, the same one whose son was married to Manduhai's so-called daughter. The commander called at Beg-Arslan's *ger* one day just as Beg-Arslan was sipping from a bowl of butter soup that he had just cooled. A large pot of the soup boiled on the fire, and smelling the rich aroma of the soup, the visiting commander said that his mouth was "thirsty for its tastiness," and he asked for some.

Beg-Arslan set aside the bowl of cool soup and, without the visitor noticing, maliciously poured boiling soup into another bowl, which he handed to the visitor. Having just seen Beg-Arslan gulping from the bowl without difficulty and not realizing the switch in bowls, the thirsty visitor eagerly took a large mouthful of the nearly boiling, greasy liquid.

Mongols pride themselves on their ability to abide both heat and cold; dropping or refusing food as too hot shows unmanly weakness. Spitting food out is an unforgivable insult. According to Carpini's report on his visit to the Mongol court in the thirteenth century, "If a piece of food is given to anyone and he cannot eat it and he spits it out of his mouth, a hole is made beneath the tent and he is drawn out through the hole and killed without mercy."

The visiting commander thought to himself: "If I swallow the soup, my heart will burn. If I spit it out I will be shamed." So he pretended that nothing untoward had happened. He held the burning soup in his mouth to let it cool, and in so doing, "the skin of his palate came away and fell off."

The commander vowed silently: "Until I die I shall never forget this hate. One day I shall think of it."

The story of Beg-Arslan's cruel disrespect for the commander circulated amid the rumors and stories of the steppe. The Three Guards joined Manduhai Khatun and Dayan Khan, and their first action was to move into the vacuum left by Beg-Arslan's rout by invading the Ordos. With their allies in control of the Ordos, Manduhai and Dayan Khan at last had the base that they needed south of the Mongolian

Plateau, from which they could launch an open attack against Beg-Arslan. Manduhai prepared for Dayan Khan to lead the expedition.

In 1479, when Dayan Khan was about fifteen or sixteen, Manduhai sent him out on his first command. Dayan Khan took "the Chakhar and the Tumed [clans], and assembled them to set out against Beg-Arslan."

He first sent a spy out west to locate Beg-Arslan. The man chosen was from the same clan as the Three Guards commander who had been burned. The spy approached the *ger* of Beg-Arslan under the pretext of being sick and needing medicine. He said to Beg-Arslan: "Alas! When this poor body of mine is peaceful, there is an enemy; when it is in good health, there is sickness." Beg-Arslan poured some alcohol in a small silver dish and gave it to him to drink.

The visitor drank it, and then in remembrance of the earlier episode when his kinsman's palate was burned, the spy put the silver dish inside his *deel.* "This is a souvenir of my drinking," he was quoted as saying, and he probably wanted to bring the stolen trophy as evidence that he had located the right person.

After the man left, Beg-Arslan became suspicious and consulted an oracle, but received an ambiguous response that left him as uncertain as before. Nevertheless, the lack of a clearly good sign from the oracle was cause enough to call for his army to gather. Because the land was dry and supported minimal vegetation, the army had been spread out over a large area, and they did not arrive in time to mount a defense for Beg-Arslan.

When he saw the dust of Dayan Khan's approaching army, Beg-Arslan raced to his horses and fled with a handful of his guards. Dayan Khan's soldiers saw him and pursued him. But before the Mongols could overtake Beg-Arslan, he removed his helmet and put it on one of his men in an effort to deceive the attackers, while he fled in the opposite direction from his men.

The Mongol force quickly caught the man in Beg-Arslan's helmet, but to save himself he pointed out the direction in which Beg-Arslan had fled. "They caught up with Beg-Arslan and seized him," according to the *Altan Tobci*, "and killed him at the depression of the Kiljir." With finality, the chronicler recorded: "It is said that salt grew at the place where he was killed."

The nomads of the steppe had an ancient tale of the wolf and a boy. The story told of a female wolf finding a human baby boy whose feet had been cut off and who had been abandoned on the steppe to die. The mother wolf nursed the boy back to health, protected him, and reared him. When the boy grew older, there was no one else to love him, so he mated with the wolf. From their offspring descended all the Turkic tribes that spread out from Mongolia. From them arose all the notable Turkic nations of history.

Dayan Khan had been born when his father, Bayan Mongke, was fourteen, but Dayan Khan passed his fourteenth, fifteenth, and sixteenth years without an active marital relationship. Manduhai had either married or, more likely, promised to marry him when she made him khan. The Mongols did not usually make a distinction between engagement and marriage. A betrothed couple was referred to as husband and wife, but the marriage was not official until the groom-to-be completed his bride service. While exempt from the formal bride service, in a sense Dayan Khan was performing it by proving himself capable to fulfill his duties as Great Khan.

Around the year 1480, Dayan Khan and Manduhai took the final step into marriage and began to live together as husband and wife. At this time he was approximately seventeen years old, and she was thirty-three. They had already been together for ten years in a formal relationship as intended spouses. Of course, no mention survives to say when or how their intimate relationship began. Unlike some societies that crush together the marriage and sexual union, even forcing both events into the same day or within a few hours of each other, the Mongols had no such artificial scheduling. Boys and girls became engaged or married as part of a social union, but their physical intimacy remained entirely private and up to their own desire and discretion.

In the many marriages where the wife was older, she led the way with her own sense of timing and appropriateness. Certainly, in the case of Manduhai and Dayan Khan, she most likely set the agenda. Because the wives are biologically more mature than their husbands, they are often ready to bear children as soon as the husband passes through puberty.

Dayan Khan did not become a father until he was nineteen years old; probably most of the young warriors of his age were already fathers by this time. By comparison, the relationship between Dayan Khan and Manduhai, no matter when it began, seemed less hurried and somewhat more mature. In 1482, two years after their marital union, the couple produced twin boys. Over the next twelve years, Manduhai gave birth to eight children, including three sets of twins.

The Mongol mother did not normally take to bed for delivery or recovery, and she was expected to get up to care for the newborn child immediately. A nomadic people, who need to move constantly in search of water and grass for the animals or in flight from human or animal predators, could not afford to allow any members of the community, even a new mother, to remain immobile in bed for long. If Manduhai's delivery followed common procedure, then immediately after birth the mother scrubbed the infant's body with wool to clean it.

As she cleaned the baby, the mother usually examined the body carefully, searching for blemishes of the skin or irregularities beneath it. She also looked for the telltale sign that marked all children of the Mongol and Turkic tribes, the blue spot. The spot, which could easily be mistaken for a large bruise by someone unfamiliar with it, appeared clearly at the base of the spine, just at the top of the crack between the buttocks, and after a few years it faded away. For the Mongols, the spot had a nearly sacred significance that marked them clearly and distinguished them from other people. It may have been caused by the blood vessels showing through the very white skin on a place in the body with little fat to obscure the vessels; or perhaps, as they were taught, the Blue Spot marked them as the children of the Eternal Blue Sky. From long interaction with other peoples, the Mongols and Turkic tribes had taken this mark on the child as a distinctive separation that made them special as the Blue Spot People.

Once she cleaned the newborn baby, the mother typically swaddled it tightly in a sheep's fleece. Most babies spent the first year of life packed snugly into the fleece that, in turn, fit into a portable cradle made of bark, twigs, or leather that fit snugly under the mother's arm when she needed to go outside the *ger*. As the child grew a little older, he or she could ride on the saddle in front of the mother and father, carefully protected by the embrace of their two arms and legs. For longer trips, such as moving camp, the parents needed both arms for other tasks, and the young children would be put in a small basket strapped to the side of a camel or horse, as Manduhai had once transported Dayan Khan.

Just as the selection of a reign title for her husband showed Manduhai's clear political agenda, the names of her children made it even clearer, proclaiming her agenda loudly. She named each of her sons Bolod, "Steel." The first two were Toro Bolod and Ulus Bolod, meaning "Steel Government" and "Steel Nation."

Manduhai and Dayan Khan now controlled all the Mongols and Oirat north of the Gobi, and south of the Gobi they had the alliance of the eastern and central clans. By 1483, Ismayil had been driven all the way to the Hami oasis at the farthest edge of the Mongol territory, almost where it turns into uninhabitable desert. With his old ally and rival Beg-Arslan removed, he was the undisputed leader of the ragtag army left behind, and at any moment he might choose to attack again. He certainly would not sit idly at Hami pursuing the life of a melon farmer or winemaker. If the Mongols showed any sign of weakness or distraction, he would return.

Ismayil's presence at Hami served as a constant alternative to the rule of Manduhai and Dayan Khan. It would be hard for them to assert much authority over the southern tribes if they faced the constant threat that those tribes might bolt to Ismayil. He had to be removed.

Of course, Dayan Khan had a much deeper and more powerful reason to go after Ismayil. After being kidnapped by Ismayil nearly twenty years earlier, Dayan Khan's mother, Siker, was still with him. Hami was located too far across a barren strip between the Gobi and the sand desert to send a large army after Ismayil. There simply would not be enough grass for the animals to get there and return safely. But sometime around 1484, Manduhai and Dayan Khan assembled a select group of men with the mission to bring back Dayan Khan's mother and to kill or capture Ismayil.

Heretofore Dayan Khan had not expressed much interest in finding his missing mother, but something in him was changing. Now that he was fully grown and had become a father, some new longing awoke in him to connect again with his original family that had been shattered so soon after his birth.

Her Jade Realm Restored

MOST OF THE MEN CHOSEN FOR THE RAID AGAINST
Ismayil came from Manduhai's Choros clan. She trusted
them, and they best knew the area that had once been ruled
by her father. Because of the difficulty of fielding and supplying an
army over vast stretches of desert, Manduhai sent out a small, but
highly skilled, detachment that probably consisted of between 200 and
250 men. A man named Togochi Sigusi commanded the raiding party
and had 22 experienced officers with him; each of them probably led a
squad of about 10 men.

Ismayil lived out in the open fresh air of the desert in a nomad's
camp of *gers* and horses, where a man could breathe free and also
freely flee if needed. The circumstances revealed in the chronicles sug-
gest that he may have lost much of his support. Though he once ruled
over vast areas, Ismayil had now been forced to flee to the distant oasis
of Hami, which he did not actually control so much as harass its
inhabitants. The desert beyond the oases certainly could not support a
large army. Therefore Ismayil's troops had been sent elsewhere at the
time, or they had deserted him. He apparently retained so few followers that he no longer had sufficient men to post an adequate guard.

The chronicler of the *Altan Tobci* described how, well before anyone could hear their hoofbeats, a servant woman in the *ger* of
Ismayil sensed the vibrations in the ground made by the approaching
horsemen. "Why is the ground shaking?" she called out in panic,

instinctively bolting from the *ger* and running to the hitching post, where several horses always stood ready.

She untied a horse for Ismayil to ride out and investigate the noise. Ismayil set out alone, perhaps suspecting these might be a returning party of some of the men who had deserted him or someone on a trading mission. Although he was seemingly concerned, there is no mention of real anxiety, and he apparently made no effort to flee.

Ismayil approached the Mongol detachment. The leader, Togochi Sigusi, had an arrow ready, but he waited until he could see clearly enough to determine the rider's identity as Ismayil. When Ismayil came within firing distance and apparently did not suspect any harm, Togochi Sigusi raised the bow, aimed at Ismayil, and released the arrow. He was an experienced marksman who judged the shot well. The first arrow found its mark, and Ismayil Taishi fell dead from his horse onto the harsh desert ground.

His death came more as a final settling of scores than as a sustained struggle between adversaries. In a certain way, the killing in the desert paralleled the killing of the Golden Prince in the Gobi.

Killing Ismayil accomplished one of the two major goals of the raid; the other was to bring back Dayan Khan's mother. The party raced to the camp before the people there could suspect the fate of Ismayil and flee. The men would take everything from the camp in a clear demonstration that not only had Ismayil been killed, but his whole property and power base had been seized and distributed by the Mongol victors.

Togochi Sigusi found the mother, Siker. She had not attempted to flee but sat down inside her *ger*, unwilling to fight, yet refusing to be rescued. In the intervening two decades, Siker had not only accepted Ismayil as her husband, she had raised two new sons, Babutai and Burnai, with him as well. She had lost her first son, Dayan Khan, but she did not want to lose these two.

She had surely expected that this day would eventually come. Perhaps she sometimes longed for it and sometimes feared it. Now that the would-be rescuers had arrived, she was not happy to see them. She seemed to hope that if she refused to cooperate, they would leave her.

Togochi Sigusi ordered Siker out of her *ger*, but she began crying. He repeated the command, telling her to mount a horse and follow him, but she obstinately refused. Her stubbornness angered him, and yet he seemed to feel some compassion for her.

As a soldier loyal to her first husband and to her still living son, he asked her if the Golden Prince had been mean to her, because he could not understand why else she would be crying instead of celebrating her liberation from the man who murdered her husband. "Was your husband the *jinong* bad?" he asked her.

She did not answer.

He reminded her of her loyalty to her son and of what an important man he had become. "Is your son the Great Khan of no importance to you?" he asked. "Do you hold your people . . . in such contempt?"

Still she would not reply. She seemed to have no words and quite possibly did not know herself which of the many emotions she should be feeling at that moment.

Her continued silence and refusal to obey or cooperate increasingly irritated Togochi Sigusi. "Why are you weeping for another man?" he demanded, "for this traitor, our enemy Ismayil?"

Togochi Sigusi pulled out his sword and threatened her with it. He would not harm her. No matter how she frustrated or angered him, she was still the birth mother of the Great Khan, and he had been sent on the assignment to rescue her. He was determined to fulfill that mission even if she did not want to cooperate.

When Siker still refused to answer or obey, the exasperated officer ordered his men to seize her and forcefully mount her on a horse to be taken away as a captive. He ordered everyone in the camp rounded up and taken prisoner, including Siker's two sons and a young woman, either an older daughter of Ismayil or a younger wife. Later, in appreciation of his successful raid, Togochi Sigusi received her as his wife.

Upon his return, Togochi Sigusi announced to the khan, "I have killed the one who was envious of you. I have subdued the one who hated you."

He presented Dayan Khan to his mother, a woman of whom the

Khan had no memory and whom he had not seen in twenty years. No chronicle mentions what she said to him—or he to her—but she was by no means happy to see him.

The convoluted kinship, political, and emotional lines between them were inordinately complex, and no one had a precedent by which to act. Even if Siker was the birth mother to Dayan Khan, Manduhai had raised him and married him. There was no more of a place for Siker in the present or the future of her son than there had been in the past.

The failed effort to reconcile with Dayan Khan's mother left him and Manduhai where they had always been, emotionally alone. They remained totally dependent on each other and bereft of relatives who might help them.

Around the time of Ismayil's defeat, and only two years after the birth of her first two sons, Manduhai gave birth to a daughter, whom she named Toroltu—a name similar to Toro, meaning "State" or "Government," but which had the more specific meaning of giving life or birth and was part of the word for humanity. Over the next decade Manduhai had three additional pregnancies, resulting in five sons. Although the chronicles disagree as to precisely which were twins, they generally agree on the names and birth order. After Toroltu's birth, Manduhai had two boys, Barsu Bolod, meaning "Steel Tiger," and Arsu Bolod, "Steel Lion." Soon after came Alju Bolod and Ochir Bolod, followed by the final single birth of Ara Bolod.

After the birth of two sons, Manduhai or Dayan Khan could straightforwardly have terminated their relationship, or if they had been so inclined, disposed of each other. With such heirs, Manduhai could have ruled as regent without sharing power. Had she wished to live with Une-Bolod for example, she could easily have rid herself of her husband and taken whomever she wished.

As he grew older, Dayan Khan also had the option to replace Manduhai with another woman; he could simply have left her with her retainers in some distant part of the country, or if he feared what she might do under those circumstances, he could easily have arranged her death. Many rising young soldiers would be anxious to curry favor with the monarch by committing such an act, by testifying against her in a trial, or by assisting in any one of a dozen other methods to dispose of an unwanted queen. Such killings of khans and *khatuns* had occurred routinely among the Mongols in the generations since the successful attacks on Genghis Khan's daughters. Despite such opportunities to each be rid of the other and have a different life, Manduhai and Dayan Khan stayed together willingly and seemingly with great affection. They had a solid political and marital union.

As the sons grew older, Manduhai sent them to live with allies in different tribes. In this way, they became acquainted with different parts of the country in preparation for their role as rulers. At the same time, each son provided Manduhai with information about the tribe where he lived and served as her link to the local population. Manduhai began using her sons as "intercessors" in much the way that Genghis Khan had used his daughters.

The Chinese had left the Mongols to fight among themselves and scarcely noticed the comings and goings of the barbarians. The court had never been a vibrant place, but with the aging of Lady Wan and her increasing attention on keeping the emperor comfortable while making her formerly impoverished relatives rich, life in the court grew stagnant and stale.

Being pregnant, giving birth, and raising children did not initially slow Manduhai's military campaigns. She and Dayan Khan continued to live the life of nomadic warriors. Like Genghis Khan, Manduhai recognized that a nation conquered on horseback had to be ruled from horseback. Genghis Khan had fought and lived in the field, but his sons and grandsons had settled down to build cities, and eventually their descendants had lost all that Genghis Khan had acquired for them.

The couple crisscrossed the land fighting border skirmishes, raiding into China, trading along the Silk Route, putting down revolts, and imposing a stronger centralized rule than Mongolia had enjoyed in the intervening centuries since Genghis Khan's death. The combination of fighting and giving birth became ever more strenuous for Manduhai. She was forty years old when she became pregnant for the fourth time, with what turned out to be her final set of twins, and when she entered into what would be almost her final battle.

Although advanced in her pregnancy, Manduhai insisted on leading her troops into battle, just as she had so often done over the past fifteen years. In a scene reminiscent of her helmet falling from her head in the middle of battle during her first campaign against the Oirat, Manduhai unexpectedly lurched in her saddle. She then swiveled awkwardly and plunged to the ground, where she lay in a twisted heap. Had she been wounded, fainted, gone into labor, or simply fallen? Was she alive or dead?

The sudden fall of the highest commander on the battlefield presents a shocking spectacle for the soldiers, and such a misfortune can easily change the outcome of an engagement by disrupting the chain of command and confusing the warriors, as well as disheartening them at a crucial moment in their struggle. If seen by the enemy, the fall will almost certainly encourage them and reinvigorate their fighting.

Such an event can also provide an unexpected opportunity for potential rivals within the commander's army, giving them an opening into which they might rush forward and seize control. The year 1488 was the Year of the Earth Monkey, a capricious creature in whose era earthshaking events like this could be expected.

Horse-herding nomads, who spent their lives in the saddle, understood well that such a fall from a horse not only could result in serious damage, paralysis, or death, it carried extra symbolic significance. For a khan or other leader, the horse can symbolize the nation, and control of the horse parallels control of the state; a rider who cannot master a horse certainly cannot master a tribe or nation of unruly people. Thus Manduhai's fall from the horse held a deeper and more sinister meaning. The death of Genghis Khan himself had been preceded only a short time earlier by a fall from his horse. Through the literate history of Mongolia, chroniclers and observers had recorded the falls of khans from horses with more avid precision than their marriages, battles, or other events to which sedentary people might attribute greater importance.

For Manduhai, the fall occurred not only at an unfortunate moment in the battle, but at a potentially devastating moment in her life. After almost two decades of struggle, she had nearly, but not yet, achieved the complete reunification of all the steppe tribes that had followed Genghis Khan. Her goal loomed tantalizingly close as she led her troops into battle that day, but this one fall could jeopardize all that she had struggled to achieve.

Manduhai no longer displayed the physical strength or emotional stamina that she had had as a younger woman. She had fought many battles on and off the field of war; she had struggled against seemingly impossible odds to unite and rule the Mongol nation. It would seem only logical that at this stage in her life, even her most ardent followers might begin to waiver in their support or to wonder how much longer her destiny would allow her to rule and to lead.

Her husband, the Great Khan, who was still in his early twenties, lacked the necessary military and leadership experience, though he had succeeded against Beg-Arslan, and he had not shown the aptitude for command needed to control the vigorous and independent Mongol tribes. He had also shown no sign of wishing to oppose his wife or to contest her leadership. Instead, he remained doggedly faithful to her, just like the thousands of men who served under her command.

If the fall incapacitated Manduhai for even a few hours, one of her powerful or popular generals might step forward to replace her. At this moment, as she lay sprawled on the battlefield, her empire could easily be dismembered, or simply crumble. All an ambitious new commander need do, if he had the backing of even a small but dedicated band of warriors, was to grab one of her young sons, declare the child to be the new ruler, and exercise power as a self-declared regent.

At this moment, four of her closest warriors quickly raced around her like a protective wall. This maneuver came habitually to the warriors from years of training in both hunting and fighting. The protective wall that they formed on their hunts served to push the game ahead of them from an expansive area into a smaller, contained area where the hunters could more easily shoot it. In fighting, the same formation became a defensive maneuver when used to shield someone from the enemy like mares protecting their foals. Only once the protective wall had been put in place with the now stationary men did another jump from his horse to pull Manduhai up. Behind the human wall, the soldiers hoisted her onto another horse and escorted the injured queen, still surrounded by the now moving wall of men, from the field.

Not only did her men save Manduhai's life, they preserved her rule without anyone making a treasonous move or showing any inclination other than following her and fighting for her. The loyalty of her men had been tested, and the effectiveness and power of her years of military training and leadership had proved itself.

The chroniclers who recorded the event carefully transcribed the name of each man who helped her in this moment of crisis, as well as a description of the yellow horse that took her to safety. More important than the names of the men, the chronicle also recorded the tribe and clan of each of them. Each man came from a different tribe, and none from Manduhai's tribe or that of her husband. The chroniclers showed clearly that the queen not only had survived the fall, she had created a fast and strong loyalty among a wide range of steppe tribes. For the first time since the collapse of the empire of Genghis Khan, she had managed to unite the tribes into a single, reconstituted nation.

Manduhai's loyal warriors fought on to victory that day, and one month later she delivered twin sons, whom she named Ochir Bolod and Alju Bolod. They, too, would one day share in the power accumulated on the battlefield by their mother, as she gave them vast stretches of land to command in the east. Each of the men who helped to protect and rescue her that day received recognition and titles for what they had done.

In Beijing's Forbidden City on February 3, 1487, at the approximate age of fifty-seven, Lady Wan died. She had been the emperor's sole comfort and the one true love of his life, and he was not able to survive the loss. Seven months later, on September 9, 1487, he followed her into death. He was thirty-nine years old.

The defeat of Ismayil, followed closely by the death of the Ming emperor, opened a new opportunity for improved relations and new trade between the Mongols and China. Manduhai Khatun and Dayan Khan sent a trade delegation to Beijing in 1488, and with it they sent a letter written in Mongolian in which Dayan Khan asserted clearly his identity as the Great Khan of the Yuan. Had it been written in Chinese, the Ming probably could not have tolerated the title claimed by Dayan Khan, but being written in Mongolian made it more tolerable, or at least more easily overlooked. With some complaining about the inelegance of the Mongolian writing, the Ming officials accepted it and permitted the trade.

The new diplomacy of that year showed some flexibility on both sides and an indication that the Mongolian and Chinese governments would tolerate each other. Without completely altering their official stances and ideology, the Mongols tacitly acknowledged that they no longer ruled China and had no plans to do so again, while the Chinese officials recognized that that they did not control the Mongols beyond the Great Wall. Future relations would still be marred by raids and skirmishes, but the two countries were beginning to move toward a mutually acceptable form of commercial and diplomatic relations.

Manduhai had finished the fighting part of her career, but she had not yet completed her mission. As Genghis Khan taught, "The good of anything is in finishing it." He had accomplished far more than

Manduhai, but the arrogant greed of his sons and grandsons had destroyed his lifetime of work. Manduhai concentrated the remainder of her life in protecting what she had accomplished and making certain that the nation could sustain itself after her departure. With the same assiduous devotion she had applied to the battlefield and the unification of the Mongol nation, Manduhai and Dayan Khan now set to the reorganization of the Mongol government and its protection in the future.

When Genghis Khan took over the leadership of his small Mongol tribe, he was installed as khan. After fighting to unite the tribes for two decades, he called the *khuriltai* of 1206 to reorganize the government and to be recognized as the ruler of all the tribes. In the same way, when Manduhai installed Batu Mongke as Dayan Khan when he was seven years old, they ruled only a very small group. After nearly three decades of struggle to unite the country and to raise a family, they were ready to formally install him as khan over the entire nation.

In 1206, most of Genghis Khan's subjects had lived north of the Gobi, but by 1500, the majority of the Mongols lived south of the Gobi. The royal couple decided that the appropriate place to re-create the united Mongol nation would be in the south, which was also the land where Manduhai had grown up prior to being sent north to marry Manduul Khan. Genghis Khan's death at the edge of the Ordos also made it a sacred place associated with his memory.

Manduhai and Dayan Khan came south to strengthen their hold on the area and possibly to move their capital there. Sometime in the previous fifty years, the collection of *gers* mounted on carts and known as the Shrine of Genghis Khan had been brought south of the Gobi for the first time since he had died nearly three hundred years earlier. The dual monarchs' control of the shrine together with the *sulde*, the banner of Genghis Khan, illustrated to everyone that they had attained the blessings of both Genghis Khan and the Eternal Sky.

Dayan Khan had not been installed in front of the Genghis Khan shrine; Manduhai had used the Shrine of the First Queen instead. Now in the 1490s, at the height of their power, Manduhai and Dayan Khan wanted to reinstitute their Mongol nation in a manner similar to the way Genghis Khan had created it in 1206. Manduhai Khatun and Dayan Khan planned to reorganize the clans, install their sons in offices over them, and enthrone Dayan Khan for a second time, recognizing that he now ruled all the tribes.

The ceremony would not merely be a renewal of Dayan Khan's office but, more important, a renewal of the Mongol nation. Since the episode of the Great Khan with the rabbit in 1399, the Mongol khans had not been the true rulers of the country. Now, nearly a century later, the power of the lineage of Genghis Khan was being restored.

In preparation, the monarchs brought gifts for the shrine, including new lamps and large incense holders. Cattle and sheep were assembled for sacrifice in sets of nine before the *sulde* of Genghis Khan. Horsemen dressed in all white, riding white horses, and horsemen dressed in all black riding black horses formed an honor guard. Drummers beat on giant kettle drums, and heralds sounded the deep-throated roar of their large, five-foot-long brass horns. Here the monarchs proclaimed the new nation amid solemn ceremonies, banquets, and the three essential Mongolian games of horse racing, archery, and wrestling.

In long, alliterative recitations, the people learned again about their Mongol history. Genghis Khan was held up as the model for everyone: "Protecting those who were of peaceful conduct, exterminating those who were of violent manners, he was glorified as fortunate emperor."

The sayings and words of Genghis Khan were recalled to his people, reminding the monarchs and their subjects of their duties: "It is necessary to accept hard and inconvenient advice, to punish bad people with merciless law, to protect the numerous subjects with kindness, to strive after a good name which is honored everywhere."

The people brought gifts of fermented mare's milk, meat, dried dairy products, and fruits to the shrine, which after being presented were then consumed by the participants in a great banquet. The crisp, fresh smell of burning juniper incense hung like a cloud over the people and their gifts. As part of each official event, singers and musicians performed songs of praise and the reverential wailing of the long song. After the feasts and the heavy drinking, songs were sung with more secular themes honoring fast horses and true love.

To consolidate power within their family, Manduhai and Dayan Khan abolished many of the old titles of the Yuan era, including *chingsang* and *taishi*, which had been given to men outside the royal family. For most of the prior century, the warlords who had occupied those positions had exercised the real power over the Mongol government and had held the so-called Great Khans as puppets, at best, and as prisoners when they wished. Ismayil would be the last foreign regent to control the Mongol khans. Henceforth the Borijin clan would hold a near monopoly on all political offices within Mongol territory.

Manduhai and Dayan Khan bestowed awards for bravery, made new marriages, gave out titles, created a new tax system, and presented gold seals to the new officeholders. Their actions deliberately and carefully recalled the deeds of Genghis Khan, but they had decided that, despite restoring the rule of his family, they would not restore exactly the same type of government he had created. In the last three hundred years, the needs had changed, and neither Manduhai nor Dayan Khan had any intention of creating an empire beyond the Mongol steppe.

In an effort to avoid future confrontations of the type that tore apart the family of Genghis Khan in the two generations following his death, Manduhai and Dayan Khan sought to abolish the title *khan*, save for the one single Great Khan. Genghis Khan permitted his children to use the titles *khan* and *khatun*, or "king" and "queen," but now there would only be one of each: Dayan Khan and Manduhai Khatun. The highest-ranking son would be *jinong*, "the crown prince," and according to their plan, he would one day be the only member of the family to take the title *khan*. All others would be called *taiji*, meaning "royal lord." The one daughter would take the title *gunj*, another term for princess. Manduahai and Dayan Khan had no need for the old title *guregen*, "imperial son-in-law," since they had only one daughter; they arranged a strategic marriage for her with a leader of the Khalkh tribe of the eastern Mongols.

Out of respect for the mother of the Great Khan, Dayan Khan and Manduhai gave Siker the title *taikhu,* "dowager empress." They thought that, if treated with respect and living in comfort, she might gradually soften her heart toward her son. However, she had grown up as a common herding girl in the southern Gobi and had lived a nomadic life of raiding. Now the life of an empress mother seemed empty to her, and she died soon thereafter.

Manduhai and Dayan Khan confronted the same problem that had created so many difficulties for Genghis Khan. Genghis Khan found that no matter how many times he fought and conquered tribes such as the Tatars, they would soon be back at war again. No permanent peace seemed possible, and alliances held only so long as the allies maintained the mood to be at peace with one another. Just as Genghis Khan had finally decided to install his daughters and sons as the heads of the various vassal nations of the empire, Manduhai and Dayan Khan reorganized all the tribes by killing or otherwise removing the enemy leaders and installing their own sons in power.

Rather than enslave or exile any of the defeated tribes, Manduhai and Dayan Khan used a combination of old and some new structures to create a Mongol nation of two wings—the Left and the Right— each of which was divided into three tribes, or *tumen,* of ten thousand. Because of this primary feature, the Mongols called this system the Six Tumen, which would come to be used as another name for their country.

The new system of clans and tribes expanded the concept of Mongol to embrace everyone living in the territory, no matter what their former ethnicity. Included were diverse and often antagonistic groups such as the Three Guards along the border with the Ming; the old imperial Ossetian and Kipchak guards from the reign of Khubilai Khan; lingering remnants of the Onggud and Tangut; and some of the Uighurs. The Six Tumen consisted of new geographic-kinship groups.

In the east were the Chakhar, Khalkh, and Khorchin, and to the west were the Ordos, Tumed, and Yungshiyebu. Each of these contained a set of *otogs,* which were something like the old clans but were comparable to an occupational caste or a geographic group as well and constituted the primary social units of allegiance for individuals.

Within the Mongols, there would no longer be a distinction between the competing lineages descended from Genghis Khan's four sons. Henceforth, they were all part of the Borijin. Other branches of the family descended from Genghis Khan's brothers were also folded into the main body, with one single exception. The descendants of Khasar, the people of Manduhai's early general and supporter Une-Bolod, were allowed to keep an independent identity within the Borijin clan.

For a people not accustomed to reading, the Mongols had to learn the new organization by means of easily learned songs such as "Zurgaan Tumen Mongol" ("The Six Tumen of the Mongols"), which listed the tribes with some pertinent information about each group's geographic location and its social function within the united Mongol nation. The Khalkh were described as "located in the Khangai Mountains, as a guard from strangers," or the Uriyanghai as "hunters of gazelle and wild animals, protectors from thieves, and diggers of wells." Through these and similar songs, the people came to know who they were or, at least, who they were expected to be in the new nation.

The monarchs devised a plan to station their sons, the Seven Steels, around the edges of the empire to protect it as a permanent wall of steel, and they established a series of permanent encampments along the Chinese border. These eventually grew to approximately thirty bases from which the Mongols could keep watch on the Chinese and from which they could launch raids into China. Each settlement had a permanent cadre of soldiers stationed there, as well as animals and food supplies if a larger army needed to be sent in to assist them.

For the Mongols, the bases required minimal cost to maintain. In addition to keeping their own herds of animals, the soldiers had ample supplies of antelope, which they hunted for meat and for hides. The bases seem to have created fear and concern in the Ming court far beyond the actual danger that they posed. The Chinese responded with a new round of wall building in order to place a permanent protection between the Chinese urban and agricultural population centers and these Mongol bases.

The new Mongol nation, or Six Tumen, included Buddhists and Muslims with a mixture of the earlier Christian groups who had long since lost all contact with the outside Christian world. Manduhai and Dayan Khan did not choose among these religions, and they let their people follow any that they wanted. The government and ruling family, however, maintained a spiritual focus on a state cult formed around Genghis Khan and his shrine.

Through the work of Manduhai and Dayan Khan, "the government was rectified and humanity was united." In this time, "peace, unity and prosperity spread throughout all the people." Yet not all of their reforms succeeded. The effort to curtail usage of the title *khan* failed as each of their sons scrambled to take the title in his own domain.

After the *khuriltai,* Manduhai Khatun and Dayan Khan maintained their capital south of the Gobi and the Mongolian Plateau, along the Chinese border, in what is today Inner Mongolia. Manduhai had abandoned the quieter northern grazing grounds of the royal family favored by her first husband, Manduul Khan. The southern area served as the source and route for the trade goods out of China, and as the ideal base for the Mongol raids. The Mongols often made their camp in the Ordos, which offered them the most varied points of access into China and the Silk Route. Their presence troubled the Chinese commanders along the border and encouraged them to raid the Mongols more frequently.

The defensive wall remained more of a plan than a reality, and the Ming officers still had to defend their territory against Mongol raids. Unable or unwilling to mount substantial campaigns against them or to engage in large battles, the Chinese army occasionally struck out against the Mongols in small raids. On one such occasion in 1501, the border authorities learned that Manduhai and Dayan Khan had set up camp in a lightly defended area in the Ordos. They launched a raid, and the pair had to flee in the middle of the night, barely escaping their pursuers.

Following their near capture in the Ordos, Manduhai and Dayan Khan recognized that despite the advantages of the location, it would always be hard to defend because they were south of the Yellow River, which they could cross only in the winter, when it froze. They had escaped this time, but the mere possibility of their entrapment or capture in the Great Loop might entice other Chinese generals to mount campaigns against them. As important as the area was strategically for the Mongols and as important as it was to Manduhai as the area where she was born and grew up, the monarchs decided to move their capital back north of the Gobi into Mongolia proper.

Because Manduhai was born in the south, she understood it, but she also understood the dangers for nomadic people living there. Eight hundred years earlier, a wise Turkish khan had cautioned the steppe tribes against staying too close to the cities. In stones carved with his words and erected near Karakorum, he told them that the steppe was the best place on Earth to live. He said that the city people "give us gold, silver, and silk in abundance," and that their words "have always been sweet and the materials of the Chinese people have always been soft." But if you settle in their area, warned Bilge Khan, "you will die!"

One of Bilge Khan's ministers, Tonyukuk, also recorded similar words on another set of stones, stating that Heaven would kill them as punishment for giving up their steppe freedom and submitting to the agricultural kingdoms. He encouraged the steppe people to remain always nomadic, to erect no buildings, and to resist the settled people at all costs. If they became too weak to resist, they should retreat into the mountains, but under no circumstances should they submit to rule from beyond the steppe.

The spirit of these men had certainly defined the prevailing attitude of the steppe tribes and had been one also accepted by Genghis Khán. The Mongols would die if they left Mongolia. The Mongol nation would die if the people gave up herding and settled in cities. With such strong ideas in their minds, Manduhai and Dayan Khan did not return to the ancient ruins of Karakorum for their capital. They would have no city with walls of stone or buildings of wood; there would be no palace, no market, and no temple.

Manduhai Khatun and Dayan Khan rejected the trappings of empire and instead withdrew to the Kherlen River near the hearth of the Borijin clan, where Genghis Khan had grown up. Along these banks, Temujin had first gathered his noble people and founded his nation in the year 1206, taking for himself the title of Genghis Khan. Most importantly, he was buried close by at a secret spot in the silence of Burkhan Khaldun. The old palace *gers* of his wife and mother still resided here, and Mongols came from everywhere to pray and to remember him and them.

This was the first tribal capital of the Mongols, not the imperial capital of the Mongol Empire. This was the place where Genghis Khan divided his empire among his sons and daughters. This was the place where he had invested Alaqai Beki with the Onggud nation and Al-Altun with the Uighurs, and where he had made his nuptial speeches to them, charging them with their responsibilities to their nation. This was the place where the *Secret History* had been written. Perhaps more than anything else that she did, this choice demonstrated Manduhai's commitment to the ancient history of the Mongols and showed her lack of interest in maintaining the pretense of an empire or of expanding into the territory of the Chinese or the Muslims. For her people and her children, she sought a secured and protected Mongol nation of herders, not a world empire of cities and foreign lands.

After Manduhai and Dayan Khan had been only a few years in their new northern capital, a delegation of the southern tribes crossed the Gobi to request their rulers' return. The southern tribes had grown tired of the constant bickering, and they had once again felt the oppressive raids of the warlords from the Silk Route oases and the Chinese. In particular, they mentioned that they had paid lower taxes under Manduhai and Dayan Khan than they were now required to pay under their new warlord.

Rather than going south themselves, the couple decided to send a son to govern for them. In their last official act together, Manduhai Khatun and Dayan Khan appointed their second son, Ulus Bolod, as the new *jinong*. Manduhai retired, turning over the control of the empire to her husband and children.

In 1508, Ulus Bolod headed south to assume his office in front of the Shrine of Genghis Khan, where his parents had created the new Mongol nation. A small group of retainers accompanied him across the Gobi, but no army seemed necessary.

Yet another warlord had begun pushing into the area. Called Ibari, or Ibrahim, he wished to replicate the power once held by Beg-Arslan and Ismayil. He and his allies incited discontent against Borijin rule. "He has come saying he will rule our country," they complained. "Has he come saying he will rule our heads?"

Ulus Bolod arrived at the Shrine of Genghis Khan and was installed the same day in his new office of *jinong* by allies there. The priests who operated the shrine seemed eager to have a descendant of Genghis Khan ruling in the territory where they were now located, since this development would only enhance their own position.

On the second day, Ulus Bolod planned a long ancestral tribute of honor to Genghis Khan, thereby stressing his direct lineal descent from him and the restoration of his family's power. This kinship connection, of course, set Ulus Bolod clearly apart from the other local leaders who did not belong to his Borijin clan. On Ulus Bolod's way to the shrine on the second morning, he could see a large crowd gathered for the ceremony which he was about to conduct.

Before he reached the entry to the *ger*, an unknown enemy stepped out of the crowd and stopped him. The man claimed that Ulus Bolod owed him a horse in payment for a wrong done by some other family member. Ulus Bolod refused to give up his horse, but the man would not let him pass. In anger, Ulus Bolod pulled out his sword and sliced off the man's head. Such a bloodletting in front of the holiest of shrines upset everyone and proved a very bad omen for Ulus Bolod.

Having arranged this confrontation, Ibari and his men rushed forward and incited the crowd against Ulus Bolod. Another man jumped out from the crowd to offer his own horse to Ulus Bolod, on which he could flee, but the conspirators already had their troops ready and they barred any escape. Ulus Bolod and the few men with him dashed into the holy tent itself for refuge, where the priests tried to protect them, but the hostile troops began shooting their arrows. In the ensuing battle at the shrine, it is said that Ulus Bolod managed to kill one of the enemy, and one of Ulus Bolod's men wounded Ibari, but the small group could not outfight the larger force attacking them. The new *jinong* Ulus Bolod was killed after only one day in office.

Dayan Khan vowed revenge for the assassination of his and Manduhai's son, calling on the Eternal Blue Sky and the spirit of Genghis Khan to help him. "May you heaven, and next, you Holy Lord know the blood which has been shed and abandoned, and the bones which lie drying."

Dayan Khan dutifully called his army and prepared to lead them south to reinstate control over the southern tribes, chase out Ibari, and install another son as *jinong*. He would henceforth rule from his base located in the central part of the Mongol territories south of the Gobi, in what is today Inner Mongolia, as head of the Chakhar clan of Mongols. His sons would occupy the lands to his left and right.

Now past sixty, Manduhai lacked the stamina to ride a horse across the Gobi one more time and charge back into battle. She had been at war for more than thirty-five years. Manduhai and Dayan Khan had scarcely been apart in those years. Ever since they came together, they had shared one life between them. Now the time had come for Dayan Khan to go on without her. He was in his early forties and had many years left ahead of him to rule, but she would not be there to see it. It seemed as though there would never be an end to the violence, that as soon as one rebel or warlord was struck down, another rose to replace him. The long struggle of Manduhai to unify her nation seemed to have been in vain.

Manduhai would never again see Dayan Khan—the crippled boy whom she had dressed in large boots and stood before the Shrine of the First Queen to make him khan, the boy whom she put in a basket and took to war, and the man whom she married and with whom she raised eight children. As Dayan Khan and his sons rode south from Manduhai's *ger*, it had been almost exactly three hundred years since Alaqai Beki had stood before her mother, Borte, and presented her cheek to be sniffed before riding south to assume her rule over the Onggud. From the same area near the Kherlen River, Manduhai sent her sons and husband back to complete the work that she had pursued throughout her life.

Whether Manduhai sniffed her sons on both cheeks or not we cannot now know, but maybe she casually demurred the offer of the second cheek. "I will sniff the other one when you come back." Of course, she would not cry. As Dayan Khan and her sons rode south toward the sun, she would pick up her pail and toss milk into the air with her *tsatsal*. They would not look back at their wife and mother, and she would stand there throwing the milk until they passed over the horizon. As long as she was able in the closing years of her life, she would arise in the mornings and repeat the ceremony of aspersing milk for her absent husband and children. Maybe she occasionally rode off into the deserted steppe to share her pain with Mother Earth.

Manduhai remained behind to die, but the nation she had resurrected did not die. She had saved the Mongols and created a government that would protect them for generations. Her Jade Realm now stretched from the Siberian tundra and Lake Baikal in the north, across the Gobi, to the edge of the Yellow River and south of it into the Ordos.

The lands extended from the forests of Manchuria in the east, beyond the Altai Mountains, and out onto the steppes of Central Asia.

More than two centuries after Genghis Khan's death, Queen Manduhai revived the dying dynasty and made it vibrant and new. When she could not defeat her enemies, Manduhai eluded them, learned from her losses, and prepared for the next battle. In keeping with the Mongolian admonition, if she did not win the first seven times, she would win on the eighth. Manduhai defiantly survived every tragedy, obstacle, and horror that befell her. Just as she gave control of her life to no man, she surrendered her army to no enemy, and she relinquished her people to no foreign nation. Heaven did not grant her a great destiny; instead, in the words of the Mongol chronicle, it allowed her to shape "the destiny of her own choosing." In history, those individuals who refuse the options presented by the circumstances of life usually end up broken. Those few who reject what life offers and still find their own path are rightfully called heroes. In creating her own destiny, she also chose the destiny for her nation.

Dayan Khan lived on and continued to lead his people down the white road of enlightenment. He restored order to the south and ruled the united Mongolia without further serious disruptions. He married two more women, and had four more sons. He led numerous campaigns. The chronicles leave a frustrating mystery in stating that his reign ended in 1517, only a few years after Manduhai's death; yet his death is not recorded until 1543, which would have been more than thirty years after her death, when he was seventy-nine years old.

In the sixteenth century, the Mongols began converting to Buddhism. In 1578, Altan Khan and Queen Noyanchu Junggen, both descendants of Queen Manduhai and Dayan Khan, bestowed on the Tibetan monk Sonam Gyatso the old Mongolian title of *dalai*, meaning "sea" or "ocean," which had first been used by Genghis Khan's son Ogodei as his title, Dalai Khan, meaning "Sea of Power." Henceforth the lama and his future reincarnations would bear the title Dalai

Lama, "Sea of Knowledge." Not long afterward, in 1592, another of Queen Manduhai and Dayan Khan's descendants was discovered to be the new Dalai Lama. Reigning under the title Dalai Lama IV, he was the only Mongolian to hold the office.

Buddhism brought Mongolia to new heights of literature, arts, and architecture. The Great Wall that divided the Mongol and Chinese nations did not guarantee peace, but it brought a new stability to the region. The foreign warlords did not return, leaving the Mongols and their neighbors to work out their own trade and commercial relations.

Manduhai and Dayan Khan's descendants managed to keep the country independent until the conquest by the Manchu in the seventeenth century. Most of the royal family continued to thrive under the Manchu and their Qing Dynasty, founded in 1644, but the country as a whole and the common people suffered wretchedly until liberation in 1911.

The lineage of Manduhai and Dayan Khan remained in power until the twentieth century. In the political turmoil of World War II, together with the prior revolution in Mongolia during the 1920s, and subsequently in China in the 1940s, most of Manduhai and Dayan Khan's identifiable descendants were deliberately killed by various factions seeking to eradicate the past for different reasons.

Almost all Mongols recognize Queen Manduhai the Wise and Dayan Khan as the two greatest monarchs in the eight centuries of Mongolian history after Genghis Khan. For Mongols, Manduhai continues to symbolize the one person who sacrificed all to save her nation and thereby to protect them, and for this reason they often call her simply Queen Manduhai the Wise. The earlier queens faded from public memory, but elements of their stories were folded into hers so that Manduhai Khatun became the quintessential Mongol queen, combining all the others into one persona and one lifetime.

No matter how assiduously the censors in the centuries that followed cut the Mongolian queens from the records and altered the texts, and no matter how much foreigners might scoff at their history, the people remembered. In their songs and poems, in their art, and in the names they gave their children and the stories that they told sitting around the fire at night, the Mongols preserved the memory of Queen Manduhai the Wise.

The Secrets of History

I N THE SUMMER OF 1492, CHRISTOPHER COLUMBUS SAILED out of Europe across the Atlantic Ocean carrying a letter from the Spanish monarchs Isabella and Ferdinand intended for the khan of the Mongols, but not knowing the name of the Asian ruler, the Spanish clerk left a blank space to be filled in upon arrival. Columbus never reached Asia to deliver the letter, and history never filled in the missing name.

In four epic voyages, Columbus searched for the Mongol khan in Cuba, Puerto Rico, Venezuela, Honduras, and small islands across the Caribbean. None of the natives could tell him the name of the Great Khan, and when Columbus died in 1506, he still had come no closer to finding the court of the Mongols or even the names of the rulers. Throughout all the years of Columbus's search, it was Manduhai Khatun and Dayan Khan for whom he was searching.

Columbus showed how seriously he and others of his time took the history of the Mongols, whom they recognized as one of the great forces of history, but one about which they knew very little. He was not the first to go in search of the Mongols. A hundred years earlier, in the fourteenth century, as Geoffrey Chaucer wrote *The Canterbury Tales*, the first book in the English language, he also launched a literary search for the elusive Genghis Khan and his daughter. Chaucer had traveled widely on diplomatic missions through Europe and had learned of Genghis Khan, whom he called Cambuyskan. In "The

Squire's Tale," Genghis Khan's daughter, the fictional Canace, acquired magical power over humans and animals; she communicated with birds and knew the use of every plant. Chaucer never finished "The Squire's Tale." The story, as much as was written, seemed much more of a European romance than anything to do with the Mongols; yet we will never know where it was going to end.

The Tatar tale was the only story Chaucer left unfinished in his book, and other writers through the centuries have occasionally sought to complete it. English poet John Milton described Chaucer's fragmentary tale as a "sage and solemn" story "where more is meant than meets the ear." In his poem "Il Penseroso," Milton called upon Orpheus, the Greek hero of music and poetry, to help him complete Chaucer's tale of contests, trophies, and enchantments in the life of bold Genghis Khan and his gifted daughter who communed with animals.

Even when learned poets such as Chaucer and Milton could not complete the accounts of these unique Mongol women, their poems constantly remind us of what is missing in our history. The poets preserved what the censors destroyed.

The memory of the Mongol queens lived on in marble as well as in literature. In 1631, after Mumtaz Mahal died during the birth of her fourteenth child, her husband, the Moghul emperor Shah Jahan, began the building of a magnificent tomb for her. The most gifted Muslim and Hindu artisans of the era brought a variety of cultural styles and motifs, and yet beneath it all the building took the simple domed shape of a Mongol *ger*. The emperor was a distant heir of Genghis Khan and Borte. His ancestors had been *guregen*, married to the women of the Borijin clan, and he was descended from those women though the line of Chaghatai. As though guided by an ancient Mongol memory, he placed the entrance to the Taj Mahal facing south like every Mongol *ger*, toward the sun. Built to honor one Moghul queen, the Taj Mahal, the most beautiful building ever erected, embodies the spirit of all the Mongol women.

In 1710, while writing the first biography of Genghis Khan, the

French scholar François Pétis de La Croix published a book of tales and fables combining Persian, Turkish, Mongol, and Arabic themes. One of his longest and best stories derived from the history of Khutulun, who rode into battle with her father and refused to marry any man who could not defeat her in wrestling. In his version, she became Turandot, meaning "Turkish Daughter," the nineteen-year-old daughter of Altoun Khan, emperor of China, but the story mostly focused on Calaf, son of Timurtasch (Timur Taishi), who was also nineteen and determined to woo her. Instead of challenging her suitors in wrestling, Pétis de La Croix had her confront them with three riddles. Instead of wagering mere horses, the suitor had to forfeit his life if he failed to answer correctly.

Pétis de La Croix wrote of Turandot: "She united with her ravishing beauty such a cultivated mind that she not only knows everything which it is customary to teach persons of her rank, but even the sciences which are only learned by men, she knows how to write the different characters of several languages, she knows arithmetic, geography, philosophy, mathematics, and above all, theology."

Fifty years later, the popular Italian playwright Carlo Gozzi saw the dramatic potential of the story for the stage, and in 1761 he premiered his play *Turandotte* in Venice, the hometown of Marco Polo. It offered the tale of a "tigerish woman" whose "greatest sin is her unrelenting pride." In a combined effort by two of the greatest literary talents of the era, Friedrich von Schiller translated the play into German as *Turandot, Prinzessin von China*, and Johann Wolfgang von Goethe directed it on the stage in Weimar in 1802.

The Italian composer Giacomo Puccini was working on his opera *Turandot* when he died in 1924, and a colleague completed it. "It's useless shouting in Sanskrit, in Chinese, or Mongolian!" Puccini wrote of his heroine who refused to marry. She challenged men because of the wrongs done to one of her female ancestors "who ruled in silence and pure joy, defying the abhorred tyranny of man with constancy and firmness." The earlier queen's reign had ended abruptly "when the King of the Tartars unfurled his seven standards," and "in that cruel night when her young voice was stifled!" The opera of the Mongol ice queen never attained the popularity of Puccini's other Asian heroine, Madame Butterfly, who lives and then must die for the love of a man.

The public memories of unusual people live on in sometimes unexpected but significant ways. Today, when Mongolian men wrestle, they wear a particular vest with long sleeves, a small back, but no shoulder covering and a completely open front. According to lore, they wear this in honor and in fear of Khutulun. To prevent being defeated by another woman, the open vest allows each wrestler to inspect his opponent's chest before wrestling and make sure that he is genuinely male.

At the end of each match, the winner stretches out his arms to display his chest again to his opponent and to the spectators, and he slowly waves his arms in the air like a bird, turning for all to see. For the winner it is a victory dance, but it is still a lingering tribute to the time when Mongolia had one princess wrestler whom no man ever defeated.

Such folk stories may or may not be accurate, but they carry a cultural truth that transcends the torn, lost, and censored documents of the past. History may have turned its back on the queens of the Mongols, but the people have never forgotten their heroines.

I first heard the name of Manduhai in 1998 while staying on the Mongolian steppe at Avarga, the place where Genghis Khan created the Mongol nation, where he installed his daughter Alaqai over the Onggud and Al-Altun over the Uighur, where the *Secret History* was written, where Borte maintained her court, and where Manduhai and Dayan Khan returned after their conquests of the south. I was there researching the Mongol Empire when, as so often happened in my work, a group gathered to give me advice, ask questions, or just enjoy their new freedom of being able to speak openly about history, religion, sex, or any other topic.

"I am only a herder," an older woman said, as though apologizing for not being a scholar. Her worn and creased face contrasted starkly with the smooth, bright blue *deel* she wore for the visit. "You should know that Genghis Khan was reincarnated as a woman. . . ." She hesitated as though unsure how her listeners might respond, then proceeded firmly in saying what she believed: "It was our Queen Manduhai."

Somewhat embarrassed, other people assured me that Genghis Khan had not been reincarnated, and it certainly would not be right for him to be a woman. The subject was closed, and we all returned to our respective *gers*.

Later that night, amid enthusiastic singing and prolonged drinking from a large porcelain bowl of fermented horse milk, people regaled me with several versions of the story of Manduhai. Much of what they said seemed too romantic or too trivial to have any use in my research. I quickly tired of the drinking, singing, and stories.

In my rush to judgment, Manduhai seemed little more than another of those mystical figures that populate the nationalist lore of every country and exercise a magical hold on the imagination of locals, but offer little attraction for foreigners. When the celebrants began singing emotional songs about Manduhai's service to the nation and her sacrifice for them, I was moved by the intensity of their feelings, but I still dismissed her. She obviously meant much to them, but little to me. I was now on the hunt for more important historical prey; I was searching for the life of Genghis Khan, not his fanciful reincarnation.

Through the years I continued to trip over Manduhai in my Mongolian travels and research, and I persisted in finding my way around her by ignoring her as a lesser character in the majestic tales of Asian history. My opinion of Manduhai did not change until I began struggling with the censored sections of the *Secret History* regarding Genghis Khan's daughters. Gradually I saw the link emerging between the omitted names of the *Secret History* and the missing name in the letter carried by Columbus. I realized that her story grew out of theirs; yet they remain unknown. Thinking that these accounts might be interesting footnotes in Mongolian history, I wanted to fill in some small pieces of these stories, but the more I discovered, the more I found missing. The holes kept growing.

As soon as I felt close, I found another cut document, garbled name, sliced page, mutilated text, changed date, or missing title. Religious clerics, political ideologues, and government bureaucrats do not have the right to change history. The truth may be hard to find, but it is out there—somewhere. If we do not continue the work, the truth remains hidden. If we stop the search, then the censor has defeated us.

Had I, at that early moment in my work, found a book that explained the role of these Mongol queens, or even had I found this book that I have now written, I doubt that I would have believed much of it. Only grudgingly and piecemeal did the story of the daughters of Genghis Khan and of Queen Manduhai the Wise arise from the dust around me, and only hesitantly and somewhat unwillingly did I acknowledge that individuals whom I had never studied in school or read about in any book could, in fact, be figures of tremendous historic importance.

What does it matter that one barbarian khan, whether male or female, replaced another as leader of the horde on some forsaken spot with an unpronounceable name in the bowels of Asia? They helped shape our world in ways that we do not see. Their influence continues on the modern map of national boundaries, in the Buddhism of the modern day, and in the legacy of the Silk Route that became the prototype for the modern world system. The story of these Mongol queens forms a secret history of the origins of the modern world; it is an unrecognized, but important part of our own story. Ultimately, the goal of rediscovering their story is to assess the unacknowledged influence they have had on our lives and the relevance they still have today.

The great queens of Mongolia protected their families throughout their lifetimes. Genghis Khan created the nation and inspired it, but the queens gave it life. Like their father, these dedicated queens did not waste time, effort, and emotion building monuments; they built a nation. Like the lingering footprints and fossils of past ages, the evidence of their lives remain, if only we are willing to search for it, willing to see it when we find it.

The censors who sliced the pages did not destroy the history; they only hampered our ability to see it. In some ways the evidence is still all around us, scarcely even hidden, merely unrecognized. There are architectural tributes to the lives and importance of these women in enduring structures as varied as the Taj Mahal of India and the Great Wall of China. The music of Puccini, the plays of Schiller, the poetry of Chaucer, and even the dances of Mongolian wrestlers keep the stories alive.

It is quite understandable that Columbus did not know the name of the Mongol monarch for whom he was searching when he sailed to America; he lived in an era of limited knowledge of an unknown world. Today we have the opportunity to know what he did not, to fill in the story that eluded Chaucer.

Amid the carefully censored documents, the conveniently lost manuscripts, and the frustratingly unfinished poems, the answers to a gripping mystery still wait to be slowly dug out again. Like the archaeologist collecting fragments from an ancient, broken mosaic, we may recover only a portion of the original portrait, but even in the faded colors of the chipped pieces we ascertain a glorious image of our history that tells us more about who we are today by seeing who they were then. We may never find the undelivered letter that Columbus carried on his momentous voyage, but it is never too late in history to fill in a missing name.

Ulaanbaatar, Mongolia
Year of the Ox, 2009

Abu-Umar-I-Usman. *Tabakat-I-Nasirir: A General History of the Muhammadan Dynasties of Asia.* Translated by H. G. Raverty. London: Gilbert & Rivington, 1881.

Al-Din, Rashid. *Rashiduddin Fazullah's Jami'u't-Tawarikh: Compendium of Chronicles.* Translated by W. M. Thackson. Cambridge, MA: Harvard University Department of Eastern Languages and Civilizations, 1998.

———. *The Successors of Genghis Khan.* Translated by John Andrew Boyle. New York: Columbia University Press, 1971.

Andrews, Peter Alford. *Felt Tents and Pavilions: The Nomadic Tradition and Its Interaction with Princely Tentage.* London: Melisende, 1999.

Atwood, Christopher P. *Encyclopedia of Mongolia and the Mongol Empire.* New York: Facts on File, 2004.

Baljinnyam, B. *Mongolchuudin Buren Tuukhiin Tovchoon.* Ulaanbaatar, Mongolia: Admon, 2006.

Barfield, Thomas J. *The Perilous Frontier: Nomadic Empires and China 221 BC to AD 1757.* Cambridge, MA: Blackwell, 1989.

Bawden, Charles, trans. *The Mongol Chronicle Altan Tobči.* Wiesbaden: Otto Harrassowitz, 1955.

Bira, Sh. "The Mongols and Their State in the Twelfth to the Thirteenth Century." In *History of Civilizations of Central Asia,* vol. 4, part 1, edited by M. S. Asimov and C. E. Bosworth. Paris: UNESCO, 243–59.

Biran, Michal. *The Empire of the Qara Khitai in Eurasian History: Between China and the Islamic World.* Cambridge, UK: Cambridge University Press, 2005.

———. *Qaidu and the Rise of the Independent Mongol State in Central Asia.* Richmond, UK: Curzon, 1997.

Bold, Bat-Ochir. *Mongolian Nomadic Society: A Reconstruction of the*

"Medieval" History of Mongolia. New York: St. Martin's, 2001.

Bretschneider, E. *Mediæval Researches from Eastern Asiatic Sources.* New York: Barnes & Noble, 1967.

Carpini, Giovanni DiPlano. *The Story of the Mongols Whom We Call the Tartars.* Translated by Erik Hildinger. Boston: Branden, 1996.

Cleaves, Francis Woodman. *The Secret History of the Mongols.* Cambridge, MA: Harvard University Press, 1982.

Elverskog, Johan, trans. *The Jewel Translucent Sūtra: Altan Khan and the Mongols in the Sixteenth Century.* Leiden, Netherlands: Brill, 2003.

Enkhbaatar, N. *Chinggis Khaan.* Ulaanbaatar: Ungut Hevlel, 2006.

Enkhtsetseg, D. *Mongolin Nuuts Tobchoo ba Emegteichuud.* Ulaanbaatar, Mongolia: Admon, 2008.

Franke, Wolfgang. *History of the Eastern Mongols During the Ming Dynasty from 1368 to 1634.* Part 2, *Addenda and Corrigenda.* Chengtu, China: Chinese Cultural Studies Research Institute of West China Union University, 1949.

Goodrich, L. Carrington, ed. *Dictionary of Ming Biography: 1368–1644.* New York: Columbia University Press, 1976.

Halbertsma, Tjalling H. F. *Early Christian Remains of Inner Mongolia: Discovery, Reconstruction and Appropriation.* Leiden, Netherlands: Brill, 2008.

Holmgren, J. "Observations on Marriage and Inheritance Practices in Early Mongol History." *Journal of Asian History* 20 (1986): 127–92.

Howorth, Henry H. *History of the Mongols from the 9th to the 19th Century.* London: Longmans, Green, 1876.

Humphrey, Caroline. "Chiefly and Shamanist Landscapes in Mongolia." In *The Anthropology of Landscapes,* edited by Eric Hirsch and Michael O'Hanlon, 135–62. Oxford: Clarendon Press, 1995.

Jagchid, Sechin, and Van Jan Symons. *Peace, War, and Trade Along the Great Wall: Nomadic-Chinese Interaction Through Two Millennia.* Bloomington: Indiana University Press, 1989.

Juvaini, Ata-Malik. *Genghis Khan: The History of the World-Conqueror.* Translated by J. Boyle. Seattle: University of Washington Press, 1997.

Krader, Lawrence. *Social Organization of the Mongol-Turkic Pastoral Nomads.* Bloomington: Indiana University Press, 1963.

Lam, Yuan-Chu. "Memoir on the Campaign Against Turfan: An Annotated Translation of Hsü Chin's *P'ing-fan shih-mo* written in 1503." *Journal of Asian History* 42 (1990): 105–60.

Linduff, Katheryn M., and Karen Sydney Rubinson. *Are All Warriors Male? Gender Roles on the Ancient Eurasian Steppe.* Plymouth, UK: Rowman & Littlefield, 2008.

Linka, Gudulda. "Nöhör (Gefährten)—Geschlechterverhältnisse bei den Mongolen im 13./14. Jahrhundert." In *Die Mongolen in Asien und Europa,* edited by Stephan Conermann and Jan Kusber, 179–205. Frankfurt: Peter Lang, 1997.

May, Timothy. *The Mongol Art of War: Chinggis Khan and the Mongol Military System.* Yardley, PA: Westholme, 2007.

Munis, Shir Muhammad Mirab, and Muhammad Riza Mirab Agahi. *Firdaws al-Iqbāl: History of Khorezm.* Translated by Yuri Bregel. Leiden, Netherlands: Brill, 1999.

Nyamaa, Badarch. *The Coins of Mongol Empire and Clan Tamgha of Khans.* Ulaanbaatar, Mongolia: private printing, 2005.

Okado, Hidehiro. "The Chakhar Shrine of Eshi Khatun." In *Aspects of Altaic Civilization III,* edited by Denis Sinor, 176–86. Bloomington: Indiana University Research Institute for Asian Studies, 1990.

———. "Dayan Khan as Yüan Emperor: The Political Legitimacy in 15th Century Mongolia." *Bulletin de l'Ecole française d'Extrême-Orient* 81 (1994): 51–58.

———. "Dayan Khan in the Battle of Dalan Terigün." In *Gedanke und Wirkung: Festscrift zum 90. Geburtstag von Nikolaus Poppe,* edited by Walther Heissig and Klaus Sagaster. Wiesbaden: Otto Harrassowitz, 1989.

———. "Dayan Khan in the *Biography of Altan Khan.*" In *Altaica Osloensia: Proceedings from the 32nd Meeting of the Permanent International Altaistic Conference,* edited by Bernt Brendemoen. Oslo: Norwegian University Press, 1990.

———. "Life of Dayan Qayan." *Acta Asiatica* 11 (1966): 46–55.

Olbricht, Peter, and Elisabeth Pinks. *Meng-Ta Pei-Lu und Hei-Ta*

Shih-Lüeh: Chinesische Gesandtenberichte über die frühen Mongolen 1221 und 1237. Wiesbaden: Otto Harrassowitz, 1980.

Onon, Urgunege, trans. *The Secret History of the Mongols: The Life and Times of Chinggis Khan.* Richmond, UK: Curzon, 2001.

Pokotilov, Dimitrii. *History of the Eastern Mongols During the Ming Dynasty from 1368 to 1634.* Translated by Rudolf Loewenthal. Chengtu, China: Chinese Cultural Studies Research Institute of West China Union University, 1947.

Polo, Marco. *The Travels of Marco Polo: The Complete Yule-Cordier Edition.* Translated by Henry Yule. New York: Dover, 1993.

Rachewiltz, Igor de, trans. *The Secret History of the Mongols.* Leiden, Netherlands: Brill, 2004.

Robinson, David M. "Banditry and the Subversion of State Authority in China: The Capital Region During the Middle Ming Period (1450–1525)." *Journal of Social History* 33 (2000): 527–63.

———. "Images of Subject Mongols Under the Ming Dynasty." *Late Imperial China* 25 (2004): 59–123.

Rockhill, William Woodville. *William of Rubruck's Account of the Mongols.* Maryland: Rana Sada, 2005.

Rossabi, Morris. *Khubilai Khan: His Life and Times.* Berkeley and Los Angeles: University of California Press, 1988.

Rybatzki, Volker. "Female Personal Names in Middle Mongolian Sources." In *The Role of Women in the Altaic World,* ed. Veronika Veit, 211–29. Wiesbaden: Harrassowitz, 2007.

Sagang Sechen. *Geschichte der Ost-Mongolen und ihres Fürstenhauses, verfasst von Ssanang Ssetsen Chungtaidschi der Ordus.* Translated by Isaac Jacob Schmidt. St. Petersburg, Russia: 1827.

———. *History of the Eastern Mongols to 1662: The Bejeweled Summary of the Origin of the Khans (Qad-un-ü ündüsün-ü Erdeni-yin Tobči.)* Translated by John R. Krueger. Bloomington, IN: Mongolia Society, 1967.

Serruys, Henry. *The Mongols and Ming China: Customs and History.* London: Variourum Reprints, 1987.

———. "Notes on a Few Mongolian Rulers of the 15th Century." *Journal of the American Oriental Society* 76 (1956): 82–90.

————. "The Office of Tayisi in Mongolia in the Fifteenth Century." *Harvard Journal of Asiatic Studies* 37 (1977): 353–80.

Thackson, W. M., trans. *Khwandamir Habibu's Siyar: The Reign of the Mongol and the Turk.* Part 1. Cambridge, MA: Harvard University Department of Near Eastern Languages and Civilizations, 1994.

————, trans. *Mirza Haydar Dughlat's* Tarikh-I-Rashide: *A History of the Khans of Moghulistan.* Cambridge, MA: Harvard University Department of Near Eastern Languages and Civilizations, 1996.

Togan, İsenbike. *Flexibility and Limitation in Steppe Formation: The Kerait Khanate and Chinggis Khan.* Leiden, Netherlands: Brill, 1998.

Urangua, J., and D. Enkhtsetseg. *Mongol Khatad.* Ulaanbaatar, Mongolia: private printing, 2000.

Wada, Sei. "A Study of Dayan Khan." *Memoirs of the Research Department of the Toyo Bunko* 19 (1960): 1–42.

Waldron, Arthur. *The Great Wall of China: From History to Myth.* Cambridge, UK: Cambridge University Press, 1990.

Weirs, Michael, ed. *Die Mongolen: Beiträge zu ihrer Geschichte und Kultur.* Darmstadt, Germany: Wissenschaftliche Buchgesellschaft, 1986.

Žamcarano, C. Ž. *The Mongol Chronicles of the Seventeenth Century,* translated by Rudolf Loewenthal. Wiesbaden: Otto Harrassowitz, 1955.

Zhao, George Qingzhi. *Marriage as Political Strategy and Cultural Expression: Mongolian Royal Marriages from World Empire to Yuan Dynasty.* New York: Peter Lang, 2008.

A NOTE ON TRANSLITERATION

Fifteenth-century Mongolian history has been one of the most confusing times for scholars because of the difficulty of establishing a clear timeline. The chronicles using the animal cycle of years are often difficult to correlate with one another or with the modern calendar. The best chronology available has been published in Mongolian in three comprehensive volumes by Professor B. Baljinnyam, and whenever possible I rely upon his dates.

English-speaking scholars use many different ways of transliterating classical and modern Mongolian names and words. The correct title for the founder of Mongolia is Chinggis Khan, pronounced CHIN-gis, but by tradition it is rendered in English as Genghis Khan. Generally, I use the spelling that is easiest for the reader rather than adhering to only one system. For example in the name Qaidu Khan, the *Q* and *Kh* represent the same guttural sound. I use the *Qaidu* spelling solely because the reader can find more additional information on him under that spelling; yet, for his daughter Khutulun, more can be found using the *Kh* spelling. For the same sound I use only an *h* as in the common spelling *Manduhai* (rather than *Mandukhai* or *Manduqai*), because it better approximates the pronunciation of *Man-du-HI*.

Similarly, I use classical and modern spellings, depending on the need, and avoid alternate spelling for the different Turkic and Mongolian dialects of different eras. Thus for simplification, *khan* is used for *khaghan, khan,* and *khagan* or the modern *khaan;* similarly, *beki* is used for *bek, beg, beghi, bägi,* and *begi.* Scholars will recognize the underlying form, but for most readers, using only a single form will be easier.

Modern Mongolian names are usually written with an initial preceding the name. In the twentieth century, the use of clan names was forbidden, and since Mongolians generally have only one name, they added the initial of the father's, or sometimes the mother's, name to distinguish them from others with the same name.

NOTES

INTRODUCTION

ix *"Let us reward our female offspring"*   Igor de Rachewiltz, trans., *The Secret History of the Mongols* (Leiden, Netherlands: Brill, 2004), §§ 214–15. The sentence is repeated in both sections, but in order to make sense of the text, many translators and editors have omitted the duplication or filled in this section with words cut from other parts of the document.

x   *"From age to age"*   Rashid al-Din, *Rashiduddin Fazullah's* Jami'u't-Tawarikh: *Compendium of Chronicles,* translated by W. M. Thackson (Cambridge, MA: Harvard University Department of Eastern Languages and Civilizations, 1998), p. 18.

xii   *"Genghis Khan loved this one"*   Ibid., p. 148.

xii   *"a great luster"*   François Pétis de la Croix, *The History of Gengizcan the Great* (Calcutta, 1816), p. 270.

PART I

1   *"There is a khan's daughter"*   Nicholas Poppe, trans., *Tsongol Folklore: The Language and Collective Farm Poetry of the Buriat Mongols of the Selenga River* (Wiesbaden: Otto Harrassowitz, 1978), p. 135.

CHAPTER 1

3   *A renegade Tatar*   Igor de Rachewiltz, trans., *The Secret History of the Mongols* (Leiden, Netherlands: Brill, 2004), § 214. His name was Qargil Šira or Khargil Shira; an alternate version of the story is found in Rashid al-Din, *Rashiduddin Fazullah's* Jami'u't-Tawarikh: *Compendium of Chronicles,* translated by W. M. Thackson (Cambridge, MA: Harvard University Department of Eastern Languages and Civilizations, 1998).

10 *baatuud*   The heroes were known collectively as the *baatuud*.

11 *"looked like so many white demons"*   N. Elias and E. Denison Ross, *A History of the Moghuls of Central Asia: Being the Tarikhi-I-Rashidi of Mirza Muhammad Haidar Dughlát* (London: Curzon, 1895), p. 81.

11 *Several Chinese commentators*   Peter Olbricht and Elisabeth Pinks, *Meng-Ta Pei-Lu und Hei-Ta Shih-Lüeh: Chinesische Gesandtenberichte über die frühen Mongolen 1221 und 1237* (Wiesbaden: Otto Harrassowitz, 1980), p. 3.

11 *"their eyes were so narrow"*   *A History of the Moghuls,* p. 81.

11 *Queen Gurbesu*   *Secret History,* § 189.

14 *"If one is concluding a marriage"*   Paul Ratchnevsky, *Genghis Khan* (Oxford, UK: Blackwell, 1991), p. 155.

16 *that his eldest daughter marry Ong Khan's grandson*   *Secret History,* § 165.

18 *"like dry horse dung in a skirt"*   *Secret History,* § 174.

18 *"looks like a frog"*   Franz von Erdmann, *Temudschin der Unerschütterliche: Nebst einer geographisch-ethnographischen Einleitung unter erfordelichen besondern Anmerkungen und Beilagen* (Leipzig: F. A. Brochkaus, 1862), p. 199.

18 *Genghis Khan killed him*   Shir Muhammad Mirab Munis and Muhammad Riza Mirab Agahi, *Firdaws al-Iqbāl: History of Khorezm,* translated by Yuri Bregel (Leiden, Netherlands: Brill, 1999), pp. 395–96.

19 *Hassan*   *Secret History,* § 182.

20 *"strength increased by Heaven and Earth"*   Ibid., § 113.

21 *Mother Earth*   Comments of D. Bold-Erdene and B. Baljinnyam, quoted in *Chinggis Khaan,* edited by Enkhbaatar Naidansod (Ulaanbaatar: Ungut Hevlel, 2006), pp. 114–17.

CHAPTER 2

28 *"I did not say that you have a bad character"*   Igor de Rachewiltz, trans., *The Secret History of the Mongols* (Leiden, Netherlands: Brill, 2004), § 208.

28 *Each wife would rule*   Hidehiro Okada, "Mongol Chronicles and Chinggisid Genealogies," *Journal of Asian and African Studies* 27 (1984): 147.

29 *He married three of his daughters*   Franz von Erdmann, *Tmudschin der Unerschütterliche* (Leipzig: F. A. Brochkaus, 1862), p. 200; Isaac Jacob Schmidt, "Die Volkstämme der Mongolien," *Jahrbücher der Literatur*, vol. 77 (Vienna: Carl Gerold, 1837), p. 22.

29 Tumelun was the daughter; Temulun was the sister.

31 *"These feasts seldom end"*   François Pétis de la Croix, *The History of Gengizcan the Great* (Calcutta, 1816), p. 270.

31 *"How shall I watch you two enjoying each other in bed?"* Hidehiro Okada, "Outer Mongolia in the Sixteenth and Seventeenth Centuries," *Journal of Asian and African Studies* 5 (1972): 70.

32 *Genghis Khan singled out only Boroghul*   *Secret History,* § 214.

33 *"If a two-shaft cart"*   Ibid., § 177.

33 *"The management of the man's fortune"*   Rashid al-Din, *Rashiduddin Fazullah's* Jami'u't-Tawarikh: *Compendium of Chronicles,* translated by W. M. Thackson (Cambridge, MA: Harvard University Department of Eastern Languages and Civilizations, 1998), p. 63.

33 *pulling one cart*   *Secret History,* §§ 186, 200.

34 *"Whoever can keep a house in order"*   Rashid al-Din, *Rashiduddin Fazullah's* Jami'u't-Tawarikh, p. 294.

34 *Ogodei summoned the wrestler*   Ibid., p. 343.

34 *"The dragon who growls in the blue clouds"*   Walther Heissig "A Contribution to the Knowledge of Eastmongolian Folkpoetry," *Folklore Studies* 9 (1950): 161.

36 *"intercessors"*   *Secret History,* § 64.

37 *Urug* also has the extended meaning of "seed," since the Mongols considered seed as the womb of a plant.

37–38 *"It happened . . . as wide as a lake"*   *Secret History,* § 254.

39 *"My wives, daughters-in-law, and daughters are as colorful"* Rashid al-Din, *Rashiduddin Fazullah's* Jami'u't-Tawarikh, pp. 298–99.

40 *"After Genghis Khan had tested his sons":* Ibid., p. 303.

CHAPTER 3

47 *Genghis Khan accepted the Oirat*   Igor de Rachewiltz, *The Secret History of the Mongols* (Leiden, Netherlands: Brill, 2004), § 239.

47 *Checheyigen* was also recorded as Tsetseikhen.

47 *"Because you are the daughter"* and related quotes to Checheyigen: George Qingzhi Zhao, *Marriage as Political Strategy and Cultural Expression: Mongolian Royal Marriages from World Empire to Yuan Dynasty* (New York: Peter Lang, 2008), p. 39.

50 *"queens as our shields"*   *Secret History,* § 64.

51 *"You should be determined"*   Zhao, *Marriage as Political Strategy,* p. 37.

52 *"Although many people can"*   Ibid., p. 37.

52 *white felt rug*   Hansgerd Göckenjan and James R. Sweeney, *Der Mongolensturm: Berichte von Augenzeugen und Zeitgenossen 1235–1250* (Graz, Austria: Verlag Styria, 1985), p. 113.

53 *The mother's blood*   Alena Oberfalzová, *Metaphors and Nomad,* translated by Derek Paton (Prague: Charles University, 2006), pp. 57–58.

53 *pail of milk*   Ibid., p. 103

59 *"It seemed to me as though the sky"*   Rashid al-Din, *Rashiduddin Fazullah's* Jami'u't-Tawarikh: *Compendium of Chronicles,* translated by W. M. Thackson (Cambridge, MA: Harvard University Department of Eastern Languages and Civilizations, 1998), p. 205.

59 *"fifth son"*   *Secret History,* § 238.

59 *a slave into a noble*   Rashid al-Din, *Rashiduddin Fazullah's* Jami'u't-Tawarikh, p. 213.

59 *"Whereas, by the Protection of Eternal Heaven"*   Francis Woodman Cleaves, "The Sino-Mongolian Inscription of 1362 in Memory of Prince Hindu," *Harvard Journal of Asiatic Studies* 12, no. 1/2 (June 1949): 31.

60 *Her nation was her first husband*   Zhao, *Marriage as Political Strategy,* p. 39.

62 *"The area has no rain or snow"*   D. Sinor, Geng Shimin, and Y. I. Kychanov, "The Uighurs, Kyrgyz and the Tangut (Eighth to the

Thirteenth Century)," in *History of Civilizations of Central Asia,* vol. 4, edited by M. S. Asimov and C. E. Bosworth (Delhi: Motilal Banarsidass Publishers, 1999), p. 203.

63 *excavations have uncovered*   Adam T. Kessler, *Empires Beyond the Great Wall: The Heritage of Genghis Khan* (Los Angeles: Natural History Museum of Los Angeles County, 1993), pp. 160–61.

64 *Karluk* are also known as Qarlu-ut, Qarluq, and Karluqs.

64 *"How can he be called Arlsan* Khan?"   Rashid al-Din, *Rashiduddin Fazullah's* Jami'u't-Tawarikh, p. 78.

65 *Tolai*   B. Baljinnyam, *Mongolchhuudin Buren Tuukhiin Tovchoon,* vol. 1 (Ulaanbaatar, Mongolia: Admon, 2006), p. 494.

CHAPTER 4

69 *killing of Ala-Qush*   Rashid al-Din, *Rashiduddin Fazullah's* Jami'u't-Tawarikh: *Compendium of Chronicles,* translated by W. M. Thackson (Cambridge, MA: Harvard University Department of Eastern Languages and Civilizations, 1998), p. 71.

69 *Jingue* is also referred to as Zhenguo, Jinkhuu, or Jinkhui.

74 *"He recognized no business but merrymaking"*   Ata-Malik Juvaini, *Genghis Khan: The History of the World-Conqueror,* translated by J. Boyle (Seattle: University of Washington Press, 1997), p. 379.

74 *"The demon of temptation"*   Ibid., p. 173.

74 *Tokuchar*   Ebülgâzî Bahadir Han, *The Shajrat Ul Atrak: Or, Genealogical Tree of the Turks and Tatars,* translated by William Miles (London: Wm. H. Allen, 1838), p. 155.

75 *"She left no trace"*   Ghiyas ad-Din Muhammad Khwandamir, *Khwandamir Habibu's Siyar: The Reign of the Mongol and the Turk,* translated by W. M. Thackson (Cambridge, MA: Harvard University Department of Near Eastern Languages and Civilizations, 1994), p. 23.

76 *"In the exaction of vengeance . . . rose gardens became furnaces"* Juvaini, *Genghis Khan,* pp. 177–78.

79 *"rhetorically ornate rhyming words"*   Rashid al-Din, *Rashiduddin Fazullah's* Jami'u't-Tawarikh, p. 180.

80 *Genghis Khan then gave the precocious Boyaohe*   Namio Egami, "Olon-Sume: The Remains of the Royal Capital of the Yuan-Period Ongut Tribe," *Orient: The Reports of the Society for Near Eastern Studies in Japan* 30/31 (1995): 2.

81 *"always obtain to wife"*   Marco Polo, *The Travels of Marco Polo: The Complete Yule-Cordier Edition,* vol. 1, translated by Henry Yule (New York: Dover, 1993), pp. 284–95.

82 *"My people of the Five Colors and Four Foreign Lands"* Charles Bawden, trans., *The Mongol Chronicle Altan Tobči* (Wiesbaden: Otto Harrossowitz, 1955), § 43.

82 *"water in the desert"*   *Altan Tobči,* § 46.

82 *"I leave you . . . one soul"*   François Pétis de la Croix, *The History of Gengizcan the Great* (Calcutta, 1816), p. 279.

84 *His four dowager queens controlled the territory*   Hidehiro Okada, "Mongol Chronicles and Chinggisid Genealogies," *Journal of Asian and African Studies* 27 (1984): 147.

PART II

87 *"As the age declined"*   Hidehiro Okada, "Dayan Khan as Yüan Emperor: The Political Legitimacy in 15th Century Mongolia," *Bulletin de l'Ecole française d'Extrême-Orient* 81 (1994): 51.

CHAPTER 5

89 *Oirat girls*   Rashid al-Din, *Rashiduddin Fazullah's* Jami'u't-Tawarikh: *Compendium of Chronicles,* translated by W. M. Thackson (Cambridge, MA: Harvard University Department of Eastern Languages and Civilizations, 1998), p. 345. Rashid al-Din identifies the girls as Oirat, but Juvaini (*Genghis Khan: The History of the World-Conqueror,* translated by J. Boyle [Seattle: University of Washington Press, 1997]) leaves the name of the tribe blank. The *Secret History* (Igor de Rachewiltz, trans., *The Secret History of the Mongols* [Leiden, Netherlands: Brill, 2004]) identifies them as belonging to Uncle Otchigen, but Ogodei would hardly have been seeking to marry the women of his own patrilineage.

90 *"Because they had jeered at the Mongols"*   Rashid al-Din,

The Successors of Genghis Khan, translated by John Andrew Boyle (New York: Columbia University Press, 1971), pp. 35–38.

90 *"star-like maidens"*　　Juvaini, *Genghis Khan,* p. 235.

93 *yeke khatun*　　Igor de Rachewiltz, "Töregene's Edict of 1240," *Papers on Far Eastern History* 23 (March 1981): 38–63.

94 *"used to weep a great deal ... Beki"*　　Rashid al-Din, *Successors of Genghis Khan,* p. 199.

95 *"became the sharer"*　　Juvaini, *Genghis Khan,* p. 245.

96 *"And the wind has pitched"*　　Ibid., p. 614.

97 *"They put to death the youngest"*　　Rashid al-Din, *Successors of Genghis Khan,* p. 121.

97 *"had killed his father ... were judged and killed"*　　Giovanni DiPlano Carpini, *The Story of the Mongols Whom We Call the Tartars,* translated by Erik Hildinger (Boston: Branden, 1996), p.111.

97 *why they killed her*　　Rashid al-Din, *Rashiduddin Fazullah's Jami'u't-Tawarikh,* p. 39.

98 *khuriltai of 1229*　　Igor de Rachewiltz, trans., *The Secret History of the Mongols* (Leiden, Netherlands, 2004), § 269.

99 *"sent us to his mother"*　　Carpini, *Story of the Mongols,* p. 107.

99 *"wives had other tents"*　　Ibid., p. 111.

99 *"He took no part in affairs of state"*　　Juvaini, *Genghis Khan,* p. 244.

100 *"Khatun to join Ogodei ... excess sensuality"*　　Abu-Umar-I-Usman, *Tabakat-I-Nasirir: A General History of the Muhammadan Dynasties of Asia,* vol. 2, translated by H. G. Raverty (London: Gilbert & Rivington, 1881), p. 1144.

100 *"And then they sent also for their ladies ... they were put to death"*　　William Woodville Rockhill, trans., *The Journey of William of Rubruck to the Eastern Parts of the World, 1253–55 as Narrated by Himself* (London: Hakylut Society, 1900), p. 164.

101 *"The affairs of the world ... they might flee"*　　Juvaini, *Genghis Khan,* p. 556.

101 *"You are a woman"*　　Rashid al-Din, *Successors of Genghis Khan,* p. 155.

103 *"You cannot have peace. . . . We shall destroy you!"*   Christopher Dawson, *The Mongol Mission: Narratives and Letters of the Franciscan Missionaries in Mongolia and China in the Thirteenth and Fourteenth Centuries* (New York: Sheed and Ward, 1955), p. xx.

103 *"As to affairs of war and peace . . . destroyed her whole family by her witchcraft"*   Rockhill, *Journey of William of Rubruck,* p. 250.

103 *praised effusively:* Morris Rossabi, *Khubilai Khan: His Life and Times* (Berkeley and Los Angeles: University of California Press, 1988), p. 12.

104–5 *"amounted to little . . . pathway of righteousness"*   Juvaini, *Genghis Khan,* pp. 264–65.

105 *increase the taxes*   Thomas T. Allsen, "The Rise of the Mongolian Empire and Mongolian Rule in North China," in *The Cambridge History of China,* vol. 6, edited by Herbert Franke and Denis Twitchett (Cambridge, UK: Cambridge University Press, 1994), p. 391.

105 *"He sent messengers"*   Rashid al-Din, *Successors of Genghis Khan,* p. 202.

106 *one of the ministers*   Ibid., p. 211.

106 *Tanggis*   George Qingzhi Zhao, *Marriage as Political Strategy and Cultural Expression* (New York: Peter Lang, 2008), p. 135.

106 *three hundred families*   George Lane, *Early Mongol Rule in Thirteenth Century Iran: A Persian Renaissance* (New York: Routledge Curzon, 2003), p. 67.

107 *"ordered her limbs to be kicked"*   Rashid al-Din, *Successors of Genghis Khan,* p. 213; also recorded in Rashid al-Din, *Rashiduddin Fazullah's* Jami'u't-Tawarikh, p. 408.

107 *"he forthwith sent to his . . . the children he had of her"*   Rockhill, *Journey of William of Rubruck,* p. 245.

107 *Menggeser Noyan*   Rashid al-Din, *Rashiduddin Fazullah's* Jami'u't-Tawarikh, p. 40; see also Christopher P. Atwood, *Encyclopedia of Mongolia and the Mongol Empire* (New York: Facts on File, 2004), p. 346.

108 *She claimed these lands*   Hidehiro Okada, "The Chakhar Shrine of Eshi Khatun," in *Aspects of Altaic Civilization III,* edited by

Denis Sinor (Bloomington: Indiana University Research Institute for Asian Studies, 1990), p. 178.

109–10 *"After sipping the unpalatable . . . Egypt and Syria"* Juvaini, *Genghis Khan,* pp. 52–53.

110 *"They shall see what they shall see"* Rashid al-Din, *Rashiduddin Fazullah's* Jami'u't-Tawarikh, p. 409.

111 *"The women of your city"* Abu-Umar-I-Usman, *Tabakat-I-Nasirir,* p. 1100.

112 *"to guard the northern frontiers"* Gombojab Hangin, "The Mongolian Titles Jinong and Sigejin," *Journal of the American Oriental Society* 100, no. 3 (1980); 259.

112 *the black sulde* Charles Bawden, trans., *The Mongol Chronicle Altan Tobči* (Wiesbaden: Otto Harrassowitz, 1955), § 85.

CHAPTER 6

113 *Mongol capital at Beijing* Khubilai Khan built his new imperial capital at the place now occupied by Beihai Park in central Beijing. The Mongols and most foreigners called it Khan Baliq, but the Chinese, who were forbidden to speak Mongolian, called it Tatu.

114 *Orghina Khatun* Rene Grousset, *The Empire of the Steppes,* translated by Naomi Walford (New Brunswick, NJ: Rutgers University Press, 1997), p. 331.

114 *he seized the courts* Rashid al-Din, *The Successors of Genghis Khan,* translated by John Andrew Boyle (New York: Columbia University Press), p. 311.

116 *"It was a large tent"* Ata-Malik Juvaini, *Genghis Khan: The History of the World-Conqueror,* translated by J. Boyle (Seattle: University of Washington Press, 1997), p. 616.

116 *"The master craftsmen"* Rashid al-Din, *Rashiduddin Fazullah's* Jami'u't-Tawarikh: *Compendium of Chronicles,* translated by W. M. Thackson (Cambridge, MA: Harvard University Department of Eastern Languages and Civilizations, 1998), p. 310.

118 *"she went around like a boy"* Rashid al-Din, *Rashiduddin Fazullah's* Jami'u't-Tawarikh, p. 309.

118 *"make a dash"*   Marco Polo, *The Travels of Marco Polo: The Complete Yule-Cordier Edition,* vol. 1, translated by Henry Yule (New York: Dover, 1993), p. 465.

118 *"People choose bays"*   Rashid al-Din, *Successors of Genghis Khan,* p. 162.

119 *"Many a man fell"*   *Travels of Marco Polo,* pp. 461–62.

121 *acted like a man*   Hansgerd Göckenjan and James R. Sweeney, *Der Mongolensturm: Berichte von Augenzeugen und Zeitgenossen 1235–1250* (Graz: Verlag Styria, 1985), p. 101.

121 *Mongol princess*   Gian Andri Bezzola, *Die Mongolen in Abendländischer Sicht: 1220–1270* (Bern, Switzerland: Francke Verlag, 1974), p. 45.

121 *Spalato*   *Der Mongolensturm,* p. 250.

121 *many women fought*   Ibid., p. 246.

122 *"young and handsome"*   *Travels of Marco Polo,* p. 464.

122 *"When both had taken"*   Ibid., p. 464.

122 *Numerous reports maintain*   Michal Biran, *Qaidu Khan and the Rise of the Independent Mongol State in Central Asia* (Richmond, UK: Curzon, 1997), p. 61.

122 *incestuous relationship*   Rashid al-Din, *Rashiduddin Fazullah's* Jami'u't-Tawarikh, p. 309.

122 *"She chose him herself"*   Ibid., p. 309.

123–24 *Qaidu Khan decided to try a deception . . . "illness into dysentery"*   Ibid.

124 *He was buried . . . "stirring up sedition and strife"*   Ibid., p. 310.

125 *novel*   Walther Heissig, "Tracing Some Oral Mongol Motifs in a Chinese Prosimetric Ming Novel of 1478," *Asian Folklore Studies* 53 (1996): 238. The novel was titled *Hua Guan Suo zhuan* (The Story of Hua Guan Suo).

126 *"When our great ancestor"*   Hidehiro Okada, "Dayan Khan as Yüan Emperor: The Political Legitimacy in 15th Century Mongolia," *Bulletin de l'Ecole française d'Extrême-Orient* 81 (1994): 51.

128–29 *Divine Demon Dancing Girls . . . "place full of obscenity"*

George Qingzhi Zhao, *Marriage as Political Strategy and Cultural Expression* (New York: Peter Lang, 2008), pp. 89–90.

129 *Erdeni-yin Tobci*   *Geschichte der Ost-Mongolen und ihres Fürstenhauses, verfasst von Ssanang Ssetsen Chungtaidschi der Ordus,* translated by Isaac Jacob Schmidt (Saint Petersburg, Russia, 1820).

CHAPTER 7

131 *Altan Tobci*   The version most often used in this book is the bilingual Mongolian-English edition, Charles Bawden, trans., *The Mongol Chronicle Altan Tobči* (Wiesbaden: Otto Harrassowitz, 1955).

131 *Erdeni-yin Tobci*   The version most often used in this book is the bilingual Mongolian-German edition prepared by command of the Russian tsar Alexander II in 1827 and published two years later as the first Mongolian book translated into a European language. *Geschichte der Ost-Mongolen und ihres Fürstenhauses, verfasst von Ssanang Ssetsen Chungtaidschi der Ordus,* translated by Isaac Jacob Schmidt (Saint Petersburg, Russia, 1829).

134 *killed the last ruling descendant of Khubilai Khan*   Hidehiro Okada, "Mongol Chronicles and Chinggisid Genealogies," *Journal of Asian and African Studies* 27 (1984): 151.

135 *the ceremony*   Rashid al-Din, *Rashiduddin Fazullah's* Jami'u't-Tawarikh: *Compendium of Chronicles,* translated by W. M. Thackson (Cambridge, MA: Harvard University Department of Eastern Languages and Civilizations, 1998), p. 260.

136 *"She is the wife of your son"*   The *Altan Tobči* identifies her as the son's wife, but the *Erdene-yin Tobči* identifies her as the wife of Elbeg's brother. The two accounts are not necessarily in disagreement since "son" and "younger brother" are often used interchangeably for junior males in the same clan. The account here combines the two texts.

136 *friendly access to senior women*   Lawrence Krader, *Social Organization of the Mongol-Turkic Pastoral Nomads* (Bloomington: Indiana University Press, 1963), p. 56.

136 *Even to bring milk*   Hidehiro Okada, "Outer Mongolia in the Sixteenth and Seventeenth Centuries," *Journal of Asian and African Studies* 5 (1972): 70.

136 *dead rabbit*   In a Tibetan chronicle, the source of the khan's problem is a monkey spirit that then led him astray. The story was presented seemingly as an excuse to denounce women and the men who love them. Georg Huth, trans., *Geschichte des Buddhismus in der Mongolei: Aus dem Tibetischen des Jigs-med nam-mk'a* (Strassburg: Karl J. Trübner, 1892), pp. 42–43.

136–37 *"when a khan behaves like a commoner"*   Hidehiro Okada, "The Bilig Literature in Chinggis Qaran-u Cadig," *Mongolica* 6 (1995): 459.

137–42 *Elbeg Khan was about to commit a crime . . . The turmoil resulting from the Great Khan's terrible deeds*   The quotes combine the accounts given in the *Altan Tobči* § 3–65, and the *Erdeni-yin Tobči*, pp. 139–143.

144 *"It is told"*   W. M. Thackson, trans., *Mirza Haydar Dughlat's* Tarikh-I-Rashide: *A History of the Khans of Moghulistan* (Cambridge, MA: Harvard University Department of Near Eastern Languages and Civilizations, 1996), p. 36.

144 *important titles*   Frederick W. Mote, "The T'u-mu Incident of 1449," *Chinese Ways in Warfare,* edited by Frank A. Kierman Jr. and John K. Fairbank (Cambridge, MA: Harvard University Press, 1974), p. 252.

148 *"If it is a girl . . . It is a girl."*   *Altan Tobči* § 95.

149 *"Do you already begin to fear"*   Henry H. Howorth, *History of the Mongols from the 9th to the 19th Century* (London: Longmans, Green, 1876), p. 364.

150–51 *"dragged his body up into a tree"*   Ibid., p. 366. The killing of Esen was placed in the year 1452 in *Erdeni-yin Tobči,* but in 1454 in the Ming records.

CHAPTER 8

155 *Beg-Arslan* was also known as Begerisün, Birirsen, Begersen, Begersün, Bigirsen, and Pai-chia-ssu-lan.

156 *He "stayed absent from" her*   Charles Bawden, trans., *The*

Mongol Chronicle Altan Tobči (Wiesbaden: Otto Harrassowitz, 1955), § 93.

160 *"elder brother"*   *Altan Tobči*, § 85.

163 deel *embroidered with gold*   Ibid., § 100.

163 *"If I receive"*   Igor de Rachewiltz, trans., *The Secret History of the Mongols* (Leiden, Netherlands: Brill, 2004), § 238.

163 *"In the blue sky"*   Quote adapted from the translation of Gombojab Hangin, "The Mongolian Titles Jinong and Sigejin," *Journal of the American Oriental Society* 100 (1980): 256.

164 *"in peace and harmony"*   *Erdeni-yin Tobči* as compiled by Isaac Jacob Schmidt in *Geschichte der Ost-Mongolen und ihres Fürstenhauses, verfasst von Ssanang Ssetsen Chungtaidschi der Ordus* (Saint Petersburg, Russia, 1829), p. 175.

164 *"They declared themselves sworn friends and loved each other"* *Secret History*, § 117.

171 *disguised as Mongol bandits*   Frederick W. Mote, "The Ch'eng-hua and Hung-chih Reigns, 1465–1505," in *The Cambridge History of China*, vol. 7, *The Ming Dynasty, 1368–1644, Part I*, edited by Frederick W. Mote and Denis Twitchett (Cambridge, UK: Cambridge University Press, 1988), p. 399.

CHAPTER 9

174 *"They marry by succession their stepmothers"*   Henry Serruys, *The Mongols and Ming China: Customs and History* (London: Variourum Reprints, 1987), p. 180.

175 *"The houses of the Tartars"*   Edward Gibbon, *The Decline and Fall of the Roman Empire* (London: J. M. Dent & Sons, 1910), p. 6.

177 *female in-law had a senior position*   Lawrence Krader, *Social Organization of the Mongol-Turkic Pastoral Nomads* (Bloomington: Indiana University Press, 1963), p. 23.

178 *Ismayil confronted the Great Khan*   *Erdeni-yin Tobči*, pp. 175–79.

179–80 *"I myself am not in good health . . . the khan became enraged*" Charles Bawden, trans., *The Mongol Chronicle Altan Tobči* (Wiesbaden: Otto Harrassowitz, 1955), § 98.

181 *Jamuka* Igor de Rachewiltz, trans., *The Secret History of the Mongols* (Leiden, Netherlands: Brill, 2004), § 201.

182 *"Have I enmity towards your kin?"* *Altan Tobči,* § 98.

183 *the prince began to style himself as the Great Khan* Chinese reports assert that Bayan Mongke claimed the title of Bayan Mongke Khan this time rather than Bolkhu Jinong, but few people recognized the young man's change of title. According to the *Erdeni-yin Tobči,* he held the title for two years, but Mongolian lists of Great Khans rarely include his name.

184 *that he might escape* *Altan Tobči,* §§ 99–100.

188–89 *"I will not go to you"* . . . *"the right to speak to me this way"* *Altan Tobči,* § 102.

PART III

CHAPTER 10

195 *sickness* Charles Bawden, trans., *The Mongol Chronicle Altan Tobči* (Wiesbaden: Harrassowitz, 1955), § 101; *hunchback-like growth*: *Erdeni-yin Tobči,* p. 179.

200 *"there was suffering"* Johan Elverskog, *The Jewel Translucent Sūtra: Altan Khan and the Mongols in the Sixteenth Century* (Leiden, Netherlands: Brill, 2003), lines 45–48.

201 *"O God! O Sky! O Earth!"* Rashid al-Din, *Rashiduddin Fazullah's* Jami'u't-Tawarikh: *Compendium of Chronicles,* translated by W. M. Thackson (Cambridge, MA: Harvard University Department of Eastern Languages and Civilizations, 1998), p. 180.

CHAPTER 11

215 *"Queen Manduhai the Good"* Charles Bawden, trans., *The Mongol Chronicle Altan Tobči* (Wiesbaden: Otto Harrassowitz, 1955), § 101.

220 *"The Queen has no helmet"* Ibid., § 102.

222 *"When it was wet"* Igor de Rachewiltz, trans., *The Secret History of the Mongols* (Leiden, Netherlands: Brill, 2004), § 214.

222 *"protected her jewel-like son"* Johan Elverskog, *The Jewel Translucent Sūtra: Altan Khan and the Mongols in the Sixteenth Century* (Leiden, Netherlands: Brill, 2003), lines 45–64.

224 *They sometimes imported horses* Denis Twitchett and Tilemann Grimm, "The Cheng-t'ung, Ching t'ai, and T'ien-shun Reigns, 1436–1464," in *The Cambridge History of China,* vol. 7, *The Ming Dynasty, 1368–1644, Part I,* edited by Frederick W. Mote and Denis Twitchett (Cambridge, UK: Cambridge University Press, 1988), p. 319.

224 *The instability of the horse trade* Morris Rossabi, "The Ming and Inner Asia," in ibid., *Part II,* p. 254–55.

225 *True civilization for the Chinese* Hidehiro Okada, "China as a Successor State to the Mongol Empire," in *The Mongol Empire and Its Legacy,* edited by Reuven Amitai-Preiss and David O. Morgan (Leiden, Netherlands: Brill, 1999), p. 261.

225 *five types of bait* Ying-shih Yü, *Trade and Expansion in Han China* (Berkeley and Los Angeles: University of California Press, 1967), p. 37.

CHAPTER 12

230 *Wang Yue proposed* Alastair Iain Johnston, *Cultural Realism: Strategic Culture and Grand Strategy in Chinese History* (Princeton, NJ: Princeton University Press, 1995), p. 220.

230 *"to dare to penetrate"* Ibid., p. 220.

233 *"I braved the snow"* Yuan-Chu Lam, "Memoir on the Campaign Against Turfan: An Annotated Translation of Hsü Chin's *P'ing-fan shih-mo* written in 1503," *Journal of Asian History* 42 (1990): 159.

236 *"When the unfortunate Mongols"* Dimitrii Pokotilov, *History of the Eastern Mongols During the Ming Dynasty from 1368–1634,* translated by Rudolf Leowenthal (Chengtu: Chinese Cultural Studies Research Institute, West China Union University, 1947), p. 77.

239 *he sighed in regret* Denis Twitchett and Frederick W. Mote, eds., *The Cambridge History of China,* vol. 7, *The Ming Dynasty,*

1368–1644, Part I (Cambridge, UK: Cambridge University Press, 1988), p. 347.

240 *pornography*   Ibid., p. 348.

242 *"thirsty for its tastiness"*   The butter soup story is from Charles Bawden, trans., *The Mongol Chronicle Altan Tobči* (Wiesbaden: Otto Harrassowitz, 1955), §§ 109–10.

242 *"If a piece of food is given"*   Giovanni DiPlano Carpini, *The Story of the Mongols Whom We Call the Tartars*, translated by Erik Hildinger (Boston: Branden, 1996), p. 45.

CHAPTER 13

248 *"Why is the ground shaking?"*   Most of the material in this chapter is taken from Charles Bawden, trans., *The Mongol Chronicle Altan Tobči* (Wiesbaden: Otto Harrassowitz, 1955), §§ 107–88.

258 *incense holders*   *Erdeni-yin Tobči*, as compiled by Isaac Jacob Schmidt in *Geschichte der Ost-Mongolen und ihres Fürsten-hauses, verfasst von Ssanang Ssetsen Chungtaidschi der Ordus*, (Saint Petersburg, Russia, 1829), p. 185.

258 *"It is necessary to accept hard and inconvenient advice"* Walther Heissig, "A Contribution to the Knowledge of Eastmongolian Folkpoetry," *Folklore Studies* 9 (1950): 158.

260 *she died soon thereafter*   Siker died at Seremeger on the Sira Mören. *Altan Tobči*, § 109.

262 *"the government was rectified and humanity was united"* *Altan Tobči*, §123.

262 *"peace, unity and prosperity spread throughout all the people."* *Erdeni-yin Tobči*, p. 195.

263 *"give us gold, silver, and silk"*   Talat Tekin, *A Grammar of Orkhon Turkic*, Uralic and Altaic Series, vol. 69 (Bloomington: Indiana University Publications, 1968), pp. 261–73.

263 *Tonyukuk*   Talat Tekin, Ibid., pp. 283–290.

265 *"He has come saying he will rule our country"*   *Altan Tobči*, §113.

266 *"May you heaven"*   *Altan Tobči*, §114.

EPILOGUE

271–72 *The Squire's Tale*   *Chaucer's Canterbury Tales,* edited by Alfred W. Pollard (London: Macmillan, 1899).

273 *"She united with her ravishing beauty"*   François Pétis de la Croix, *The Thousand and One Days: Persian Tales,* translated by Justin Huntly McCarthy (London: Chatto & Windus, 1892) p. 195.

273 *"tigerish woman"*   Carlo Gozzi, *Turandotte,* Act I, scene i.

273–74 *"in that cruel night"*   Puccini, *Turandot,* Act II, scene ii.

ACKNOWLEDGMENTS

THE GLORY OF MONGOLIA IS BEST APPRECIATED THROUGH the three treasures that bring the Mongols the greatest joy and pride: the splendor of their landscape, the magnificence of their history, and the grandeur of their music. While writing this book, I spent as much time as possible in the Mongolian countryside with my wife, Walker Pearce. When we could not be there, I relied upon the music to re-create the landscape and to summon the images of the past.

Throughout the writing of this book, I repeatedly found inspiration in the songs written about Manduhai and, most important, in the symphony written in her honor by N. Jantsannorov, one of the greatest composers of our time. In researching this project, I realized how much the Mongolian people have preserved their history through song, despite the historical censorship of documents. Sometimes, they were not allowed to publicly perform the songs, as in the case of a beautiful song written in tribute to Manduhai Khatun by composer and musician D. Jargalsaikhan in the 1970s. Like many musicians working under censorship, he had to leave out her name and change the words slightly to disguise the song's subject matter.

I received great inspiration from the voices of Shurankhai: B. Nomin-Erden, D. Uriintuya, and G. Erdenchimeg, and I benefited greatly from the performances of D. Odsuren and T. Batbayasgalan.

The portrait of Queen Manduhai on the cover of the book was made by Kikutake Yuji. Throughout the writing of this book I used it as the screensaver on my computer because it represents the dynamic nature of Manduhai while also reminding me that, like the artist, I too am a foreigner trying to interpret Mongolian culture.

It is not surprising that with so much censorship of the written history of the Mongol queens, no portraits of them are known to exist from their lifetimes. For Mongols, however, the essence of a person persists not so much in the physical features of the body as in the sound of the spoken name and the appearance of the written name. They summon this fundamental nature through calligraphic drawings that simultaneously record the name and the general form of the person. The artist N. Bat-Erdene made the name drawings that illustrate this book. Borte appears at the opening of Part One, Sorkhokhtani Beki of Part Two, and Queen Manduhai of Part Three.

The symbol on the epigraph page is a *tamgha* designed and given to me as a gift by Z. Purev, who also sculpted it in metal for use as a brand. It, too, is a special form of Mongolian calligraphy, and represents the three basic letters of my first name. All of the images and symbols used in the book were combined through the creative design of Leonard Henderson.

I appreciate the support of my daughter, Walker Buxton, and son, Roy Maybank, as well as their spouses, J. Edward Buxton and Amanda R. Maybank, and my granddaughter Walker Buxton during sometimes difficult circumstances in Mongolia. I look forward to one day traveling in Mongolia with our other granddaughters, Pearce Buxton, Lavinia Maybank, and Rhett Maybank, as well as our grandsons, Edward Buxton and Roy Maybank.

At Macalester College, Professor Sonia Patten was one of the consistently most helpful and encouraging supporters of this project from its inception. I benefited tremendously from the tireless service of the DeWitt Wallace Library staff, as well as from my colleagues Naran Bilik, Dianna Shandy, Arjun Guneratne, Martin Gunderson, David McCurdy, Mahnaz Kousha, Karen Nakamura, Olga Gonzalez, David Lanegran, Ahmed Samatar, Mary Lou Byrne, Juanita Garciagodoy, Wang Ping, and Lee Olson.

In Mongolia, the faculty and staff of the Chinggis Khaan University, under the direction of Kh. Lkhagvasuren, diligently assisted in my work. I was aided by the enlightened work of Professors T. Bold, D. Bold-Erdene, Davaadulam, O. Sukhbaatar, B. Baljinnyam, Oi. Daghadorj, T. Namjil, Kh. Shagdar, A. Shagdarsuren, and J. Saruulbuyan, as well as

Mr. Barudas of the South Gobi. Also in Mongolia, I very much value the support and encouragement that I received from O. Batnairamdal, Lauren Bonilla, Roger Chilton, Martha Crunkleton, E. Enerelt, D. Enkhchuluun, S. Erdenebold, B. Erdenesanaa, B. Ganhuyag, U. Gereltod, Tjalling Halbertsma, D. Javkhlan, William Kennedy, Bijani Mizell, A. Mungunzul, Susan Murphy, B. Narankhuu, Axel Odelberg, Catherine Sepulveda, S. Soyoljin, E. Soyombo, Robert Stroozas, and Rochelle and Rebecca Tschida. Merely listing their names can in no way express the appreciation I have for what they have done for me or the emotional bonds that I share with each of them in a different way.

Producing a book depends on far more than writing. It is a group endeavor in which dozens of people contribute crucial pieces, but, in the end, the author, somewhat unfairly, gets the credit. In thirty years of work together, my agent, Lois Wallace, has always guided and encouraged my work. I have been with Crown Publishers almost as long as I have been with Lois Wallace. I have benefited from working with some of the finest talents I have known in my career. In our generation together, many have married, given birth, or adopted children, and some have retired or moved on to new challenges. Yet they all remain a part of my work. Rachel Klayman took a chance in accepting this book for publication, and Lucinda Bartley put in tremendous work to edit it repeatedly. Their diligence and enthusiasm made it possible for me to complete this project.

The nation of Alan Goa, Genghis Khan, Manduhai Khatun, and Dayan Khan still lives today. As in any democracy, the people have different views and ideologies, yet they are all united in honoring the history and culture of their Mongol ancestors. They have helped me in seemingly every way that they could. From the guards at the doors to the ministers of parliament, from teachers in the rural classrooms to the ministers of state in Ulaanbaatar, and from library clerks to the president, first lady, and prime minister—all encouraged and assisted me throughout the six years of work on this project. They made my work possible, and, more important, they are the ones who give it meaning.

From herders to parliament members, Mongolians never tired of teaching me about their culture and place of birth, *torson nutag,* within Mongolia. Because of the subject of my investigations, individuals frequently wanted me to tell the story of a particular queen, hero, or divinity for whom their mother or daughter was named. Sometimes they encouraged me to meet their grandmother as the best living example of the true ideal of Mongol womanhood. They wanted to highlight the importance of their home area or to stress the neglected virtues of a special type of camel or way of singing. They had a preferred spelling or pronunciation of a name, or hoped I could explain that the milk of their district had just the right amount of fat and the best flavor, and was used in the past by doctors to cure certain diseases. I treasure each of these accounts in my memory even if, in the end, I was not able to incorporate them into this book.

Throughout my research, I relied upon scholars whom I never met and who often work in anonymity without receiving the attention and honor that they deserve. They glean the historic and linguistic fields searching for grains of information about Mongolian life, history, and culture. They study, translate, catalog, and preserve the texts and manuscript fragments of the past. They analyze archaic scripts, compare spellings, and chase down the etymologies of unusual suffix combinations. I greatly admire and appreciate their scholarship.

I hope that the readers of this book will go on to explore the many works about Mongolia, listen to the music of its great artists, and perhaps one day find the white road that leads them to visit the beautiful land and taste the pure water of Mongolia.

INDEX

Note: Familial relationships in parentheses are to Genghis Khan unless otherwise noted.

Mongol Empire (*cont.*)
Guyuk as Great Khan, 98–99
imperial era (1206–1368), xv
inauguration of Great Khan, 196
Karakorum as capital, 71, 95–96, 98–99, 118, 119, 123, 159, 208, 263, 264
Karluk Turks in, 64–65, 66
Khubilai Khan as Great Khan, 112
Khutulun and Qaidu Khan, rule of, 116–21
kingdoms of, 84, 98
knowledge and flow of information, xii, xiii
in Korea, 126–27
as largest empire in history, 39, 51, 78
literacy, 104, 131
Manduhai Khatun and restoration of, xv–xvi 210–21, 257–62
Manduul as Great Khan, 156–59
medallion of office (*gergee*), 117
merciless retaliation by, 68–69
Ogodei as Great Khan, 85
Oirat in, 47–48, 54, 65, 66
Onggud lands, 57–58, 64
postal stations across Eurasia, 89–91
seals (*tamghas*) of authority, 117
sexual terrorism employed by, 90
Silk Route and trade, 48, 64–67, 72, 77–79, 92, 114, 125, 213
Six Tumen, 257–62
Sorkhokhtani's retribution, 107–10
story of women fighting women, 110–11
strongmen takeover, 143–44
taishi (prime minister), 163
Temuge Otchigen put in control of, 72
as Thirteen Ordos or Thirteen Hordes, 84
torture employed by, 100–101, 105–7, 109
Uighurs and, 58–64, 67, 79
wives of Genghis Khan as rulers, 28–29
women warriors, xiv, 117, 120–22, 214–21, 252–56
written language (Mongol script), 69, 79–80
zenith of, 112, 113
Mongol epic poem, 1
Mongolia (Mongolian Plateau), 40, 41, 44. *See also* Mongol Empire
environmental devastation of, 133, 140–41
first European envoy to, 98–99
Gobi desert and, 194 (*see also* Gobi desert)
homeland in, xv, 19, 28, 51, 66, 83, 112, 114, 117, 130–34, 160, 211, 213
reunited under Esen, 145, 154
reunited under Manduhai Khatun, 210–21, 254–70
Silk Route (Silk Road) and, 44–45, 115
southern, 228, 240, 257–67 (*see also* China, Inner Mongolia)
twentieth century, 269
warlords of, 154–55, 221–22, 223

Western, 82, 120, 142, 143, 194, 205, 212–13, 227
Zavkhan province, 218, 221
Mongol queens (*khatun*)
Alajin Beki, 97–98
Al-Altun, 62–64, 65, 83, 97
Alaqai Beki, 50–52, 54–58, 67–69, 83, 92, 153
attacked by male khans, 91–112
Borte Khatun, 28
bred to rule, 50
Checheyigen, 47–48, 54, 65, 66, 83
choice of husbands, xiv–xv
commercial system devised by, 78–79
consorts of, 35–36, 54
coronations of, 52
daughters-in-law of Genghis Khan as, 36–37, 93–112
daughters of Genghis Khan, xiv, 29, 58, 98 (*see also* specific daughters)
decline of women in power, 125–26
defeat of by Borijin men, 125
devastation of Nishapur and, 75–76
dual leadership of men and women and, 33–34
Ebuskun, 94, 98
Fatima as *khatun*, 95
female descendants of Genghis Khan as rulers of the Mongol Empire, xv, 38–39, 50–52, 54–64, 83
government of empire created by, 70–71
granddaughters of Genghis Khan as, 97–98, 102, 114
headdress, xiv, 214–15
historical evidence of, xiii–xiv, xvi, 274–77
Ibaka as, post-divorce, 28
influence today, 276
Khulan Khatun, 28
Khutulun, 116–25, 203, 273–74
Korean, 126–27
in literature, 271–74
Manduhai the Wise, 152–54, 156–65, 172, 175–76, 185–89, 191, 193, 195, 196–209, 210–27, 237, 239, 240–47, 248–70, 274–77
marriage of Genghis Khan's daughters as a union of dragons and peacocks, 34
Noguk of Korea, 127
nuptial decrees/speeches by Genghis Khan and, 32–33, 34, 47–48, 60
Oghul Ghaimish Khatun, 102–6
ordo (court) of, 28
Orghina Khatun, 114
power curtailed by Mongke Khan, 110
Samur Gunj, 141–51
as shields to defend the empire, 50, 60, 66
signs of authority, 117
Silk Route and, 65–66, 67, 72, 77–79, 92, 125, 210, 223–27, 228

Jack Weatherford holds the DeWitt Wallace Chair of Anthropology at Macalester College in Minnesota and an honorary position at Chinggis Khaan University in Mongolia. In 2007 he received the Order of the Polar Star, the highest award for service to the Mongol nation.